Ruptures

Ruptures

Anthropologies of Discontinuity in Times of Turmoil

Edited by Martin Holbraad, Bruce Kapferer and Julia F. Sauma

First published in 2019 by
UCL Press
University College London
Gower Street
London WC1E 6BT

Available to download free: www.ucl.ac.uk/ucl-press

ISBN: 978-1-78735-620-7 (Hbk.)
ISBN: 978-1-78735-619-1 (Pbk.)
ISBN: 978-1-78735-618-4 (PDF)
ISBN: 978-1-78735-621-4 (epub)
ISBN: 978-1-78735-622-1 (mobi)
ISBN: 978-1-78735-623-8 (html)
DOI: https://doi.org/10.14324/111.9781787356184

Contents

List of figures   vii
List of contributors   viii
Acknowledgements   xi

Introduction: Critical Ruptures   1
Martin Holbraad, Bruce Kapferer and Julia F. Sauma

1. The Guillotine: Reflections on Violent Revolutionary
   Rupture   27
   Caroline Humphrey

2. Rupture and Repair: A Museum of the Red Age
   Confronts Historical Nihilism   52
   Michael Rowlands, Stephan Feuchtwang and Lisheng Zhang

3. Times Like the Present: Political Rupture and the Heat
   of the Moment   70
   Carol J. Greenhouse

4. Inner Revolution: Reaction and Rupture in a Danish
   Lutheran Movement   93
   Morten Axel Pedersen

5. Blurring Rupture: Frames of Conversion in
   Japanese Catholicism   116
   Tobia Farnetti

6. Writing as Rupture: On Prophetic Invention
   in Central Africa   140
   Ramon Sarró

7. Slow Rupture: The Art of Sneaking in an Occupied Forest   157
   Stine Krøijer

8. The Rhythm of Rupture: Attunement among
   Danish Jihadists   174
   Anja Kublitz

9. Earthquake Citizens: Disaster and Aftermath Politics
   in India and Nepal   193
   Edward Simpson and Michele Serafini

Afterword: Some Reflections on Rupture   218
Joel Robbins

Index   233

List of figures

Figure 1.1   Placard of the head of Robespierre. (Bibli-
              othèque nationale de France, département
              Estampes et photographie,
              RESERVE QB-370 (48)-FT4)   43
Figure 2.1   Gongxiaoshe (supply and marketing coop-
              erative) diorama in the Museum of Red Age
              Everyday Objects. Photo by Lisheng Zhang   65
Figure 2.2   Porcelain teapots, Museum of Red Age
              Porcelain Artwork. Photo by Lisheng Zhang   65
Figure 2.3   Mao effigies, Museum of Red Age Porcelain
              Artwork. Photo by Lisheng Zhang   66
Figure 2.4   Plate and chopsticks decorated with Maoist
              slogans, Museum of Red Age Everyday
              Objects. Photo by Lisheng Zhang   66
Figure 5.1   Outdoor service under the cherry tree on
              Palm Sunday. Photo by the author   123
Figure 5.2   A Christian cemetery at the edges of Tokyo.
              Photo by the author   126
Figure 5.3   Fukuzawa and her friends, holding a picture
              of themselves on holiday a few decades ago.
              Photo by the author   128

List of contributors

Tobia Farnetti is Honorary Research Associate at University College London, where he completed his PhD. His main areas of research are Japan and the intersection of religion, politics and aesthetics.

Stephan Feuchtwang is Emeritus Professor of Anthropology at the London School of Economics. His publications include *After the Event: The Transmission of Grievous Loss in Germany, China and Taiwan* (Berghahn Books, 2011); and *The Anthropology of Religion, Charisma and Ghosts: Chinese Lessons for Adequate Theory* (De Gruyter, 2010).

Carol J. Greenhouse is Arthur W. Marks '19 Professor of Anthropology at Princeton University. Her publications include *The Paradox of Relevance: Ethnography and Citizenship in the United States* (University of Pennsylvania Press, 2011); *A Moment's Notice: Time Politics across Cultures* (Cornell University Press, 1996); and *Praying for Justice: Faith, Order, and Community in an American Town* (Cornell University Press, 1994).

Martin Holbraad is Professor of Anthropology at University College London. His publications include *The Ontological Turn: An Anthropological Exposition* (Cambridge University Press, 2016, co-authored); *Truth in Motion: The Recursive Anthropology of Cuban Divination* (University of Chicago Press, 2012); and *Thinking through Things: Theorising Artefacts Ethnographically* (Routledge, 2007, co-edited).

Caroline Humphrey is Emeritus Professor of Social Anthropology at the University of Cambridge. Her publications include *The Unmaking of Soviet Life: Everyday Economies after Socialism* (Cornell University Press, 2002, Heldt Prize); *Marx Went Away, but Karl Stayed Behind* (University of Michigan Press, 1998); and *Karl Marx Collective: Economy, Society and Religion in a Siberian Collective Farm* (Cambridge University Press, 1983).

Bruce Kapferer is Emeritus Professor of Social Anthropology at the University of Bergen (Norway). His publications include *2001 and Counting: Kubrick, Nietzsche and Anthropology* (University of Chicago Press, 2014); *Legends of People, Myths of State: Violence, Intolerance and Political Culture in Sri Lanka and Australia* (Berghahn, 2011; Smithsonian, 1998); *The Feast of the Sorcerer: Practices of Consciousness and Power* (Chicago, 1997); *A Celebration of Demons: Exorcism and the Aesthetics of Healing in Sri Lanka* (University of Indiana Press, 1987 and 1991); and *Strategy and Transaction in an African Factory* (Manchester University Press, 1972).

Stine Krøijer is Associate Professor of Anthropology at the University of Copenhagen. Her publications include *Figurations of the Future: Forms and Temporalities of Left Radical Politics in Europe* (Berghahn, 2015).

Anja Kublitz is Associate Professor of Anthropology at the University of Aalborg. Her publications include 'Escalations: Theorizing Sudden Accelerating Change' (*Anthropological Theory*, 2018, co-authored) and 'From Revolutionaries to Muslims: Liminal Becomings across Palestinian Generations in Denmark' (*International Journal of Middle East Studies*, 2016). She is currently working on a monograph entitled *Life of Catastrophes: Mutable Conflicts among Palestinians in Denmark*.

Morten Axel Pedersen is Professor of Anthropology at the University of Copenhagen. His publications include *Urban Hunters: Dealing and Dreaming in Times of Transition* (Yale University Press, 2019, co-authored); *The Ontological Turn: An Anthropological Exposition* (Cambridge University Press, 2016, co-authored); and *Not Quite Shamans: Spirit Worlds and Political Lives in Northern Mongolia* (Cornell University Press, 2011).

Joel Robbins is Professor of Social Anthropology at Cambridge University. His research interests include the study of religion, cultural change, values and ethics. Among numerous other books and articles, he is author of *Becoming Sinners: Christianity and Moral Torment in a Papua New Guinea Society* (University of California Press, 2004), and 'Continuity Thinking and the Problem of Christian Culture: Belief, Time, and the Anthropology of Christianity' (*Current Anthropology*, 2007).

Michael Rowlands is Emeritus Professor of Material Culture at University College London. His publications include a chapter in *De la Mascarade au Film Video: transmettre le diaboloque en Afrique de l'Ouest* (Editions de la Maison des Sciences de l'Homme, 2012); *Reclaiming Heritage: Alternative*

Imaginaries of Memory in West Africa (Left Coast Press, 2007, co-edited); and *Social Transformations in Archaeology: Global and Local Perspectives* (Routledge, 1998).

Ramon Sarró is Associate Professor in Social Anthropology at the University of Oxford. His publications include *The Politics of Religious Change on the Upper Guinea Coast: Iconoclasm Done and Undone* (Edinburgh University Press, 2009).

Julia F. Sauma is Senior Researcher in the Department of Anthropology at the University of Bergen. Her publications include 'Carnal Words: On Re-Membering and Re-Forgetting, Being and Not Being, among the Children of the Erepecuru' (*Revista de Antropologia*, 2016); and 'Mutual Engagements, an Afroindigenous Ethnographic Reflection' (*Cadernos de Campo*, 2014). She is currently preparing a monograph entitled *Collective: A Maroon Sociology*.

Michele Serafini is a PhD candidate in Anthropology at the School of Oriental and African Studies in London. His research areas are Nepal and the anthropology of politics and play.

Edward Simpson is a Professor of Anthropology at the School of Oriental and African Studies in London. His publications include *The Political Biography of an Earthquake: Aftermath and Amnesia in Gujarat, India* (Hurst, 2013); and *Muslim Society and the Western Indian Ocean: The Seafarers of Kachchh* (Routledge, 2006).

Lisheng Zhang is a PhD candidate in the Institute of Archaeology at University College London, whose main areas of research are China and Heritage.

Acknowledgements

This book is the result of the sustained interaction between the research teams of two projects funded by the European Research Council: *Egalitarianism: Forms, Processes, Comparisons*, led by Bruce Kapferer (ERC-2013-ADG, 340673), and *Making Selves, Making Revolutions: Comparative Anthropologies of Revolutionary Politics*, led by Martin Holbraad (ERC-2013-CoG, 617970, CARP). Most of the chapters of the volume were presented at our event *Rupture*, which was held at University College London in February 2017 and co-sponsored by the research project *Escalations: A Comparative Ethnographic Study of Accelerating Change*, led by Lars Højer and funded by the Danish Research Council. We thank all of the participants in that event for their contributions. We are also grateful to Chris Penfold for chaperoning the book through to publication so skilfully.

Introduction: Critical Ruptures

Martin Holbraad, Bruce Kapferer and Julia F. Sauma

The unsettling effects of rupture, understood as a radical and often force-ful form of discontinuity, are central to current perceptions of a world in turmoil. How far might a sense of rupture – of a world that is serially breaking with itself – be an occasion to transform conceptions of social and political transformation? And how might the ruptures and fissures that lie at the heart of such experiences of turmoil instigate a break in the way we think about them? This volume casts a sharp focus on rupture as the active ingredient in some of the most defining experiences of our time, including the rise of populist politics, the corollary impulse towards protest and even revolutionary change, as well as moves towards violence and terror, and the responses that these moves elicit. The volume's cen-tral contention is that a concern with different experiences of rupture lies at the heart of these diverse phenomena. Gaining a handle on the ways the world around us is changing, therefore, demands paying attention to how burgeoning forms of rupture, some of them familiar (e.g. populism, protest, revolution), others apparently new (e.g. global/virtual specta-cles of terror, natural disasters, responses to environmental catastrophe) are constituted, experienced, and even desired for their own sake.

One of this volume's prime concerns is therefore to expose what, after Spinoza, we call the 'dual aspect' of rupture: while rupture oper-ates as an inherently negative moment – a critical cut or 'switch-point' (Weber 1930)[1] that instigates a significant break with existing con-ditions – by the same token it can act as a positive or dynamic impulse towards escape, redirection, reconstitution and sometimes renewal. In our conceptualization, then, ruptures are moments at which value emerges through a break with something. Focusing on the co-implication of emergence and negation in times of rupture, we suggest, allows us to break away from conventional functionalist orientations (e.g. that link continuity with change) or those of a dialectical or transformational kind that beg questions as to the values of what is to come. It also allows us to steer in a new direction analyses that tend to view change as a piecemeal affair undergirded by continuities of structure and process (e.g. Sahlins 1985; Latour 1999), as well as a more recent inclination to celebrate discontinuity as the moment in which the new might emerge (e.g. Badiou 2003; Robbins 2004, 2007, 2010; cf. Humphrey 2008).

By thematizing rupture as a radical, sometimes violent and even brutal form of discontinuity, the volume lends a harder edge to contemporary discourses, both in social theory and public debate and policy, couched in terms of novelty, collaborative creativity and emergence. At the same time, sharpening the analytical focus onto questions of rupture serves to counter the politically freighted tendency to view contemporary upheavals through the prism of 'crisis' (see also Roitman 2013). Taking a longer view, the volume's emphasis on the dual aspect of rupture resonates with Victor Turner's focal concern with the mutual relationship between disruption and reconstitution in the phenomena he treated as 'liminal' (Turner 1969; 1975) – a notion that continues to hold a spell over generations of anthropologists, albeit sometimes as something of a conceptual catch-all. Furthermore, attention to the mutual constitution of discontinuity and renewal in specific ethnographic settings allows us to offer alternatives to the revival of Joseph Schumpeter's notion of 'creative destruction' (1994) in sometimes wide-eyed contemporary debates about 'disruptive innovation' (e.g. Christensen et al. 2015). Indeed, our orientation towards the concept of rupture implies no judgement as to its value, suggesting neither a pessimistic nor an optimistic assessment of its impact. How ruptures are evaluated by the people caught up in them, and how these evaluations emerge and interact with one another, are for us open ethnographic questions.

In the rest of this introduction we make two moves towards substantiating the volume's perspective on rupture as a concept and concern peculiarly attuned – indeed pressing and necessary – for the contemporary juncture. First, we place the idea of rupture in the intellectual landscape not only of the development of anthropology – the discipline from which the chapters of this volume speak – but also of broader social and political theoretical trends in recent decades. Most crucially, we address the apparent aversion towards the negative moment of rupture in a lot of the writing that has been associated with the late twentieth-century shift away from the certainties of 'modernity'. Following on from that, our second move will be to explore how an anthropological multiplication and reformulation of rupture as a variable object of ethnographic inquiry could serve to rescue the harder edge of rupture that, we feel, is so needed to make sense of the tumultuous transformations of the contemporary world. Is it possible to take seriously the criticisms that have been made of standard 'modern' conceptions of rupture – for example, its association with the violence of revolutionary politics, or the closure of dialectical progressions – without losing the analytical power of the very concept of rupture? To make an argument that such a move is not only possible but necessary, we draw substantially on the chapters in this volume, which, taken together, demonstrate the critical power of rupture as a concept of and for our times.

Old and new ruptures

Anthropology itself, as a discipline, saw its beginnings in a moment of profound rupture, making some of its greatest contributions by witnessing and recording the violent emergence and global expansion of European and North American power. Shifts in anthropological focus and thought throughout the discipline's development have been no less conditioned in the rupture of what some might describe as the decline of the West. While anthropology is in many ways the discipline of rupturing moments, however, its traditional point of departure has been normative in orientation, examining societies as more or less completed systems, often presented as closed, self-reproducing orders. The forces of rupture connected to Western expansion were therefore viewed as principally disruptive and destructive of a static unchanging traditional order that was brought in from out of the cold, as it were.

Attempts were made by some to make change more central to anthropological analysis, and Gluckman (e.g. 1955; 1963) and the Manchester School were arguably at the forefront of this reorientation (Evens and Handelman 2006; Meinert and Kapferer 2015). For them change was the condition of existence, normative consistency was the exception. Gluckman and his colleagues therefore made process the centre of their methodological innovations, developing around the concept of situational analysis, which concentrated on events or moments of rupture, disruption and disturbance in the ongoing activities of everyday and not so everyday life. Events in this approach exhibited what Gluckman and his colleagues discussed to be the logics of practice relative to the situations in which they were provoked. They were windows on the continually emerging structures of existence that were highly variant – dependent on the problem at hand – in their situated practice, rather than being consistent or normative in the ideal typical sense apparent in many ethnographies to this day. Anthropological description as abstracted empiricism (Mills 2000) was what characterized the bulk of ethnography at the time: the event not as a dynamic or process of the continual construction and reconstruction of value – in which the diverse and differentiating potential of value in practice was revealed – but as an illustration of overarching value of a normative sort. In this perspective, events were generally treated as moments of conflict, and breaks and disruptions in the ongoing flow of life – ruptures, in effect – were integral to the continuity of existence.

The Manchester group conceived of rupturing moments as integral to what had been conceived as stasis, as well as to transformations in the orders of sociocultural existence. The dichotomy between the modern and the traditional – an ideologically legitimating move for Western dominance, consequent of the irruption of its emergence to power, and these days much thrown into question – was problematized. Furthermore, the tendency at that time for anthropologists to regard the societies they studied as closed systems was criticized as a limited analytical strategy. Rupturing events were reconceived as born of the structural contradictions in idea, structure and practice, as always in some way or another produced by their entanglement with historical forces in larger global realities.

However, in more recent decades it feels as if the concept of rupture has somehow fallen by the wayside for some, outmoded by a putative shift from the age of extremes of the twentieth century to a twenty-first century of multitudes and assemblies, to take Hobsbawm's (1995) and Hardt and Negri's (2004) books' titles as somehow representative. Rupture, to be sure, connotes radical change, and the desire for sundry forms of transformation, including truly radical ones, has hardly gone away. Yet rupture also connotes negativity – breaking away from things as well as changing them, tearing things apart as well as encouraging them to flourish in new directions, brutally razing things to the ground as well as sowing the seeds for their emergent flourishing. If the hegemony of what, for the purposes of this broad exposition, we will be tagging as a contemporary ethos of the 'life-affirmative' is anything to go by, however, it would seem that these kinds of investments in the moment of the negative have been out for a good while in social theory at large. Process is preferable to essence (Braidotti 2006; Stengers 2014); relations go before entities (Barad 2007; Latour 2005); assemblages obviate social groups (DeLanda 2006); difference trumps identity (cf. Laruelle 2010); exceptions rule over rules (Agamben 2005); the multiple trumps the negative (Deleuze and Guattari 1987).

Particularly towards the end of the twentieth century, when these choices were most hotly debated, the shift from the negativity of rupture to the affirmation of life was glossed as a transition from modernity to postmodernity. It is significant for our purposes here to note how close to the surface of those debates the concept of rupture lay. For example, one of the concerns that rode on these critiques of modernity was the apparent demise of 'grand narratives' (Lyotard 1984). Certainly, the very idea of rupture seems 'grand' in just that sense. Imagined as momentous, one-off events that change the course of history, ruptures are, as Reinhardt Koselleck (2005) wrote in relation to the modern concept of revolution in particular, 'metahistorical': they provide the definitive temporal structure of the open, forward-moving thrust of chronological time that the grand narratives of modernity take as their premise. Indeed, if ruptures also connote a moment of temporal evacuation – the void that the hiatus of their break opens up – they rehearse also the definitive ontological structure of what is perhaps the grandest narrative of all, namely the Judaeo-Christian conception of creation *ex nihilo* (Rubenstein 2012).

Plenty of anthropologists have taken these critiques of the grand narratives of modernity to heart, contributing substantially to them or, often, adopting them as a diffuse theoretical aesthetic. The logical priority of relations over entities, for example, has been developed systematically out of first structuralist principles into a powerful post-structural analytical paradigm for both feminist (Strathern 1988; 1995) and post-colonial purposes (Viveiros de Castro 2003; 2013), giving rise to what today is discussed in the discipline as a 'relational' approach (Holbraad and Pedersen 2017). Similarly, the conceptual ammunition provided by the emphasis in social theory on the contingency and porousness of all identities, giving logical priority to becoming over being (e.g. Ingold 2011), has for some time now been deployed by anthropologists against the threat of essentialism, which, it is felt, dogged earlier generations' accounts of social and cultural diversity (e.g. Herzfeld 1997). Still, partly owing to the analytical traction of these approaches, no doubt, and partly owing to the general philosophical atmosphere connoted by the prefix 'post-', which still holds so much sway, an aversion to entities, essences, fixity, permanence and any hard and fast way of distinguishing one thing from another seems to have become normative in anthropology today. The logic of both/and, to put it figuratively, is now simply *better* than that of either/or.

Critical assessments of the effects these developments in contemporary anthropology (and social theory more broadly) have been growing in recent years, exploring ways in which this life-affirmative theoretical aesthetic stands in the way of getting an analytical handle on such phenomena as individual subjectivity (e.g. Humphrey 2008; Laidlaw et al. 2018), forms of 'detachment' (Candea et al. 2015) and other phenomena that in one way or another could be described as 'non-relational' (cf. Venkatesan et al. 2012). At the same time, the 'endurance' (Stoler 2016) and therefore relational dimensions of the negative – structures of racial exclusion and 'zones of non-being' (Fanon 2007) established through violent and undesired instances of rupture, such as the transatlantic slave trade (Sojoyner 2017; Alves 2018) and the European colonization of Native American lands (Simpson 2014) – have been brought to the fore of anthropological thinking. Powerfully describing how the ideals that emerged from modern instances of 'rupture' – such as freedom, the individual and democracy – are entwined with the violent breaches created and maintained by an ongoing, fundamentally racist Euro-American colonial project, these texts push us to consider how the practices of refusal and escape that emerge as a result of such breaches can reorient anthropology's analysis of structures of power, of strategies of resistance and instances of radical autonomy. Crucially, it is from their dual capacity to both theoretically unmask 'the field of racial annihilation we call civil society' (Alves 2018, 13) and consider forms of black and indigenous agency that often appear as contradictory – such as black youths' involvement with crime in Brazil or Native American claims to 'nested sovereignty' (Simpson 2014) – that these authors take the impetus to question the unexamined, often heroically charged deployment of the concept of resistance, and invite further ethnographic research.

Building on this work, in relation to the conceptualization of rupture in particular, we make two critical comments about the broader implications of the hegemony of the life-affirmative – one political, the other theoretical. On the politics, it is important to note that the normative rise of life-affirmation in anthropology and elsewhere has been something of a double-edged sword. On one side, it has been fuelled by a desire to break down the certainties upon which structures of power and domination are built. If colonialism, nationalism or the patriarchy, say, are social constructs, then resisting them must involve deconstructing their claims to essences that hold sway over time, critically exposing their fluidity and contingency, rendering them more fragile and reversible in the process. In such a context, any insistence on essence or attempt to fix an identity smacks of violence – a power-move to be resisted (even when that power-move is itself framed as a form of resistance to the life-affirming hegemony of what the populist far-Right in the USA, for example, deride as 'the liberal establishment').

The other side of the sword, however, cuts in the opposite direction. If all that is solid melts into air in this particular way (Berman 1988), then experiences of exclusion and alternative political projects or proposals are also subject to de-essentializing deconstruction. Indeed, one way to think of the passage from an age of extremes to one of multitudes and assemblies is as a transition from a politics of clashing proposals for the good life (e.g. free market versus state socialism) to a politics of difference, in which keeping the horizon for such proposals open becomes the prime political objective (e.g. Holbraad et al. 2014). While potentially welcome, positive assertions in favour of an alternative political order must be themselves founded on essentializing assumptions that close down the scope for multiplying diversities. Affirming just that scope, then, by turning the process of an open politics into a political project in its own right, is the point at which otherwise contrasting hues of liberalism, libertarianism and Left radicalism meet in the cause of autonomy, freedom, diversity, inclusion, creativity and so on. What is lost in this (or overcome, depending on the view one takes) is what David Scott (2004, 96) calls the 'heroic figuration' of a politics centred on overthrowing one political order in favour of another. Such a view of politics, Scott suggests, following Hannah Arendt (1965) as well as Koselleck (2005), is distinctly modern, and bound up with a post-Enlightenment conception of revolution in particular, seen as 'a form of change that looks forward into an unknown and novel future' (Scott 2004, 89). What is lost or overcome, in other words, is a politics of opposition, antagonism, clash and mutual exclusion, including the mutual negation of opposites – a politics of either/or, of down with this and up with that; in short, a politics of rupture.

In fact, ongoing Left-radical debates regarding the relevance – indeed the possibility – of revolutionary action (as distinct, say, from political activism) are telling of the apparent demise of rupture as a political option. Invested in violence and heroic class struggle, revolution is now often seen as a cipher of failure, the failure of modernity's failure as it were; an outmoded aspiration wedded to outmoded grand narratives about wholesale social and historical transformation. As in the much-cited adage, pronounced with mournful irony by Marxist critics of postmodern images of life-affirmative emancipation, in the post-Fordist, post-Soviet era it is easier to imagine the end of the world than the end of capitalism (Jameson 2003). Indeed, while icons of the contemporary Left such as Slavoj Žižek and Alain Badiou may proclaim the virtues of a revolutionary action that '"resignif[ies]" terror, the ruthless exercise of power, the spirit of sacrifice' (Žižek 2000, 326), the deliberately rearguard character of such provocations (invoking Lenin, Stalin and Mao over and again) bears out the notion that debates about emancipatory politics on the Left have left grandstanding rhetoric of 'historical rupture' behind. As the German environmental protesters discussed in Stine Krøijer's chapter (this volume) also testify, Left-radical calls to emancipation in the era of multitudes (as opposed to the era, say, of class struggle) are much more likely to take the form of pre-figuring assemblies (Juris 2008), temporary autonomous zones (Bey 1991), deterritorialized nomads and migrants (Hardt and Negri 2000), and other such forms of decentred insurrection performed contingently and on a local scale (see also Graeber 2018). Revolutions, on this kind of view, are to be celebrated not as violent overthrows of existing orders of power, but rather as festivals of carnivalesque expressions of desire. Gilles Deleuze's link between his philosophy of difference and affirma-tion with the repudiation of the politics of revolutionary rupture in the final pages of *Difference and Repetition* delivers the point pithily:

> History progresses not by negation and the negation of negation, but by deciding problems and affirming differences. It is no less bloody and cruel as a result. Only the shadows of history live by negation: the good enter into it with all the power of a posited dif-ferential or a difference affirmed … That is why real revolutions have the atmosphere of fêtes. (1994, 268)

This leads us to our second point, which concerns the deeper philosophical roots of the bracketing of rupture in favour of life-affirming processes of dif-ferentiation and creativity. At issue here is the philosophical fate of negation in particular, understood as a constitutive feature of the either/or logic that seems to have fallen out of philosophical favour, being seen now as a cipher of a peculiarly modern tendency to treat change as a matter of dialectics. Marxist social theorists John Holloway, Fernando Matamoros and Sergio Tischle (2009) see this as a general characteristic of post-structuralist philos-ophy in the wake of the experience of state socialist 'dialectical materialism' in the USSR and elsewhere, which they see as rooted in Hegel's 'apologetic' dialectics (as opposed to Theodore Adorno's 'critical' negative dialectics – Bonnet 2009: 42; cf. Adorno 1990). To state the charge they cite Michael Hardt and *Colectivo Situaciones* (in a somewhat rough translation):

> The dialectical operation consists of putting an end to that which has none, giving a defined orientation to that which has no final-ity, taking (overcoming) the previous moments by rescuing what is

useful (preserving) in the service of a new affirmation, prohibiting every consciousness of an irreducible diversity, of an excess that is not retaken. (2007, cited in Holloway et al. 2009, 4)

The problem with dialectics, then, is that it impoverishes difference, turning it into contradiction, replacing the openness of affirmation with the closure of negation. On such a view, Holloway et al. suggest:

> Life becomes a positive concept rather than the struggle against the negation of life. There is in general a positivization of thought. Struggles are seen as struggles for, rather than being principally struggles against. The centrality of crisis (a negative concept) is lost and replaced by an emphasis on restructuring (a positive concept) … This has not only theoretical but also political consequences: it can lead to a blurring of the distinction between negation and synthesis, between refusal and reconciliation, between an uprising and the reconciling government that follows the uprising. (2009, 6)

From their trenchantly critical theoretical perspective, Holloway et al. lament the loss of critical potential that negation affords. They write:

> What we need is not to reject dialectics as such, but only the synthetic understanding of it: to insist, in other words, on a negative dialectics, a restless movement of negation that does not lead necessarily to a happy ending. History is seen not as a series of stages, but as the movement of endless revolt. (2009, 7)

It is not our intention here to take sides on these controversies – neither the political question of whether revolution is still possible or desirable, nor the related philosophical question of whether negation and the dialectical view of history that it supports ought to be rescued or abandoned. Instead, distinctively anthropological, our purpose is to unhook the concept of rupture from these debates by multiplying it in line with the variety of contingent ethnographic situations in which, as the chapters of the book show, rupture features as a matter of concern.

To be sure, this is in part the standard anthropological response to any normative controversy: take a concept that in a given debate features as normative premise, stand back from it critically and then multiply it ethnographically to show that other ways of conceiving it and experiencing it are possible – anthropology as the vantage of the 'otherwise' (Povinelli 2012). Indeed, our interest in making such a move on rupture is expressed in the plural of our title: *ruptures*. In this connection, a book in political philosophy by literary and cultural theorists Paul Eisenstein and Todd McGowan (2012), titled *Rupture* in the singular, serves as useful foil by the contrast it presents. Having defined rupture as 'the occurrence of the impossible, when the very ground under our feet shifts in order to transform the point from which we see' (2012, 4), the authors go on to scope the remit of a new political philosophy that, rather than concerning itself with the 'distribution of power' (2012, 3), takes rupture as its starting point:

> The fundamental question of politics is in not how to assume or contest power but how one relates to rupture ... Within the logic of rupture, all subjects are irreducibly singular and free. The rupture frees individuals from the despotic rule or nature or tradition, and it constitutes them as singular subjects. But it also introduces a principle of equality that binds subjects to one another in an experience of human solidarity. Belief, universality, solidarity, equality, freedom, singularity, and humanity are neither natural values nor the achievements of culture. They are the product of the rupture that causes culture to arise out of nature or the rupture that causes a new social order to emerge from an older one. Rupture marks the creation of value out of nothing, and the paradigm for this creation is the emergence of signification itself. (2012, 11)

From our anthropological point of view, the problem with this way of approaching rupture is not just how it enshrines within it so many of the cardinal principles of an emblematically modern conception – culture rising out of nature, freedom from the despotism of tradition, and the emergence of new social orders as a matter of breaking with old ones. The issue is rather how the concept of rupture here is pressed to the service of a normatively conceived political programme, based now not just on cardinal principles but also on cardinal virtues, expressing an image of the good life consisting of solidarity, equality, freedom and so forth. Our anthropological tack here, by contrast, is to place such normative points of departure between brackets in order to explore how far conceptions and experiences of rupture can be multiplied ethnographically, rendered contingent in a way that might display alternative sets of possibilities for thinking, including for thinking politically.

Still, our desire for ethnographic multiplication also has a more pointed critical purpose, namely that of disentangling the concept of rupture from its putative modernity, to render it capacious enough to address the contemporary circumstance of turmoil. As we have seen, one reason why the notion of rupture is sidelined in much contemporary social and political writing is that it is seen as bound up with both political and philosophical projects that now seem outmoded – revolution and dialectics being prime examples of projects that, with the advent of the 'post' era of the late twentieth century seemed exactly the kinds of things one ought to be 'post' about. Regardless of whether it is fair, the idea that rupture is somehow stuck in the twentieth century raises the question of whether it could yet be unstuck from it, for use in the twenty-first. Can the baby of rupture (if such it is) be rescued from the bathwater of modernity (ditto)? Can one maintain one's interest in rupture as a constitutive element of social reality – indeed a potent political force – without thereby also committing to the baggage of the grand narratives it has so typically carried in the past? Can one think rupture *without* the heroic politics or revolution, the closed *telos* of self-transcending dialectics, the monotheistic mould of *ex nihilo* creation, and all the *Sturm und Drang* of the forward thrust of history?

To bring rupture back into the fray in this way, we suggest, is necessary when confronted with a world experienced as turmoil. We may remain agnostic as to whether something called modernity has indeed been surpassed. What seems patently obvious to us, however, is that any notion that negativity, contradiction, fissure and violence have somehow been on the wane, and that the world around us is now better understood in terms of the affirmation of life in and as difference, is just wrong. If there is something in the common sense, not only of commentators but also of ordinary people as well as protagonists across the globe, that new forms of terror, authoritarianism and populism, not to mention rising inequality and pending environmental catastrophe, are all encroaching, then a place for rupture must be found in our thinking about these circumstances. We can indeed sidestep the grand narratives that earlier versions of rupture-thinking supported, and open ourselves up to the shifts in attention that writings thinking after (if not post) modernity have produced – new 'arts of noticing', as Anna Tsing calls them (2015). Yet in doing so we need to retain the capacity for thinking with a harder edge – forms of understanding and analysis that can countenance the brutality of what is going on, and the perhaps irreducible conflicts and fissures that seem to be erupting in so many registers of life today.

The point, we should be clear, is not to use the concept of rupture as a lever for erecting new grand narratives of history, politics or human life in the round. Nor is our aim to use rupture in order to articulate a new political theory, fit for our times, as Slavoj Žižek (e.g. 2010) and

Alain Badiou (2007) have sought to do in recent years – indeed, the traction their attempts to do so have gained in broader debates is itself telling of the renewed relevance of rupture in the contemporary setting. In fact, even philosophical projects that deploy notions of radical rupture to undo attempts to found politics on prior principles (God, Nature, Reason, Justice or indeed Conflict), tend to capitulate to the basic expectation that a political philosophy, as such, must provide some kind of normative criterion about what counts as 'political' in the first place (e.g. Marchart 2007). As anthropologists, we are more interested in political cosmologies of rupture than we are in its political philosophy – if by 'cosmologies' we designate the long-standing anthropological concern with charting the entities and relations that compose people's conception of the worlds they inhabit (Kapferer 2010; Abramson and Holbraad 2014; Sauma 2016). Ethnographic scrutiny of how ruptures of different kinds and in different senses are constituted and lived in varying social (as well as political) settings, we suggest, may provide the resources for exploring what alternatives to modern conceptions of rupture might look like. With reference to the chapters that follow, in the next section we set out some programmatic thoughts on how this might be done.

On ethnographic ruptures

Given the dangers involved in reintroducing the negative into anthropological analysis, and the significant shifts in attention brought with postmodernist vitalism, how can we proceed? Our answer is to treat ruptures as a way of doing and describing, rather than as an explanatory lens, as offering a method of cutting through rather than resisting grand narratives, since resistance itself can so easily become yet another 'grand' axiom. This shift can be delineated by looking at the effects that thinking with rupture can have on the very different materials presented by the contributors to this volume, effects that we would distinguish into a series of possible forms of interference in the production of grand narratives. The first of these effects reveals the multiple dynamics that lie underneath the surface gloss of heroic, emblematic events or contexts of rupture: the ethnographies and/or anthropological analyses contained here therefore pluralize singular moments of rupture, looking to the breaks within them. By describing what is produced at the moment of revolution, of populist electoral upheaval, of spiritual awakening as rupture rather than transformation, the authors can therefore point to the unexpected consequences of these significant moments for those who bear witness to them. Through this multiplying dynamic we therefore find heroism's more qualitative foundations: the radical uncertainty upon which its varying, impressive structures are built.

There are probably no grander instances of this than the great revolutions that open our volume, in Caroline Humphrey's analysis of the different scales of the rupture caused by the Terror during the French Revolution, and in Michael Rowlands, Stephan Feuchtwang and Lisheng Zhang's description of the cyclical relation between radical rupture and necessary repair in relation to the Chinese Communist Revolution and New Era. In the first of these meditations on the underside of heroic transformation, Humphrey's significant distinction between revolution and rupture is guided by the guillotine itself, and the temporal cut that it makes in our capacity to look at the French Revolution as a linear process. This emblematic killing machine produces something very different, not the replacement of one political whole with another – monarchy with republic – but the dismemberment of something previously considered whole, the body politic: a cut that contains not just a before and after but also the singular moment in which it happens. Witnesses to Louis XVI's decapitation and the ensuing period of the Terror are therefore seen to carry within them not only revolutionary fervour and national vitalism but 'new sensations, excitements, fears and strangely productive pathologies' (Humphrey, this volume) caused by the physical cut and gush of blood produced by the guillotine. Blood that repulses and royal blood that is collected and kept as keepsake, undoing the revolutionary neutralization of the royal body, producing numerous breaks within the revolutionary self, the revolution itself and the retelling of it: ruptures between those who were present and became energized by blood, and those who fell apart in witnessing the decapitations; between those who defended and those who criticized the violence. The 'we' of the Terror contains a rupture that is 'a shifting, temporary and multiple entity', that places the radical nature of the revolution in question by 'that spectral "thing" which had been cut off' (Humphrey, this volume) and in doing so also produces a break in the heroic 'we' of the most primordial of Euro-American revolutions.

While in the French case rupture and revolution are made distinct by the guillotine, in the Chinese case Rowlands, Feuchtwang and Zhang point in this volume to how revolutionary objects can also enact rupture – a break with the humiliation and repression of the past – not as a cleavage, not as a cut, but as a repair of the human: the re-establishment of some form of continuity with the potential of the people, something that is both new and ancient. Rupture, in this case, is not multiple but cyclical, not spectral but practised. The private museum collection analysed by the authors conveys this ethnographic instance of rupture, with its artful simultaneous claim to both a commitment to historical restoration and to support Xin Jinping's New Era. Adeptly negotiating potential accusations of 'historical nihilism' and therefore censorship – aimed at those who would deny the Party's revolutionary accomplishments, 'the historical inevitability of China's socialist path', through claims to historical objectivity – Fan Jianchuan's controversial and celebrated private collection of everyday objects, the waste of the Cultural Revolution, conjures the correct balance between facticity, patriotism and personal remembrance of revolutionary suffering. In doing so, these discarded, broken objects ensure that an obsolete past – and the people of that past – are given new life within Xi Jinping's drive to project a new global China. Rupture as repair can be seen as the non-narrative exposition of a revolutionary past – and loss – in a fast-paced, consumer-driven present that breaks with it: rupture as cyclical – it has happened before and will happen again but not in the same way – rather than as linear or singular, conjures an ambivalent history 'more fractured and open [to the] coincidence of norms and histories ... in which realities can be questioned and alternative futures can be seen enacted and propagated' (Rowlands, Feuchtwang and Zhang, this volume).

In both of these reflections about the multiple ruptures that lie beneath the veneer of singular revolutionary moments, we find the motile play between the different spatio-temporal scales of the events witnessed, experienced, portrayed and enacted, the play between rupture as past, present and future, as personal, national and universal phenomenon. This conforms to the suggestion made by Daniel Knight and Charles Stewart in a comparative study of recent experiences of 'economic crisis' in Southern Europe, that 'in moments of extreme crisis, time becomes elastic', and 'crises turn ordinary daily routine inside out and expose the seams of temporality to view' (2016, 3). Drawing on works in the philosophy and anthropology of time (e.g. Deleuze 1991; Serres and Latour 1995; Hirsch and Stewart 2005; Hodges 2010), Knight and Stewart explore how moments of crisis put the very notions of time and history in crisis. Familiar distinctions between past, present and future are compressed, collapsed or suspended in different ways, and people's historicity – their 'sense of the historical continuity grounding the present' (Knight and Stewart 2016) – becomes connected with scales of experience that may in ordinary times feel removed. Such temporal torsions, along with spatial and scalar ones with which they are often related, are certainly characteristic of the situations of rupture we examine in this book. Treating rupture as an object of ethnographic inquiry therefore implies also treating the constitution of time and history in each case as an ethnographic variable, much as Knight and Stewart do in their study of crisis.

To the extent that the concept of crisis is itself constitutive to the 'grand narrative' of modern historical reckoning, however, and has become a prominent ingredient of ideological formations of contemporary global capitalism (Roitman 2013; Masco 2017), we prefer to parse these temporal dimensions in terms of the concept of rupture, which carries less of this political and economic baggage. As an analytical concept, we suggest, crisis connotes the very grand narratives it diagnoses as unstable, while rupture has the potential to cut through them. Our emphasis on the cut here also allows us to relate to important bodies of work on memory, in anthropology and beyond that pre-date current emphases on crises and that have long reflected on the ways in which experiences of traumatic collective loss or breach (whether historical or not) inform everyday practice. Through numerous descriptions of the ways in which collective memory is maintained by repetition – that which allows regeneration and also 'continually "cuts" back to the start' (Snead, cited in Hartman 1997) – and takes place even when there is an 'inability to occupy an imagined prior condition or to bridge the divide of the split subject' (Hartman 1997, 75), such works push us to consider the different ways in which the temporal 'elasticity' of rupture is related to specific experiences of reconstitution, of re-encountering something previously known, and perhaps purposefully forgotten or taken away.

Nowhere is this more anthropologically and politically poignant in this volume, perhaps, than in Carol Greenhouse's description and analysis of Donald Trump's electoral victory in 2016 and its immediate aftermath: the way in which it 'unsettles habits of time, place, scale and standpoint'. Using the metaphor of temporal heat to characterize the sudden realizations and encounters, the sparks that occur at the moment of political rupture and of its unforeseeable consequences – such as the realization of having knowledge that one was not aware of before – Greenhouse challenges us to acknowledge the untenable continuity of relativism's 'cool indifference'. The destabilization of the political field and of anthropology's social distance is thus conjoined. In the gaps produced by this fissure, the author reveals the production of a different temporality and relativity, one more suited to the heat of this moment, so that 'ethnographic knowledge is inseparable from self-knowledge, knowledge of others in the world, others in oneself' (Greenhouse, this volume). In this context, Greenhouse experiments with other ways of knowing power, with identifying political agency through the signs constituted by people's experience of power and of powerlessness, with the personal, subjective dimensions of political rupture. In doing so hers is a call for anthropology to understand 'the diversity of people's practical experience of democracy (or lack of it) in their own lives' (Greenhouse, this volume). This is a call for full ethnographic relativity – a commitment to the multiple directions that rupture takes – widening a parallel space and time for the anthropologist's personal convictions as a visible source of insight.

The subjective or personal scale of political agency in the face of rupture is also a concern for Morten Pedersen's interlocutors in his chapter on the significant political influence of the Danish Protestant movement, but in a directly opposing way – usefully highlighting the multiplying effects of rupture at an ethnographic and analytical level. Pedersen's ethnography of a Lutheran movement in Denmark, in conjunction with his analysis of the ideas of key figures within it – such as the Danish philosopher and theologian Søren Kierkegaard – reflects specifically on the significance of the experience of subjective rupture. However, in this case it is not political but existential rupture that is at stake: 'leaps' that arise from 'genuine faith' and, significantly, oppose all forms of political and societal upheaval. This is subjective rupture not as a future and outward-oriented break with the past, but as the inward re-entrance into the kingdom of God. As it is individualized, rupture is a conscious or indeed desired change, a transformation premised in everyday actions that, taken together, intone one's leap of faith, one's relation to God and therefore one's freedom. Rupture as leap, rupture as action rather than as historical event, transforms this notion spatio-temporally: rupture not in hindsight or as future promise, but as a constant present, as the condition of humans as detached or fallen parts of the kingdom of God. In this view, the attempt to 'change or improve this primordial fall or rupture in the form of progressive reforms, let alone political revolutions, are ... evil and ungodly', for '[s]ince God is not of this world, you are in this world *not* supposed to relate to society and politics in a god-like and absolute way' (Krarup, 1987). In the Lutheran movement in Tidehverv, as described by Pedersen, we therefore find an explicit preoccupation with the different scales of rupture, with its multiplying capacity and as such a concern with how to keep it within a 'radically introspective' individual: apprehensions that have had a direct impact on the modern Danish nation state.

The individual, internalized rupture that defines the Danish Lutheran movement is probably something that the priest in Tobia Farnetti's chapter in this volume on conversion in Japanese Catholicism would repudiate to a certain degree; the life of his church is after all in its community activities. However, it is also the case that his flock, in converting to Catholicism, must struggle with rupture on a daily basis; as a result of internal and external impositions – from the priest himself and from Japanese society – they are being made to break with previous cultural forms and therefore with previous relations, past and present. In response to this demand for rupture, which also figures so prominently in anthropology's treatment of Christian conversion (Robbins 2004; 2007), Farnetti's interlocutors practise the blurring of the clear distinctions set from within and without, between previous and current lives. In personal histories Christian conversion figures as 'a flavour or an afterthought', as a gradual process lacking any sense of crisis and calling. In their apparently transgressive weekly drinking sessions particularly, there is no sense in which they are flouting Christian values, but instead seem to mark, as Farnetti notes, 'a particular affective way of engaging rupture' (Farnetti, this volume), by blurring the distinct lines that it draws. The result is that for a few fleeting hours, during evenings of drinking that are in a continuum with church life – since drunken conversations are dominated by church activities and people – the clear distinction between Christian and Japanese life, drawn by priest and by society, is collapsed, so that it seems that each encompasses the other simultaneously, without 'a definite direction or outcome' aside from establishing the indispensability between the two. Rupture in this sense can not only be multiple, but is also temporarily erasable; it can somehow also be refused.

If the erasability of rupture is particularly vivid in Farnetti's ethnography, it would be incorrect to say that this is the first time we encounter it in this volume, or indeed the last. From the very first two chapters we see, in relation to the French Revolution and to cyclical socialist reinventions in China, how the invention of powerful collective narratives is premised on the erasure of rupture, the erasure of terror and suffering. It also emerges, in a very different way, in Ramon Sarró's contribution to this volume, with the double rupture required for prophetic invention in West and Central Africa. If, in the Japanese case described by Farnetti, rupture is deliberately blurred, here putative ruptures are created through careful works of erasure. What emerges is an 'as if' rupture, which is very important for the inventor's claim to be an instrument of God, a prophet, but which is actually founded on a much more piecemeal and combinative basis, which needs to be 'erased' for invention to be recognized as such. So in Sarró's description of the creation of the language and 'graphemes' of Mandombe by Wabeladio Payi we encounter with tremendous precision the double aspect of rupture: destruction as tantamount to creation. In the case described by the author, double rupture occurs through the decontextualization of geometric elements from their tangible foundations, and then the disconnection of the final product from traditional influences – such as the inventor's conversations with Kinshasa artists, mathematicians, linguists and theologians. Invention is therefore the pragmatic use and breaking with material and immaterial origins, which must be erased or forgotten to denote originality: a process of synthesis, the capacity to 'connect the seemingly unconnectable', which allows Wabeladio to 'simultaneously introduce the new and revalue the old' (Sarró, this volume).

The interference involved in this creative process, and the effect that it can have on dominant narratives, leads us to focus on another way in which rupture emerges as an effective ethnographic device: not only does it render emblematic, unifying events multiple or invisible, by shifting the spatio-temporal coordinates and scales at stake, it can also create fissures in the concepts commonly used to oppose Euro-American grand narratives. We are thinking here specifically of notions such as resistance, which as other authors have noted (for example, Abu-Lhugod 1990; Kapferer and Taylor 2012; Mitchell 1990; Ortner 1995; Mbembe 2001) has the potential to be a stultifying grand narrative of subaltern/minority political agency. Rupture, we believe, can act instead to reveal instances in which interference in dominant narratives is more strategic than resistance. In this way, the concept of rupture indicates the voids or gaps produced by acts that we might superficially identify as those of resistance, and the unexpected strategies of interference that fill those gaps. In thinking about her own work in this way, one of the volume's editors, Julia Sauma, suggests that perhaps the most powerful interference for us (the editors) to think with here comes not from prominent political events or religious practice but from apparently more peripheral examples: from what is generally considered to be the collateral damage of contemporary capitalist societies, as yet to be resolved by liberal practices of 'social justice'. Looking to her previous work with street children in Brazilian metropolises, for example, she argues that it is such non-axiomatic contexts that the plentiful gaps produced by thinking with ruptures are most explicit.

Sauma notes that there is a reflex reach for the apparently self-evident idea of socio-economic failure and the need for protective liberal framings when anthropologists are faced with such contexts. Childhood can do this to us. It is a powerful construct, sedimented in our minds and actions by law and everyday collective practice. So what does the ethnographer do when street children themselves persistently break with and escape from the notion that childhood is a spatially and temporally delimited, and therefore subordinate, condition – that the best place for children is under an adult gaze, and that childhood will inevitably end? The enduring return of children to violent streets even when other options are made available, and their practised escape from the end of childhood – such as by dissimulating their ages or forgetting birthdays (Sauma 2007) – are powerful examples of how rupture can be persistently enacted: as recurrent escape from and interference in dominant anti-Black contemporary ideals in Brazil, such as the virtues of security, labour and individual responsibility. Among the street children that she worked with for almost a decade, this interference took the form of performative play, through which they oscillated constantly between the position of dangerous criminal, lost child and responsible workers, to name a few. The interfering rupture that they sought, and that they sought to fill with questions, was thus not with the notion that being a street child was a dangerous condition – none of them could doubt that – but that being an adult and participating in an adult world was a solution: that that world, a world in which their blackness is persistently used as a marker for limiting presents and futures and yet is ideologically denied, was necessarily as coherent, as non-violent as the adults around them tried to make out.

Interference in the coherence of dominant anti-black narratives and ideals does not push against them with an opposing force, as the notion of revolutionary resistance suggests, but rather cuts through them, refusing their logic, their mode of operation, and this can occur in many different ways – as a growing body of literature on indigenous and Black political and cultural expression can attest (e.g. Alves 2018; Hartman 1997, 2007; Moten 2008; Simpson 2014; Sojoyner 2017; Sauma, in preparation). In the case of the street children, rupture with the adult world opens up a prohibited space *in* that world – the street – from where they can identify, observe, experience and manipulate the oscillation that occurs alongside coherence in a 'normal' anti-Black world.

In a similar way, the environmental activists described by Stine Krøijer in her contribution to this volume seek to create internal breaks within a totalizing capitalist system by enacting a slowing down of life and a reconnection with the non-human, a building of alternative structures and practices in the very centre of that system: the 'carbon bombs', the mines, the often unseen and brutally extractive spaces that support capitalist speed and growth. This anti-heroic form of activism, as Krøijer notes, has grown as a response to the perceived failure of approaches historically favoured by the radical Left: the inability of effecting change through protest. In place of the 'spectacular confrontations and clashes with the police and the heroic narratives about it' (Krøijer, this volume), the activists with whom she works see the need to change strategies, to produce a rupture with capitalist structure of domination by doing exactly that which capitalism (and revolution) will not do: by slowing down, by sneaking, dwelling in trees and becoming animal. By doing so her interlocutors seek to create a radical break *within* capitalism, a rupture within the rupture of resistance. This form of rupture is premised on the idea that mundane acts can scale up, potentially creating 'large-scale or delayed systemic effects', reminding us of the potential heat of the moment raised by Carol Greenhouse in her contribution (Krøijer, this volume). The subjective scale of this form of political agency also brings with it uncertainties about what lies ahead, about the ability to endure in this form of rupture, in the internal gaps that this type of activism creates within the system that it is attempting to implode. Once again, we see how thinking with rupture changes the scale and spatio-temporal dimensions of political agency, shifting the focus of activism from grand scale, macho and aggressive political events premised on unwavering certainty to the construction of 'new more-than-human political subjectivities' that abandon male and human vanguardism, enabling avoidance and hesitation rather than resistance, and in doing so awakening 'the brutal realization that something must change' (Krøijer, this volume).

This form of rupture, one in which parallel spatio-temporal coordinates are revealed, can also be identified in Anja Kublitz's description, in this volume, of what happens in the process of becoming a Danish jihadist. In this case, however, it is not oscillation but underlying divine harmony that becomes apparent to the young men who answer the call to fight against a fractured, violent existence of recurrent rupture. Her description therefore shows how the montage of jihadi anasheed (militant Islamist hymns) YouTube videos that her interlocutors watch, which pointedly display the repetitive nature of Muslim suffering and inspire them to travel to Syria, appears to open a portal to them: access to an underlying world of harmony that they can tap into in their daily lives, through which they might be able to transform a history of suffering on repeat, and at the same time experience what their parents and grandparents might have felt once before. This portal is built on the powerful affects produced by the recursive ruptures that are 'always new again', of the everyday lives of peoples profoundly marked by changes such as forced migration and racial discrimination: broken continuities that 'make [the past] reappear, reflecting and intensifying the present' (Kublitz, this volume). In this way, Kublitz argues against a traditional Christian view of rupture as a singular break in a linear continuity, to show how the radical transformative events upon which rupture is based can take various forms and, in the case of her interlocutors, as 'intersecting rhythms' between past, present and future: 'as a continuous repetition of extraordinary transformative events' (Kublitz, this volume). These rhythms are powerful in that they are able not to resist but cut through an 'existing spatio-temporal colonial order', offering a glimpse to an underlying world of harmony 'perfectly made' and ready to be joined, ready to be enacted in the everyday.

The gaps produced by such actions require new descriptive forms, that is clear: if not resistance, for example, then what might be our means to describe the instances of turning away from, breaking with, refusing that we are raising here. As we have seen, the spatio-temporal coordinates and scales evoked to describe these very different moments of rupture are motile, but rupture also has an effect on the metaphors that we might use to describe these instances of interference, multiplication and/or cutting through. The contributors to this volume provide us with a range of new images with which to consider rupture, and this is part of the ethnographic premise of our proposal. We therefore have rupture as the gush of blood, the need for repair, the heat of the moment, leaping, blurring, sneaking and rhythm. In relation to the most cataclysmic events described in this volume, in Edward Simpson and Michele Serafini's analysis of the aftermaths of earthquakes in India and Nepal, rupture is therefore used by the authors to identify the different levels – the physical and emotional, familial and material, political and religious – of the shock caused by these disasters, and how they establish the condition for new possibilities. The breaking apart of land might appear as one of the most powerful images that we can conjure, but in its stead it is rupture that the authors use to identify the different levels – the physical and emotional, familial and material, political and religious – of the shock caused by these disasters, and how they establish the condition for new possibilities.

Significantly it is the aftermath of rupture that concerns the authors, who can therefore directly answer any doubts that we might have over the unforeseeable consequences of the cataclysmic events described by some of our other contributors: that in the long term rupture not only leads to new forms of cooperation but also to conflict and to the restoration of older patterns; destruction does not wipe the slate clean. In describing moments in which there is a 'general sense ... that history had imploded into a rumbling moment and meaning had collapsed' (Simpson and Serafini, this volume), it is therefore notable that the authors describe how – much as in the aftermath of ritual liminal moments of *communitas* (Turner 1969) – in the aftermath of earthquakes relations are renewed between people and the state, leading to a renegotiation of these relations, to the appearance of new vocabularies and solutions. However, it is also interesting to note how the tools for this renegotiation do not just emerge from the places and peoples at stake, but the way disaster marks the influx of intervention of various kinds, the bureaucratic, financial, infrastructural and divine, which are sought out to impose some form of control over what these chaotic moments are able to produce.

Fissures and openings

Taken alongside the preceding chapters, then, Simpson and Serafini bear out our emphasis throughout this volume on conceptualizing rupture as a creative/destructive dynamic, which operates in many ways as what is currently being discussed as a 'singularity' (see Stengers 2000). Seen in the light of the chapters of this volume, rupture can be understood as a moment of differentiating and generating intensity, creatively emergent from the destructive force either of a natural sort (earthquakes, floods, volcanic eruptions) or of human manufacture, though always specifically as a dynamic of sociocultural formation. If destruction is a vital dimension of rupture, such destruction has immanent *within it* a creative and regenerative potential that is never the reproduction of the same but always of difference. As Deleuze might have said (1994), it is a dynamic energy of repetition or the continuity of the existential terms of human life – always a sociocultural phenomenon – through creative regenerative (re)construction. It is in rupturing moments and in the reverberations of rupturing effect (their aftershocks as it were) in which the social and cultural nature of human being as constant unfolding potential is revealed, in multilinear and multidirectional ways. In a sense, the nature of human being can never be known in any causally originating sense – a particular essentialism in anthropology that has largely been discarded – but only through the way in which human beings create the terms (or objectifications) of their existence and action (Kapferer 2014).

Such an emphasis on the capacity of rupture to reformulate the coordinates of people's existence raises the broader methodological question of how such a forcefully regenerative potential can be described without fear of reducing it to the very terms with which it seeks by its nature to break, this being a feature that our conception of rupture as a singularity shares with Alain Badiou's conception of the 'event' (2007). Indeed, the question of how anthropological language is affected by the kinds of ruptures we present in this volume is central to our proposition.

The ruptures presented here do not only point to previously unseen fissures in the emblematic images of rupture we inherit from the grand narratives of modernity, interfering with and cutting into the putative heroism of rupture as grand Event (a heroism that Badiou's theorization, incidentally, ratifies entirely – see also Humphrey 2008; Laidlaw et al. 2018 – and from which we seek to find ethnographically driven routes of escape in the present volume). The chapters also explore new descriptive forms that can get to grips with the kinds of situations ruptures engender, and the forms of life they format, doing justice to the character of rupture as at once destructive and generative – its dual aspect, as we call it, which makes it irreducible to standard social scientific dilemmas between, for example, continuity and change.

The question we are left with, then, is whether, as anthropologists working in the current historical juncture, we are ready to break with the legitimating controls of the discipline, which demand that we always end our analyses with the aplomb of certainty as the signature of analytical success – of our job well done. Perhaps a test of this lies in how we might conclude this brief introduction to the chapters that follow. Our sense is that breaking with the academic compulsion toward producing grand narratives must involve breaking also with the linearity of such arguments and forms of thinking. This feels particularly important at this present moment of turmoil and rupture – one that, as so many of the chapters show explicitly, defies any sense of linearity (e.g. Humphrey, Greenhouse, Sarró) or indeed clarity and consistency of scale (e.g. Krøjer; Kublitz; Simpson and Serafini). Such a focus, we suggest, necessarily stands against any ultimate kind of unifying narrative about the forcefulness of rupture. Instead, what we have here are also a series of attempts to trace in the narrative form of ethnographic engagement how what we have to say about rupture can break with itself at every turn, demonstrating its violently incisive power in its very action.

Note

1. Max Weber was consciously using a railway metaphor to indicate a radical change of direction. Weber was interested in those moments in history that were new directions and ultimately irreducible to the past with which they are continuous. Thus, he was interested in what are referred to as axial moments, for example the advent of Christianity and of Islam that have related but different and major implications for history. It is noteworthy that Weber used a railway metaphor, appropriate to the technological era of modernity with which his sociology was largely concerned, and which focused on the redirections and turning points in the heterogeneous 'tracks' along which history unfolds.

References

Abramson, Allen, and Martin Holbraad, eds. 2014. *Framing Cosmologies: The Anthropology of Worlds*. Manchester: Manchester University Press.

Abu-Lughod, Lila. 1990. 'The Romance of Resistance: Tracing Transformations of Power through Bedouin Women'. *American Ethnologist* 17 (1): 41–55.

Adorno, Theodor W. 1990. *Negative Dialectics*. London: Routledge.

Agamben, Giorgio. 2005. *State of Exception*. Chicago: University of Chicago Press.

Alves, Jaime Amparo. 2018. *The Anti-Black City: Police Terror and Black Urban Life in Brazil*. Minneapolis: University of Minnesota Press.

Arendt, Hannah. 1965. *On Revolution*. London: Penguin Books.

Badiou, Alain. 2003. *Saint Paul: The Foundations of Universalism*. Translated by Ray Brassier. Stanford, CA: Stanford University Press.

Badiou, Alain. 2007. *Being and Event*. Translated by Oliver Feltham. London: Continuum.

Barad, Karen. 2007. *Meeting the Universe Halfway: Quantum Physics and the Entanglement of Matter and Meaning*. Durham, NC: Duke University Press.

Berman, Marshall. 1988. *All That is Solid Melts into Air: The Experience of Modernity*. New York: Penguin Books.

Bey, Hakim. 1991. *TAZ: The Temporary Autonomous Zone, Ontological Anarchy, Poetic Terrorism*. Brooklyn, NY: Autonomedia.

Bonnet, Alberto R. 2009. 'Antagonism and Difference: Negative Dialectics and Poststructuralism in View of the Critique of Modern Capitalism'. In *Negativity and Revolution: Adorno and Political Activism*, edited by John Holloway, Fernando Matamoros, and Sergio Tischle, 41–78. London: Pluto Press.

Braidotti, Rosi. 2006. 'Post Human, All Too Human: Towards a New Process Ontology'. *Theory, Culture, and Society* 23 (7–8): 197–208.

Candea, Matei, Joanna Cook, Catherine Trundle and Thomas Yarrow. 2015. *Detachment: Essays on the Limits of Relational Thinking*. Manchester: Manchester University Press.

Christensen, Clayton M., Michael E. Raynor and Rory McDonald. 2015. 'What is Disruptive Innovation?' *Harvard Business Review* 93: 44–53.

DeLanda, Manuel. 2006. *A New Philosophy of Society: Assemblage Theory and Social Complexity*. London and New York: Continuum.

Deleuze, Gilles. 1991. *Bergsonism*. New York: Zone.

Deleuze, Gilles. 1994. *Difference and Repetition*. Translated by Paul Patton. London: Athlone Press.

Deleuze, Gilles, and Felix Guattari. 1987. *A Thousand Plateaus*. Minneapolis: University of Minnesota Press.

Eisenstein, Paul, and Todd McGowan. 2012. *Rupture: On the Emergence of the Political*. Evanston, IL: Northwestern University Press.

Evens, T.M.S., and Don Handelman. 2006. *The Manchester School: Practice and Ethnographic Praxis in Anthropology*. New York: Berghahn Books.

Fanon, Frantz. 2007. *Black Skins, White Masks*. New York: Grove Press.

Gluckman, Max. 1955. *Custom and Conflict in Africa*. Oxford: Blackwell.

Gluckman, Max. 1963. *Order and Rebellion in Tribal Africa*. London: Cohen and West.

Graeber, David. 2018. 'The "Yellow Vests" Show How Much the Ground Moves under our Feet'. Accessed 9 December. http://criticallegalthinking.com/2018/12/09/the-yellow-vests-show-how-much-the-ground-moves-under-our-feet/

Hardt, Michael, and Colectivo Situaciones. 2007. 'Leer a Macherey'. In *Hegel o Spinoza*, Pierre Macherey, 5–16. Buenos Aires: Tinta Limón.

Hardt, Michael, and Antonio Negri. 2000. *Empire*. Cambridge, MA, and London: Harvard University Press.

Hardt, Michael, and Antonio Negri. 2004. *Multitude: War and Democracy in the Age of Empire*. London: Penguin Books.

Hartman, Saidiya V. 1997. *Scenes of Subjection: Terror, Slavery and Self-Making in Nineteenth-Century America*. Oxford: Oxford University Press.

Hartman, Saidiya V. 2007. *Lose Your Mother: A Journey along the Atlantic Slave Route*. New York: Farrar, Strauss & Giroux.

Herzfeld, Michael. 1997. *Cultural Intimacy: Social Poetics in the Nation-State*. London and New York: Routledge.

Hirsch, Eric, and Charles Stewart. 2005. 'Introduction: Ethnographies of Historicity'. *History and Anthropology* 16 (3): 261–74.

Hobsbawm, Eric. 1995. *Age of Extremes: The Short Twentieth Century, 1914–1991*. London: Abacus.

Hodges, Matt. 2010. 'The Time of the Interval: Historicity, Modernity, and Epoch in Rural France'. *American Ethnologist* 37 (1): 115–31.

Holbraad, Martin, and Morten A. Pedersen. 2017. *The Ontological Turn: An Anthropological Exposition*. Cambridge: Cambridge University Press.

Holbraad, Martin, Morten A. Pedersen and Eduardo Viveiros de Castro. 2014. 'The Politics of Ontology: Anthropological Positions'. Accessed 13 January. http://culanth.org/fieldsights/462-the-politics-of-ontology-anthropological-positions.

Holloway, John, Fernando Matamoros and Sergio Tischle, eds. 2009. *Negativity and Revolution: Adorno and Political Activism*. London: Pluto Press.

Humphrey, Caroline. 2008. 'Reassembling the Individual Subject: Events and Decisions in Troubled Times'. *Anthropological Theory* 8 (4): 357–80.

Ingold, Tim. 2011. *Being Alive: Essays on Movement, Knowledge and Description*. London and New York: Routledge.

Jameson, Fredric. 2003. 'Future City'. *New Left Review* 21: 65–79.

Juris, Jeffrey S. 2008. *Networking Futures: The Movements against Corporate Globalization*. Durham, NC, and London: Duke University Press.

Kapferer, Bruce. 2010. *Legends of People, Myths of State: Violence, Intolerance, and Political Culture in Sri Lanka and Australia*. Oxford: Berghahn Books.

Kapferer, Bruce. 2014. *2001 and Counting: Kubrick, Nietzsche, and Anthropology*. Chicago: University of Chicago Press.

Kapferer, B., and C. Taylor. 2012. 'Introduction: Forces in the Production of the State'. In *Contesting the State: The Dynamics of Resistance and Control*, edited by Angela Hobart and Bruce Kapferer, 1–20. Herefordshire: Sean Kingston Publishing.

Knight, Daniel M., and Charles Stewart. 2016. 'Ethnographies of Austerity: Temporality, Crisis and Affect in Southern Europe'. *History and Anthropology* 27 (1): 1–18.

Kosellek, Reinhart. 2005. *Futures Past: On the Semantics of Historical Time*. Translated by Keith Tribe. New York: Columbia University Press.

Laidlaw, James, Barbara Bodenhorn and Martin Holbraad, eds. 2018. *Recovering the Human Subject: Freedom, Creativity and Decision*. Cambridge: Cambridge University Press.

Laruelle, François. 2010. *Philosophies of Difference: A Critical Introduction to Non-Philosophy*. Translated by Rocco Gangle. New York: Continuum.

Latour, Bruno. 1999. *Pandora's Hope: Essays on the Reality of Science Studies*. Cambridge, MA: Harvard University Press.

Latour, Bruno. 2005. *Reassembling the Social: An Introduction to Actor-Network-Theory*. Oxford: Oxford University Press.

Lyotard, Jean-François. 1984. *The Postmodern Condition: A Report on Knowledge*. Manchester: Manchester University Press.

Marchart, Oliver. 2007. *Post-Foundational Political Thought: Political Difference in Nancy, Lefort, Badiou and Laclau*. Edinburgh: Edinburgh University Press.

Masco, Joseph. 2017. 'The Crisis in Crisis'. *Current Anthropology* 58 (S15): S65–S76.

Mbembe, Achille. 2001. *On the Postcolony*. Berkeley: University of California Press.

Meinert, Lotte, and Bruce Kapferer, eds. 2015. *In the Event: Toward an Anthropology of Generic Moments*. Oxford: Berghahn Books.

Mills, C. Wright. 2000. *The Sociological Imagination (The 40th Anniversary Edition)*. Oxford: Oxford University Press.

Mitchell, Timothy. 1990. 'Everyday Metaphors of Power'. *Theory and Society* 19 (5): 545–77.

Moten, Fred. 2008. 'The Case of Blackness'. *Criticism* 50 (2): 177–218.

Ortner, Sherry. 1995. 'Resistance and the Problem of Ethnographic Refusal'. *Comparative Studies in Society and History* 37 (1): 173–93.

Povinelli, Elizabeth. 2012. 'The Will to be Otherwise / The Effort of Endurance'. *South Atlantic Quarterly* 111: 453–7.

Robbins, Joel. 2004. *Becoming Sinners: Christianity and Moral Torment in a Papua New Guinea Society*. Berkeley: University of California Press.

Robbins, Joel. 2007. 'Continuity Thinking and the Problem of Christian Culture'. *Current Anthropology* 48: 5–38.

Robbins, Joel. 2010. 'Anthropology, Pentecostalism and the New Paul: Conversion, Event and Social Transformation'. *South Atlantic Quarterly* 109 (4): 633–52.

Roitman, Janet. 2013. *Anti-Crisis*. Durham, NC: Duke University Press.

Rubenstein, Mary-Jane. 2012. 'Cosmic Singularities: On the Nothing and the Sovereign'. *Journal of the American Academy of Religion* 80 (2): 485–517.

Sahlins, Marshall. 1985. *Islands of History*. Chicago: University of Chicago Press.

Sauma, Julia. 2007. 'Encontros Cartografados: reflexões sobre encontros entre meninos e educadores de rua'. *Cadernos de Campo* 15 (14–15): 41–63.

Sauma, Julia. 2016. 'Palavras carnais: sobre re-lembrar e re-esquecer, ser e não ser, entre os Filhos do Erepecuru'. *Revista de Antropologia* 59 (3): 150–73.

Sauma, Julia. In preparation. *Collective: A Maroon Sociology*. Monograph.

Schumpeter, Joseph A. 1994. *Capitalism, Socialism and Democracy*. London: Routledge.

Scott, David. 2004. *Conscripts of Modernity: The Tragedy of Colonial Enlightenment*. Durham, NC, and London: Duke University Press.

Serres, Michel, and Bruno Latour. 1995. *Conversations on Science, Culture, and Time*. Ann Arbor: University of Michigan Press.

Simpson, Audra. 2014. *Mohawk Interruptus: Political Life across the Borders of Settler States*. Durham, NC: Duke University Press.

Sojoyner, Damien M. 2017. *First Strike: Educational Enclosures in Black Los Angeles*. Minneapolis: University of Minnesota Press.

Stengers, Isabelle. 2000. *The Invention of Modern Science*. Minneapolis: University of Minnesota Press.

Stengers, Isabelle. 2014. *Thinking with Whitehead: A Free and Wild Creation of Concepts*. Translated by Michael Chase. Cambridge, MA: Harvard University Press.

Stoler, Ana Laura. 2016. *Duress: Imperial Durabilities in Our Times*. Durham, NC: Duke University Press.

Strathern, Marilyn. 1988. *The Gender of the Gift: Problems with Women and Problems with Society in Melanesia*. Berkeley: University of California Press.

Strathern, Marilyn. 1995. *The Relation: Issues in Complexity and Scale*. Cambridge: Prickly Pear Pamphlet no. 6.

Tsing, Anna. 2015. *The Mushroom at the End of the World: On the Possibility of Life in Capitalist Ruins*. Princeton: Princeton University Press.

Turner, Victor. 1969. *The Ritual Process*. London: Routledge, Kegan and Paul.

Turner, Victor. 1975. *Revelation and Divination in Ndembu Ritual*. Ithaca, NY: Cornell University Press.

Venkatesan, Soumhya, Matei Candea, Casper Bruun Jensen, Morten Axel Pedersen, James Leach, and Gillian Evans. 2012. 'The Task of Anthropology is to Invent Relations: 2010 Meeting of the Group for Debates in Anthropological Theory'. *Critique of Anthropology* 32 (1): 43–86.

Viveiros de Castro, Eduardo. 2003. *AND*. Manchester Papers in Social Anthropology 7.

Viveiros de Castro, Eduardo. 2013. 'The Relative Native'. *Hau: Journal of Ethnographic Theory* 3 (3): 473–502.

Weber, Max. 1930. *The Protestant Ethic and the Spirit of Capitalism*. London: George Allen & Unwin.

Žižek, Slavoj. 2000. 'Holding the Place'. In *Contingency, Hegemony, Universality: Contemporary Dialogues on the Left*, edited by Judith Butler, Ernesto Laclau and Slavoj Žižek, 308–29. London and New York: Verso.

Žižek, Slavoj. 2010. *On Violence: Six Sideways Reflections*. London: Profile Books.

1

The Guillotine: Reflections on Violent Revolutionary Rupture

Caroline Humphrey

Introduction

The guillotine is routinely associated with the French Revolution, but I shall suggest that one value of thinking about the killing machine itself is that it forces us to realize that 'rupture' is not the same as 'revolution' and requires its own analysis. Crucially, the two have a different relation to time, or more exactly they have different 'time-forms'. While most revolutions begin, or their actors imagine they begin, with rupture, this is but the initiatory moment in their onward process of transforming politics and society (Holbraad 2018). Along the way they face opposition, confusion and internal divisions, and the need to work out on the go what the new arrangements are to be. Hence revolutions occur in stages, a sequence of bursts and retreats, and it is often difficult to tell when they begin and when they end (Herrmann 2011). Rupture, as I use the word, has a different shape: by definition it is a splitting apart of something that was previously joined or a whole, and it is conceived as a singular moment. It will be argued here that a moment of political rupture has to be bidirectional, in that actors inhabiting that point in time have to face the past as well as the future. In other words, rupture is a radical cut that is at the same time a 'break from' and a 'break towards'. There is nothing simple about this idea. Since the event of rupture includes not only the time of the severance itself but also the visions by which both the before and the after are imagined, it contains a notional internal trifurcation. There is a further complexity, namely that it is only amid political strife and with imaginative strain that something vividly present now can be turned into a thing of the past, while elaborate efforts are simultaneously made to call into being the things of the future. The split is in practice convoluted, since each of the elements as they are understood on the spot affects the character of the others. This chapter will suggest that the trifurcation and convolution of rupture are evident not only in political events but also appears in the subjectivities of the actors in diverse ways. The guillotining of Louis XVI in January 1793 is a moment of rupture that exemplifies these points.

Studies of French politics at that time suggest that the past as then conceived was coloured as tyranny precisely by the ways in which it contravened the virtues of the new society being initiated. The glowing 'future coming into being' was relational too – it was bringing into existence institutions that glimmered not only with a forward but also with a vengeful backward-looking light. The time now starting was still coloured to a great extent negatively, by the dark features of the betrayals, insults and injustices that must immediately be punished. Yet at the same time, this future also shone with the pure light from a deeper past, since the break was conceived by many revolutionary leaders as a return to once existing 'natural rights' – the rights to life, liberty and property that Rousseau had claimed natural to humanity before it was deformed by the evolution of society. This was a world view (though not the only one) through which the existential break at the juncture of these complicated and mutually influenced pasts and futures – the execution of the king – was conceived to be fertile. Starkly, the killing cut itself was politically 'life-giving': the display of the king's severed head was followed by silence, then the cries 'Long live the Republic! Long live the nation!' Robespierre had expressed the thought when he declared: 'It is with regret I pronounce this fatal truth: Louis must die so that the nation may live' (Robespierre 1958, 130). As this chapter will show, however, this idea of 'national life' was far from the only way in which execution by guillotine was imagined by the population to produce vitality. Indeed, over a wider compass of time, it was prolific with new sensations, excitements, fears and strangely productive pathologies.

There is a question that should be addressed first: can the guillotining of the king be said to be *the* rupture of the French Revolution? Historians, the populace and the state have named other revolutionary events as the moment of rupture. In particular, 14 July 1789, the date of the storming of the Bastille prison, was a day that became The Day. It came to signify the founding moment of the Revolution and therefore a historical rupture. Already a grand public festival on its first anniversary, in 1794 it became the *Fête de l'Etre Suprême* at which Robespierre declaimed: 'Nature, how sublime, how delightful thy power! How the tyrants must turn pale at the thought of this Festival' – though Christopher Prendergast commenting on this declaration remarks that the tyrants 'were more likely to turn pale at the thought of the guillotine, which for the duration of the festival has been discreetly moved from view to – of all places – the site of the now demolished Bastille' (Prendergast 2008, 17).

It was 14 July that was taken up by the French state as the cardinal national holiday, a point I will return to later, but meanwhile it should be noted that several other events have been claimed by historians as just as significant, even more truly ruptural in a political sense. For as it was happening the attack on the Bastille was not conceived as a project of ending monarchy (it was mainly a rush to acquire arms from the prison's store for self-protection against royal troops). The achievements claimed for it – the capitulation of the king, its designation as an act of the people's sovereign will that would transform the political system, the invention of a new concept of revolution – were all conferred on the event after it had happened (Sewell 1996); whereas the meeting of the Estates General in May 1789, the Declaration of the Rights of Man and the Citizen in August that year, the reinvention of dates itself and declaration of a new calendar in November 1793, the official end of the monarchy on 21 September 1793, and the founding of the Republic on the 22nd, were all regime changers in themselves. I can see no problem with acknowledging that a revolution might contain within itself several crucial breaks that might metaphorically be called ruptures. But the beheading of the king in January 1793, and more broadly the Terror, the period between September 1793 and July 1794 when thousands were guillotined, was rupture in the most direct sense. It was understood to be a rending apart *in itself*, as it happened and not by virtue of some subsequent designation. It combined – uneasily – the three elements of how 'rupture' can be thought: the biological-material, the ideational-symbolic and the political. Further, as a devastating experience for participants and onlookers, it had an unexpected psychic afterlife, a bizarre and diverse existence in subsequent decades that has something important to say about the ongoing social implications of violence.

Matters at stake

It is very difficult to discuss the Terror as a point of rupture without a brief preliminary survey of the turbulent intellectual debates about what the Terror *was* as a political event. The beheading of the king curdled radically opposed political philosophies and thus it represented, and still to some extent represents, rifts in social and moral judgement. I provide a short outline – indeed outrageously brief in view of the mass of writing on this subject – in order to acquaint readers with what at least some of the stakes are. Even for contemporaries in the eighteenth century, the guillotine stood for several sharply conflicting positions. For radical Republicans, it was the just and efficient instrument that demonstrated *égalité* and the will of the people (kings and workmen, they all die in exactly the same way); indeed, the clean cut of the guillotine was regarded as humanitarian, in comparison to earlier frantic mob carnage. For conservatives, the guillotine represented the barbaric bloody violence that destroyed the 'natural bonds' of society and religion; while for moderate Republicans it stood for an impending tyranny that threatened progressive ideals of democracy and liberty.

Later interpretations that influenced the way the Revolution is understood today have been set out by one of the most renowned historians of the Revolution, Francois Furet. As he explains (1998), most nineteenth-century historians were champions of the Revolution and adhered to Rousseau's theory of the general will; that is, the idea that politics is largely about the process of discovering the will of the nation. This later solidified into a Marxist orthodoxy according to which the Revolution was not just a battle to overcome evil (absolute monarchy) and replace it with good (republican democracy), but was also a deeper transformation through class conflict, in which feudalism gave way to capitalism. After the overthrow of the monarchy, the conflict shifted to pit the capitalist bourgeoisie against the urban political movement led by the sans-culottes with their vision of a truly social revolution. With this overall positive view historians could nevertheless understand the Terror in different ways. The Revolution was divided into phases. For loyalists of the Revolution, the Terror had to be separated off as a temporary aberration in the general trajectory. It was the consequence of 'the intentional villainy of historical actors', or alternatively it was elevated to the cosmological-theological, being understood as the outcome of the design of Providence (Furet 1998, 55). For some writers, far from being consubstantial with the Revolution, the Terror manifested, on the contrary, 'the emergence of its antithesis, its anti-principle, the resurrection of the [despotic] Ancien Régime and the corruption of the new by the old' (1998, 56).

Radical Jacobin republicans, on the other hand, did not reject the Terror. They explained it as necessary, since the revolutionaries faced both internal and external enemies. In their view, according to Furet, the Terror was nevertheless separable from the Revolution, being not intrinsic but merely one of its risks, and if the killing phase was particularly 'heroic' this was because it achieved victory, not because of the means it used to do so. Furet himself attacked the 'Marxist catechism' of the class struggle reading, and returned to political theory and intellectual-cultural history; he refused to separate the Terror from the Revolution, seeing it as the logical result of the reconceptualization of politics, which was now based on popular sovereignty. The Terror was the Revolution's culmination, quite plainly an abuse of power, achieved through demagoguery in the name of the people.

The American historian Arno Mayer (2001) has developed Furet's argument to discuss terror comparatively in the French and Russian revolutions. He argues, in summary, that there is no true revolution without violence and terror; that terror takes several forms, both 'wild' and 'would-be legitimate'; that its initiation stems from the radical breakdown of political authority; that terror is driven by a dialectical interaction between revolution and counter-revolution; and that a key element in this interaction is religious confrontation (in the case of France between secular millenarianism and the fanaticism of folk Catholicism). However, Mayer, unlike Furet, downplays the importance of revolutionary ideology. He argues that terror directly emerges out of the revolutionary process itself, from the confrontation with the real threat of counter-revolution.[1] This conclusion is supported by Timothy Tackett (2001, 570–2), who emphasizes more than Mayer the stimulant of fear among the revolutionaries and the emergence among them of an obsession with conspiracy and hidden counterplots. This is splendidly illustrated by a revolutionary poster in which the aristocracy is depicted as a Janus-like figure: a demonic, knife-wielding priest and a simpering lady are bound together by a serpent, while a cloven hoof and a claw appear from under their gowns. The legend reads: 'The aristocracy unmasked. Beware of its caresses, its thousand arms are ready to strike you' (Tackett 2000, 690).

Most germane to this chapter, however, is the work of Sophie Wahnich (2003; 2009; 2012), a writer of the Left who nevertheless eschews a directly Marxist account. She argues that the Terror can only be understood, and its political import comprehended, by thinking about the emotions that compelled it and which it generated. For her, the Terror was not a rational recourse of government, the only way to maintain order (i.e. through imposing fear) when all civic institutions had been overturned, as the revolutionary Saint-Just had argued (Sonenscher 2008, 404). Rather, it came about as an emotional reaction to insult, the aristocracy's refusal to accord sovereign right to the new Republic, surging first as frenzied vengeance for the assassination of the revolutionary hero Marat in July 1793. This vengeance was not that of an individual psychological kind, nor the expression of primitive animal instinct, nor was it a displacement of religious ideas into politics; rather this vengeance was a *foundational violence*, one that gave a new possibility for bringing men together, and it is best understood in the light of the dismantling and remaking of social relations, and of sacrificial ritual and sacred violence (Wahnich 2003, 21–2). Other writers, such as William Sewell in his magisterial study of the Bastille, reserve the notion of foundational violence for the glorious 14 July (Sewell 1996, 859); but Wahnich refuses to dissociate 1789 from 1793, and thus in effect she defends the Terror, characterizing it as a *response* to the counter-revolutionaries' threat to terrorize the people. This idea of relational responses is why she advances the idea of an economy of emotions – in which initiatory actions were imagined as 'paybacks' in return for the anger of an enemy. What is important, she writes, is to understand which political sacra were the foundation of the circulation of emotions that led to the Terror (2003, 24–6). They were justice, honour and the masses' identity as 'the people' and as the victors. Thus, the Terror in Wahnich's account appears as a form of constitutive justice corresponding to a new social configuration, that of the sovereign people (2003, 43–4).

Wahnich's works contain important discussions of how her interpretation relates to the argument that the Terror was the precedent for twentieth-century totalitarianism, to Agamben's theory of *Homo sacer* and the sovereign exception, and above all to contemporary terrorism (Wahnich 2009). But for now I will leave these questions aside in order to focus on the anthropology and ethnography of the Terror as rupture.

Anthropologizing a historical event

Given these conflicting understandings of what the Terror and the Revolution were (ontologically), it seems to me that anthropologists could best approach them as 'matters of concern' (Latour 2004). Latour advocated against deconstructing swirling debate, facts, opinions and emotion to get at the truth. Rather he was aiming at a new realism concerned with 'things', in which 'a thing is in one sense an object out there and, in another sense, an *issue* very much *in* there', in a gathering of participants (2004, 233, emphasis in original). 'The critic is not the one who lifts the rugs from under the feet of the naïve believers, but the one who offers participants arenas in which to gather' (Tafarella 2012).

In our case, the contents of any 'arena' offered by anthropologists will be filled in – short of becoming a historian oneself – by the materials supplied by social historians, with their accumulation of painstaking research on places, dates, persons and eyewitness accounts. Some of their work also raises what we can readily see as anthropological issues – that is, interpretations, using concepts developed by the authors that would be alien to eighteenth-century participants but make sense in terms of the intellectual history of their discipline. An example is Lynn Hunt's Freudian influenced argument (2013) that the French Revolution was imagined through a new conceptualization of patriarchy and the familial order. And as Thomassen points out (2012), there are many classical theories developed in anthropology that could be turned to analysing revolution, such as Van Gennep on ritual, Simmel on crowd behaviour, Turner on liminality and Bateson on schismogenesis. However potentially productive these ideas might be, I do not propose to return to them in this chapter, which is concerned specifically with rupture. Instead I turn to the newer anthropology focused on the event, ontology and experience, hoping in this way to offer an 'arena' for gathering that is indeed composed as far as possible of contemporary participants, rather than retrospective analysts. Such anthropology, I am convinced, is needed to deal with the singular *physical and conceptual* moment of rupture that the guillotine brings so vividly before us.

Admittedly, the guillotine is a grim object around which to enable a gathering. But it is a brilliantly 'contrary' kind of case if we are thinking about the co-presence of the physical and conceptual that I am arguing for; the point may appear glib, or even obvious, but it is worth pointing out that arguing for it goes against the grain – runs contrary to countless descriptions, narratives and rhetorical statements from the time of the Terror that separated body from mind. For the cut effected by the guillotine was not the splitting of an object into two similar parts, like slicing an apple in half. It was the separation of a person's *head*, with all of its connotations of mind and personality, from their *body*, with its implied merely physical nature. The decapitation of Louis XVI was a particular point of concentration that brought into focus and then threw up and multiplied many antinomies: on top of mind and body there tottered an edifice of sacred king versus mere man, monarchy versus republic, tyranny versus freedom, abstract reason versus history and indeed life versus death. 'Rupture' is a capacious idea that can accommodate the splitting that took place on so many 'levels', or rather within so many kinds of discourse. Yet it is a properly anthropological task to *query* this capaciousness, to inquire about the grounds for the proliferation of conceptual bifurcations, and in particular to investigate the idea that politically conceived oppositions might be placed in relational tension by physical/mental combinations thrown up in the actual experience of beheading. Actually, if we consider the philosophy, political and social history, psychology and psychoanalysis, art history and indeed subsequent revolutionary activist theory that has been devoted to the French Revolution, I do not think that anthropology can provide anything more than a partial view of the event of rupture. Still, it is worth trying to think about what that might be.

The historical 'we' of the Terror

That being said, I hope readers will forgive me for preparing the ground by starting with Hegel and Kant. Although of different generations, they were contemporaries of the Terror and both had interesting things to say about the Revolution that can orient an anthropological view of rupture, in particular if the aim is not just to write another anthropologically inflected social history but also to 'gather in' the philosophical ruminations that gave meaning to such a brutal happening. Hegel in *The Philosophy of Spirit* is concerned to understand how a finite event, the French Revolution, could take on a universal, transcendental character ('spirit'), such that it could be conceived as having in some sense happened to us all. His critique of the Terror was that in their efforts to institute a new conception of human freedom – absolute ahistorical human freedom – the Republicans were forced to turn on themselves and to destroy the very institutions of freedom they had created. As David Ciavatta argues, this meant that for Hegel the Revolution was a failed attempt to efface its own character as a *historical* event, its actual contingency and spatio-temporal contingency. As the voice of timeless reason, the Revolution was inherently incapable of owning up to its own historicity (Ciavatta 2014, 579).[2] This argument is crucial for Hegel because it reveals the impossibility of a rationality that is wholly detached from history. The event of the Terror, by which the Revolution annihilated itself, thus becomes for Hegel a decisive revelation of the historical nature of reason itself. The Terror cannot be understood as the vehicle of a rationality that exists independently or prior to these events, but must be understood as having its own thought process that gives efficacy and compelling authority to a rationality that could not exist at any other moment (Ciavatta 2014, 580).

Kant, older by a generation, makes a not dissimilar argument, though in a completely different way. In his work on enlightenment and revolution, as described by Foucault, Kant's question is: what is this 'now', which we all inhabit and which defines the moment in which I am writing? What is there in this present that can have contemporary meaning for philosophical reflection? Kant's response is that this meaningful element manifests itself in the bearer of a process of thought, someone who forms part of this same process, figuring in it. To be a philosopher is not a question of adherence to an ideology, nor belonging to the human community in general, but of membership in a particular 'we', corresponding to a cultural ensemble characteristic of his own contemporaneity. The French Revolution, like the Enlightenment, was an event in the history of thought that created such a 'we'. It does not consist of its successes or failures, its overturning of institutions or its crimes. Rather, its meaning lies in its operation as a spectacle and in its re-memorable, demonstrative and diagnostic character as an event. In effect, the bearers of this meaning are all the people who may not have taken part in it but allow themselves to be swept away by it. According to Kant such approbation emerges from a moral disposition of humanity: to provide a government for itself that seems good to itself, virtuous and renouncing external war. This is why the Revolution, which reveals this thought, can never be forgotten, even if the actual result was to slump back into something like the old rut (Foucault 1986, 92–4).

Hegel and Kant both suggest, at least to my mind, that understanding the Terror requires placing the philosopher *in the middle of it*, as a necessarily historical actor experiencing its particular reasoning and enthusiasm. So what could this have meant in an event as ghastly as rupture effected specifically by the use of the guillotine? Perhaps the best way to think about this is to consider the similarities and differences between the so-called 'September massacres' of 1792 and the Terror proper initiated by the guillotining of the king in January 1793. In September crowds had attacked virtually the entire prison population of Paris, in the fear that the inmates would break out and join the enemies then invading France. The subsequent decision to employ the guillotine by the revolutionary regime, in public and surrounded by thousands of soldiers, was rationalized as the terrible but orderly justice of the state. The contrast between the two episodes of violence can be seen in the killing of the Princess de Lamballe, whose ghastly end also has some interesting things to say to us.[3]

On 3 September 1792, the princess was extracted from prison, and 'gasping for breath, held at arm's length, almost unconscious' she was led before a hurriedly improvised Tribune of the People.[4] She was sentenced to death, to be 'sent away' (*élargie*) in the euphemistic language of the Tribune. Two men carried her into the street; she was struck with sabres on her head and neck, stabbed in the eye. She tried to fall down to die, but the crowd forced her onto her feet. A certain Charlat knocked her senseless with a log, and then the crowd attacked her body until it was a shapeless, bloody, unrecognizable thing. A butcher's boy named Grison cut off her head. A procession then set off dragging the macabre trophies, pulling a rope attached to the princess's feet. It visited her family's Paris residence, then the place of imprisonment of the royal family. The head, people said, was brought to make a bow to Marie-Antoinette, before parading both head and body in the streets of Paris. In the words of an observer:

> We heard tumultuous and prolonged shouts: they were here! Two individuals dragged a naked body by its legs, headless, its back on the ground and its abdomen laid open to the chest. The cortege halts. On a shaky platform, the corpse is ceremoniously spread out, and the limbs arranged with a kind of art, and, above all, a *sang froid*, which leaves a vast field to the meditations of the wise. To my right, at the end of a lance, was a head that often brushed against my face because of the movements the bearer made when he gesticulated. To my left, another one, more horrible, held in one hand the intestines of the victim against his chest, and in the other a large knife. Behind them, a large collier hung from a lance, above my forehead, a scrap of camisole soaked with blood and mire. (De Baecque 2003, 62)[5]

The crowd demanded the presence of the royal family at the window to witness the body and hear the shouts demanding the head of Marie-Antoinette; the corpse was then taken to be presented to the Duc d'Orléans, the princess's brother-in-law, amid constant tumult, oaths and roars of triumph. The crowd disposed of the body at a construction site near Chatelet, where it was left naked all night, and next day taken to be buried at the Foundlings' Cemetery.

What is common to the execution of the king and that of Lamballe is that the dismembered physical parts were not ignored as embodiments of the rejected past, but instead became a matter of extraordinary attention. The revolutionary future and the abhorred past were both kept in full view. In fact, it is not just that the 'revealed, paraded, exhibited, tortured body is like the support of the judiciary procedure … that must become readable for everyone' (Foucault 1977, 47–8), the corpse also became an object of hatred and wild phantasmagoric visions released during or immediately after the killing.

The death of the princess, like that of the king, can be seen as a 'thing' in the Latourian sense, in which participants gather to maintain its existence by their conflicting accounts (Latour 2004, 246). De Baecque underlines the probable embroidery of the popular narratives, pointing out that official reports did not support the eyewitness accounts cited above: the body was left clothed; trinkets in the pockets were preserved; the corpse was probably carried in a wagon, not dragged through the streets at the end of a rope; decapitation did occur, but the head was not damaged. No mention was made in these sober reports of mutilation or the sexual outrages that appeared almost obsessively in outraged Royalist narratives, such as cutting off the genitals or plucking the pubic hair to be worn by a soldier as a mocking moustache. It is clear, however, that the public needed to project backwards some kind of imagined past. It had been animated by rumours about the despicable and depraved life the princess had led: she was a courtesan, rumoured to be an intriguer at court; and through her the crowd took aim not only at a friend of hated Marie-Antoinette but also at her as a woman and her alleged homosexuality (De Baecque 2003, 71).

Whatever the truth of the treatment of this particular body, it is evident that the corpse, representing all that was rejected by the Revolution, was at the very least an equal in the imagination of the crowd to the vision of a socially just future. In this respect, the same was true of the guillotining of the king, as I shall show. Yet the crucial difference is that there was no contemporary 'we' of the September massacres. In the following months, citizens advised one another to 'cover with a veil' this terrible event (Tackett 2015, 217). No public body took responsibility for those killings, unlike in the case of the king, when the Convention, which argued for days, took several close-run votes to arrive at the sentence for the monarch. The decision that prevailed emerged through reasoned arguments: the king had committed treason by earlier attempting to flee France, and his inviolability accorded by the Constitution of 1791 was subordinate to the principle of equality embodied in the revolutionary Rights of Man and the Citizen. Almost all social groups followed the debates in the Convention closely. The participants themselves took collective responsibility for the decision to kill the king, and even an anxious member had no doubt that the story of the execution 'would reverberate to the far corners of the earth and through the end of time' (Tackett 2015, 239–42). Thus, unlike the case of the princess, the execution of the king became a political-social rupture as I have defined it; that is, as a conscious making of a momentous historical break.

The decision was based not only on new political principles but also on its own distinctive idea of virtue. It was in its light that members of the Assembly solemnly voted to execute Louis XVI and later to enable the Terror. Virtue was now defined, especially by Robespierre, as unshakeable and selfless devotion to the public good. Furthermore, 'being virtuous' had to be demonstrated by action, for fear of accusations of hypocrisy (Linton 2013). Thus, it had become 'necessary to be inhuman', to wound sensibility by offering violence to the body of the enemy, 'a violence that was infinite, exceptional and legitimate, since it was offered through the sentiment of doing good' (Wahnich 2003, 20).[6]

The fertile blood of rupture

The 'we' of the execution of the king was, however, a shifting, temporary and multiple entity, as I attempt to describe in the following sections. The shape of a political rupture that takes place in history can be notionally divided into a before, now and an after. Yet in this case, the trifurcation is more like a constantly moving immaterial coupling that has a recursive form, in that the attempt to make a radical rift is constantly placed under question by the unpredicted reattachment to the present of that spectral 'thing' which had been cut off – yet this is a rejoining that is given a new, productive meaning by the actors as it happens. Revolutionary rupture in such a 'social form' may be mobile in the sense that it becomes a new part of a culture (Robbins, this volume) to which people can have recourse, and may re-enact in different places and periods. But I would like to differentiate the 're-memorative' revolutionary fervour extolled by Kant, which reappeared for example in the Paris Commune of 1870 and the Russian Revolution in 1917 (adumbrated also by Rowlands et al. for the Chinese case in this volume), from the imaginative shape surrounding a subject 'in the middle' of rupture, the subjectivity of the one who takes part if only in his or her mind. In the abstract, the guillotine seems to bring about a simple relation – that of a whole entity that becomes two separate parts. But it did more than that. The very instant of severance brought before a viewer's eyes a third active element. Mechanically more efficient than other methods of execution it may have been, but beheading by the guillotine caused a gush of blood; this was something ambiguous and unearthly, a messy flow that was neither 'the head' nor 'the body' and that somehow had to be conceptualized with the cultural means of the time. As I shall now explain, the spilling of blood became an element, at once tangible and symbolic, in the creation of social identities (the various 'us') attached to revolutionary events.

Let us turn to the execution of Louis XVI, or Louis Capet as he was then known. At this point, in January 1793, the political breaks had already happened: the monarchy was over and the Republic had been founded. So the decision to guillotine the former ruler shows that something not purely political had come to the fore: the issue of *physically* ending the threat posed by the continued life of the heir of the Bourbons. Blood-metaphor was the language of the day, and now real blood was to become its physical instantiation. As he stood on the scaffold, Louis's last words were, 'People, I die an innocent man. I pardon those who have decided my death. I pray God that my blood will not come down on France' (Tackett 2015, 241). And during the subsequent Terror, Louis-Marie Prudhomme repeated like a litany, 'They [enemies of the Revolution] want our blood. Well then, since it's blood they want, let the blood flow' (Tackett 2015, 278–9).

The killing of the king on 21 January 1793 was the first and most important act of the Terror and everyone realized its symbolic significance. The platform of the guillotine was surrounded by around 20,000 spectators and 80,000 armed guards. The tension in the air was extraordinary, for the king was seen by all to have been the apex of an entire social order. Even though he had by now become Louis Capet and thus his body was in principle no longer held sacred, at his trial the 'sacred body' of the king was invoked, since, as de Baecque argues, the person of the king had to be 'excepted' from ordinary humanity as the body and soul of the monarchy, the better to turn it into a monstrosity 'outside the nation' (De Baecque 2003, 90).[7] The Divine Right of the Kings of France had rested greatly on the rites of internment whereby the sacred power was transmitted to a successor-descendant (Kantorowicz 1997). In 1793 the elaborate rites and constantly reiterated masses, designed to proclaim that the kingship never dies, were abruptly cut short and the royal mausoleum of Saint-Denis was desecrated along with the other repositories of royal remains. This was the context in which Louis's execution was designed to draw attention to a void – his blanked-out royal ancestry. The revolutionaries deliberately moved the platform of the guillotine so that it faced the empty pedestal that had earlier supported a statue of the previous king, Louis XV. The whole religious funerary hand-over scenario was now abolished by the 'rational' decapitation of the king.[8] The revolutionaries insisted on the ordinariness of the body, on the sober demeanour of the crowd. There was to be no sacralization of the corpse, no insult, no desecration. 'Let them take his body where they like! What does it matter to us?' exclaimed *Le Républicain* (De Baecque 2003, 98). *Révolutions de Paris* wrote: 'The head of a king, in falling, must not make more noise than that of any other scoundrel' (2003, 99). In other words, once it had happened the execution was to be a non-event, a true annihilation.

But meanwhile there was the blood, and this, it seems, turned people to a frenzy. Again, the official reports denied or downplayed any such happening. But almost immediately graphic representations of the Medusa-like severed head (Louis's head held up by an anonymous arm, copiously dripping) appeared everywhere, prominently featuring blood.

De Baecque writes:

> The properties of royal blood are rich, as we know, and by a very strange spatiotemporal phenomenon, seem to stretch out in time and dilate in space the Republican representation of the death of the king: the blood flows out from the royal corpse, spreads out, and Republican narratives soon begin to swell, making the ordinariness and silence at first associated with the description of the execution implode. (2003, 102)

Eyewitness accounts of the execution appeared in the same month. The people wanted the king's hair, others rushed to soak their handkerchiefs in the blood, dip their lances and bayonets in it, taste it; there was crying with joy. According to Prudhomme, one man climbed up onto the guillotine, plunged his bare arm into Capet's blood, filled his hand with it and three times showered the crowd of attendants who pressed up to the foot of the scaffold to receive drops on their foreheads (quoted in de Baecque 2003, 107). People were reported to have paid to get hold of traces of blood, and pieces of bloodied cloth, hair, and fragments of the king's clothing were sold. The impression is inescapable that the blood of the king was not just plain blood; rhetorically impure as it might be, but had become somehow vitalizing, like an injection of a dangerous drug, giving a burst of energy to the popular spirit of the Revolution itself.[9] Blood-soaked, tiny scraps of material had become magic charms.[10] Indeed, among such a (perhaps formerly, but still…) Christian people as the French in the eighteenth century, it would not be surprising if *being anointed* by the king's blood was experienced by many participants as a new subjectivity, something like a baptism – perhaps a kind of transformation of the self, via the overcoming of revulsion.

The 'we' thus created by acquiring blood relics, or participating in the enthusiasm for them, was replicated in similar form a few months later, following the assassination of the 'Friend of the People', Jean-Paul Marat in July 1793. What is interesting about this is first that it was the exceptionality/sacredness of the blood that seems to have mattered most, rather than judgement of its character (that of a traitor king in one case, of a revolutionary hero in the other), and second that the liquid, absorbable nature of blood enabled the creation of a immediate 'we' of a socially dispersed kind. Marat's body, already decomposing and turning green, was paraded through Paris, with the chest naked, exposing the bloody knife wound. According to eye-witness accounts, people fainted at the ghastly sight. Men turned away to look at the orators, but women gazed firmly at the bier, threw flowers on it, and in great numbers gathered the blood that seemed to flow from the corpse. The body remained more or less entire, but the blood was disseminated – into Marat's shirt, his gown, the pages of the journal he had been holding, and onto those who were attending him (Guilhaumou 1986, 71). This powerful blood took on a biologically life-giving, or hero-creating, vitality. Women were anointed with it to the cry, 'Let the blood of Marat become the seed of intrepid republicans'. They replied, swearing to 'people the earth with as many Marats as they could' (Guilhaumou 1986, 71; Hunt 2013, 76).

However, the antinomy intrinsic to rupture, that of the discarded, the horrible, the impure, being re-attached as a vitalization of the future good life, is most starkly seen in the case of the king. In later generations, the 'we' of the Revolution found this difficult to bear. Indeed, the contradiction turned the king's blood into an archetypal Latourean 'thing' of contention. One issue was about impurity. At the time, republicans began to identify Louis's earlier life with evil blood. 'Scarcely had he emerged from infancy when the germ of that ferocious perversity that characterizes a despot was seen to develop in him. His first games were games of blood, and his brutality increasing with age, he took delight in satisfying it on all the animals that he encountered', wrote the *Comité des Secours Publics* (De Baecque 2003, 103). In the poster, the king's blood drips directly onto the caption ('May an impure blood water our furrows'), a visual statement that the 'impure blood' is that of the king, with the understanding that it is impure because he was a vicious enemy. However, this caption is a line from the refrain of an army song, the *Marseillaise*, which shortly became the republican, and then the French national, anthem. National sentiment changes over time, and later on the idea of glorifying in the blood of the defeated enemy began to evoke alarmed responses. Could such a bloodthirsty sentiment represent France, and anyway, was this interpretation not ignorantly anachronistic? Latter-day observers pointed out that in eighteenth-century agrarian France the sans-culottes were of lowly, often peasant, origin, that the king's blood was pure by definition, and therefore that it must be *our* blood, the honest impure blood of ordinary people, that would fructify the furrows. Thus, it is concluded, the caption refers symbolically to our sacrifice, that of republicans proud to give their blood on the field of honour (Peretti 2012). Something of a sleight of hand perhaps, yet it is only in such ways that jarring antinomies can be circumvented and the 'we' of the Terror morphed into the glorious 'we' of the Revolution taken as a whole.

This revised interpretation of the placard reflects, of course, the political and moral ambivalence that simmered beneath the surface among many of those who had publicly acclaimed the Terror. It was only a year later, in July 1794, that the radical Committee of Public Safety was ousted in the coup of 9 Thermidor (in the new dating system), and in 1795 Robespierre was arrested and guillotined. A poster of Robespierre's cut-off head now appeared. Visually, this undoubtedly referenced the one of Louis XVI, but the caption was changed to reflect the new sentiment of revulsion: "'I've played the French and divinity … I die on the scaffold, [which] I have well merited.'"

People who had earlier fervently supported the guillotining of the king and queen as a necessary part of the Revolution, now turned against the Terror, many afraid for their own lives. If there can be no Revolution without its Thermidorian reaction, more germane to this chapter is the thought that rupture may contain its own inner rupture, the splitting apart, or transmutation, of the formerly seemingly implacable 'we' (or even 'I') that had formed around it. The placard has Robespierre himself abjuring his acts, and while this was an external imputation, it is clear that there were many advocates of the Terror who soon disowned it in person – abdicating from its 'we'. One such was Prudhomme, who had first called for bloodletting but from 1794–5 devoted himself obsessively to collecting and disseminating the names of all the victims and then to publishing an 'impartial' multi-volume history of the faults and crimes committed during the Revolution (Prudhomme 1796).

The widespread recantation is a main reason why, in my view, it would be mistaken to approach the killing of Louis XVI, in terms of sacrifice. This observation does not apply to revolution as a whole. Indeed, the language of sacrifice was used widely, in many different circumstances, during the French Revolution, usually in the sense of self-denying sacrifice of property and even one's own life for the sake of the *patrie*, using the idiom of virtue. Membership of the community of the faithful was to a

Figure 1.1 Placard of the head of Robespierre. (Bibliothèque nationale de France, département Estampes et photographie, RESERVE QB-370 (48)-FT4).

great extent defined by evidence of this kind of sacrifice. Analytical works have drawn on a different notion of sacrifice – as expiatory violence, the revolutionary 'transfer of the sacred' from monarch to nation – an example somewhat hazily drawn is Wahnich (2003) (for a thoughtful and extensive survey of this literature, see Zizek 2016). Nevertheless, I would argue that the rupture of the killing of Louis XVI was not a sacrifice in the classical anthropological sense (Hocart 1954; Hubert and Mauss 1964; Hertz 1960). As theorized by Maurice Bloch (1991), for example, the ritual of sacrifice is an attempt to bring about the very opposite of rupture – the continuity of a transcendent social-cosmological vision. The executors of a killing that is sacrifice in this sense desire to sustain, by this means, the continuation of the immortal social and political subjecthood of all those who had carried out this sacrifice in previous generations. This was not the case with the guillotining of Louis XVI. In that killing the aim was radical change, of both the object (now *not* a king) and the actor-subject (an entirely new body, the Jacobin republicans). Although the act could be subsumed as an episode in the overall revolutionary process, for which the overarching idea of 'revolutionary sacrifice' may well be appropriate, I would submit that it was *in itself* not a sacrifice, if only because the executants cut themselves off from their cosmological past, and were riven in the way that rupture itself is riven.

This was a deeply ambivalent position and its fragility (prone to factions and disintegration) is one reason why I suggest, contra Wahnich, that the historical descendants in France of the 'we' of the guillotining of the king could not be the same as for the French Revolution. It would be interesting, though I cannot take the point further here, to compare this situation with the ferocious factionalism inside the Soviet Communist Party at the initiating of the 1930s purges, which indeed appropriated some of the language of the French Terror.[11] But politically this was a different situation and a dissimilar, more long-drawn-out rupture. In the French case, the latter-day inheritors of the Terror were mostly the victims; far removed from the state, they appeared in strange, displaced and shattered forms.

The afterlife of rupture

Early in the Revolution, in 1790, the physician Philippe Pinel observed the 'salutary effects of the progress of liberty'. The national mind was flooded with vigour 'as though by some electric virtue, the system of nerves and muscles of a new life'. Earnestly committed to the Revolution, he gave up his Christian faith and decided to become a doctor. By 1793, however, the massacres appalled him, and the execution of Louis XVI provided the occasion for him to draw up his own judgement:

> As a physician and philosopher accustomed to meditating on governments, ancient and modern, and on human nature, I can foresee only anarchy, factions, and wars that will be disastrous even for the victors, now that I truly know [Paris] and the full value of the pygmies making so much noise. (quoted in Murat 2014, 42–3)

In August 1793 Citizen Pinel was appointed to the post of physician at Bicêtre, a combined prison, hospital and hospice of appalling squalor that housed some 4,000 people of all kinds, some 200 of them insane, along with vagabonds, epileptics, criminals, the senile and the venereal. Pinel drew up a chart of the 200 under his care, noting the large number of cases, some 33 per cent, whose mental distress was not caused by economic or domestic misfortune, nor by love, nor by religious fanaticism (his other categories), but by 'events connected by the Revolution' (2014, 49–50). For him, 'madness' was a 'disease of human sensitivity, whose causes are to be found in the torments of life – mourning, despair, jealousy, desire for fame, excessive bookishness or religion' (2014, 43). Pinel thus understood his patients to be in a common pool with the rest of humanity and to be curable. He wrote:

> The idea of madness should by no means imply a total abolition of the mental faculties. On the contrary, the disorder usually attacks only one partial faculty, such as the perception of ideas or judgement, reasoning, imagination, memory or psychological sensitivity. A madman who died this year and who thought he was Louis XVI was a living example of the nonconformity of ideas with the objects that occasioned them, since he saw all persons who entered the hospice as so many Pages or Guardsmen come to receive his orders. (quoted in Murat 2014, 44)

Pinel thought that there was a substrate of reason that the doctor should try to reawaken, and that this should be done first by protecting patients, earning their trust, and then shocking them into an unambiguous break with their delusions – this last to be done by a 'formidable show of terror'.

How could Pinel, who despaired of revolutionary excesses, have used such an expression? As Murat observes, it was not a coincidence. The semantic spread of the word 'terror' – the arbitrariness of violence as a policy of necessary virtue, that is to say as 'all at once attribute, method and system of government – was in fact perfectly suited to the ambivalence of the birth of psychiatry, its structure and ideological options' (2014, 45). The point I would like to make is that Pinel, by using both sympathy and terror, was *entering into* the mental world of the people affected by 'events connected to the Revolution'.

According to Pinel's accounts, what prisoners awaiting their execution by guillotine dreaded most was not death but the public dismemberment, the end to the integrity of the body in a gush of blood. Many people had this same dread even if they had not been sentenced. One was a tailor who had one day freely expressed his opinion about the beheading of Louis XVI, and thereafter lived in perpetual fear of arrest and execution. In 'trembling and dark consternation' he lost the ability to eat and sleep, until he lost his mind. Sent to the Hotel-Dieu, he failed to improve from the usual treatment (blood-letting) and was then transferred to Bicêtre. The idea of his death haunted him day and night. Pinel applied his usual sympathetic treatment, encouraging the man to take up his usual trade of tailoring inside the asylum. But after some months of improvement, the patient had a relapse. Then Pinel applied the terror. This consisted of a mock trial set up by the doctors, at which after a serious questioning of the 'accused', the 'prosecutor' in a loud voice, so as to make a deep impression on his imagination, pronounced the citizen duly examined according to law and found him to be a true patriot and not guilty. The stratagem worked for a while; the tailor went back to work, though he relapsed into depression when someone told him that the trial had been a jest (Murat 2014, 58–60).

If this case shows the thoughtful doctor as well as the patient taking subjective positions in relation to the threat posed by the guillotine, another case is more direct evidence of a subjectivity of rupture. A watchmaker patient believed he had lost his head on the scaffold; that it had been thrown in the basket indiscriminately among the heads of other victims; that the judges, repenting their cruel sentences, ordered these heads to be restored to the owners and placed on their shoulders; but that in consequence of an unfortunate mistake the head of a different victim had been placed on his own shoulders. The idea of this change of head occupied his thoughts night and day, which caused his relatives to consign him to Hotel-Dieu and thence to Bicêtre. The watchmaker had an outrageous and jovial humour. 'Look at these teeth', he would cry; 'mine were exceedingly handsome, but these are rotten. What a difference between this hair and mine before my head was changed!' (from Pinel, quoted by Murat 2014, 61).

Here the political rupture is transmuted into personal mental-physical experience, but something has gone terribly wrong with the clean split: instead of dismembered death on one side and a completely new being on the other, this imaginary saw only a jumble, a mistake, a loss of the person's true identity. This case is different from the public preoccupation with blood discussed earlier, for that was always blood that was in some way symbolic, which because it represented an idea could then appear as an external agent with efficacious powers. Here, the watchmaker can only have been one among countless other witnesses whose imagination fixed on the real bodily separation: my body, my head, and on the unthinkable of existence after decapitation. The rupture of the body politic was transmuted into the rupture of me as a whole and continuous human being, someone who now hosts 'the wrong head'.

Conclusion

Extracting the pivotal moment of 'rupture' from the revolutionary process, as I have tried to do here, is a theoretical exercise. It has left aside consideration of many themes usually regarded as essential to understanding the French Revolution: the great changes of structures of government and the new language of political legitimacy (Sewell 1996), the strategic manoeuvring of leaders, and the occupation of the space of power, which Furet saw as filled up with democratic rhetoric but other writers such as Jean-Clément Martin and Lynn Hunt have described as sucking in gender, religious, social, economic and regional differences, allowing these strands to combine, disaggregate, and then recombine in explosive fashion.[12] A more comprehensive understanding would have to incorporate the new 'practical filiations' to which both Martin and Wahnich draw attention, the new social groupings and sensibilities that suddenly appeared (from the aesthetic taste for ruins, the fashion for mesmerism, changes in familial relations, new perception of bodily smells, the vogue for pornography, to the appreciation of the horrific 'sublime'). Still, in support of advancing a skeletal picture of rupture in order better to delineate it, there is the key argument made by Wahnich, which is relevant both to the Terror and to the political violence of our own time. Addressing anyone who might think to draw a parallel between the Terror and 9/11, she states: 'Revolutionary violence is not terrorism. To make a moral equivalence between the Revolution's year II and September 2001 is historical and philosophical nonsense … The violence exercised in September 2001 aimed neither at equality nor liberty.'[13]

The 'we' of the Revolution consisted of those who upheld the values of equality, liberty and justice. And perhaps the elevation of values declared to be universal and human has to be true of all revolutionary movements, in order to form the resolute 'us' against which the rotten enemy is conceived. Martin Holbraad, for example, has drawn attention to how people in Cuba are encouraged by official discourse to think of 'our revolution' as an ongoing project that has continued to develop since the event of the revolution's 'Triumph' in 1959. He argues that the notion of 'having been formed in the revolution' and the feeling of still in some way caring about it continues to be common, even normal (2018, 1–2). Castro's proclamation: 'Within the Revolution – everything; against it – nothing', made revolution into a container, with the shape of a totality outside of which contrary forces had no right to exist. This shape was developmental, forward-looking, a totalizing current (2016, 7–8). In the case of the

French Revolution, the great social changes that gave evidence of the 'love of humanity' extolled by Robespierre also took years to unroll. The rationale of state, as well as much retrospective historical judgement (e.g. Sewell 1996), heaped them together as the achievements initiated by Bastille Day. But by this move the systematic slaughter of the guillotine was cast aside, without an owner. Was there then no 'we' of the Terror?

Arguing that there was, I have come to the conclusion that this 'we' was a subjectivity of a specific and conflicted kind – one formed by historical rupture. If we are to call any moment rupture, there has to be a bursting of bonds; there has to be a new sensibility, the definition of a reviled object from which to be separated, and the abrupt violence that actually achieves the split. This combination evoked the extraordinary antimonies of feeling, the necessary cruelty, that Robespierre called for: 'Citizens, the last proof of devotion that representatives owe to the fatherland is to immolate the stirrings of natural sensibility in a salute to a great people and to oppressed humanity! … The clemency that complies with tyranny is barbaric.'[14] Loyalty to transcendent and absolute principles meant that sympathy with the designated enemies was anathema. They were 'beyond the law' because they did not recognize the rules of the now regenerated 'humanity'; that is, the purified people who had recuperated humanity's original nature. Yet, after all, what could be more human than the blood that reddened the king's shirt? Thus, as Wahnich observes with magisterial understatement, a 'theoretical humanism' was inextricably tied to an 'anti-humanism of the situation' whereby a human life was worthless if it was decided that it had traduced its 'humanity' as that ought to be (Wahnich 2009, 220). We see from this that in the highly theorized terms employed by Wahnich, the 'we' that took ownership of the Terror was one founded on an antithesis.

As I hope this chapter has shown, the shape of rupture outlined at the beginning – namely a tripartite splitting into two opposite-facing parts with an unfathomable liminal fulcrum – was reproduced subjectively among the people who were participants or witnesses of the guillotine in action, and who quite soon found it unbearable. In the end the shared intentionality disintegrated into diverse and eccentric forms of memory (of which I have been able to give only a brief impression here). The 'revolution as a whole', which secreted the Terror into a dark fold, gave rise to a far more robust and productive kind of 'we', since it could be given the appearance of a transition from one holistic polity to another. But the 'rupture' created and revealed internal divisions, inconstant re-attachments, and desperate metaphors: along with the revolutionary mothers who swore to give birth to 'republican babies' there were also the people broken by contemplation of the idea of killing to give (political) life.

Acknowledgements

Research for this article was supported through my participation in an ERC Consolidator Grant on comparative anthropologies of revolutionary politics (ERC-2013-CoG, 617970, CARP).

Notes

1. See discussion of these points in Tackett (2001, 570–2).
2. Ciavatta writes that the Republican calendar is an excellent example to show the ambivalent relation to history at the heart of the Revolution: (a) a radical new beginning, itself – not Christ's birth – is now the foundational orienting point; and (b) we can detect in the calendar an attempt to efface the inescapable situatedness of its own institution, since its express goal was to rid itself of any trace of historical origins, for example the use of new names and a decimal system as the most rational (Ciavatta 2014, 580–81).
3. In the aftermath of the storming of the Bastille, members of the Assembly made a similar contrast between mob violence and the 'justified violence' inspired by the 'annihilation of despotism and the birth of liberty', quoted in Sewell (1996, 858).
4. The tribune 'had been pronouncing swift, often hasty judgments, handing prisoners over to a few slaughterers officiating in front of the prison, in the street, surrounded by a large crowd with sabres, lances and bludgeons. In four days, 1,300 people were thus massacred in Paris, at the Abbaye, La Force, and the Conciergerie, including nonjuring priests, aristocrats and common prisoners' (De Baecque 2003, 61–2).
5. The quotation is from a manuscript of 1792 first cited in Bertin (1888, 323–36).
6. It should be noted that Wahnich herself extends her support of the Terror to the September massacres, which she includes in the framework of constitutive vengeance, seeing them as a means of 'manifesting irrevocably the identity of the sovereign people by the act of public justice' (2003, 45). However, the merely tepid acceptance of that violence by the revolutionary leaders suggests that Wahnich's judgement has to be seen as retrospective rather than one current at the time.
7. The corpses of the kings of France had always been 'excepted' from those of ordinary humanity. Since the seventh century they had been inhumed in the royal necropolis of Saint-Denis and provided with effigies. From mediaeval times, they were subject to embalming and ritualized dismemberment: with the custom of 'tripartition' the entrails and heart were separated from the body and taken to further, strategically located sacred repositories (Migeon 2018, 48–9).
8. The Republican newspaper *Journal des homes libres de tous les pays* wrote: 'Today the great truth that the prejudiced ones of so many centuries had stifled has been clearly shown; today we have been convinced that a king is nothing but a man, and that no man is above death. Capet is no more. People of the earth! Contemplate thrones and see that they are nothing but dust.' Quoted in De Baecque (2003, 98).
9. 'One zealot sprinkled blood on the crowd shouting, "Brothers, they tell us that the blood of Louis Capet will fall again on our heads; well, so be it, let it fall … Republicans, the blood of a king brings happiness"' (Hunt 2013, 10).
10. To this day, certain families in France retain vessels containing scraps of material said to be soaked in the king's blood (Biancamaria Fontana, personal communication).
11. In Soviet Marxist circles 'Thermidor' was a synonym for betrayal of the Party line from within. Further divisions into 'right' and 'left' Thermidorians were used in confusing accusations against enemy factions in the Party (Greeman 2015, 220).
12. See discussion in Hunt (2007).
13. Quoted in Ruth Scurr's review of Wahnich's book *In Defence of the Terror: Liberty or Death in the French Revolution. The Guardian*, 17 August 2012.
14. Parliamentary speech 1792, quoted in Wahnich 2009, 215; my translation.

References

Bertin, Georges. 1888. *La Princesse de Lamballe d'après des documents inédits*. Paris: Flammarion.

Bloch, Maurice. 1991. *Prey into Hunter: The Politics of Religious Experience*. Cambridge: Cambridge University Press.

Ciavatta, David. 2014. 'The Event of Absolute Freedom: Hegel on the French Revolution and its Calendar'. *Philosophy and Social Criticism* 40 (6): 577–605.

De Baecque, Antoine. 2003. *Glory and Terror: Seven Deaths under the French Revolution*. Translated by Charlotte Mandell. London and New York: Routledge.

Foucault, Michel. 1977. *Discipline and Punish: The Birth of the Prison*. Translated by Alan Sheridan. New York: Pantheon Books.

Foucault, Michel. 1986. 'Kant on Enlightenment and Revolution'. *Economy and Society* 15 (1): 88–96.

Furet, François. 1998. 'The French Revolution Revisited'. In *The French Revolution: Recent Debates and New Controversies*, edited by Gary Kates, 53–67. London: Routledge.

Greeman, Richard. 2015. 'Introduction' and 'Glossary'. In *Midnight in the Century*, Victor Serge, translated by Richard Greeman, 10–41 and 476–99. New York: New York Review of Books.

Guilhaumou, Jacques. 1986. 'La mort de Marat à Paris'. In *La Mort de Marat*, edited by Jean-Claude Bonnet, 39–80. Paris: Flammarion.

Herrmann, Irene. 2011. 'Introduction: Ruptures in Revolution'. In *La Révolution Française*. Accessed 9 December. http://journals.openedition.org/lrf/319.

Hertz, Robert. 1960. 'A Contribution to the Study of the Collective Representation of Death'. In *Death and the Right Hand*, translated by Rodney and Claudia Needham, 27–88. Glencoe, IL: Free Press.

Hocart, Arthur M. 1954. *Social Origins*. London: Watts.

Holbraad, Martin. 2018. '"I Have Been Formed in this Revolution": Revolution as Infrastructure, and the People it Creates in Cuba'. *Journal of Latin American and Caribbean Anthropology*. Accessed 22 May. https://anthrosource.onlinelibrary.wiley.com/doi/full/10.1111/jlca.12344.

Hubert, Henri, and Marcel Mauss. 1964. *Sacrifice, its Nature and Function*. Chicago: University of Chicago Press.

Hunt, Lynn. 1988. 'The Sacred and the French Revolution'. In *Durkheimian Sociology*, Jeffrey Alexander, 25–43. Cambridge: Cambridge University Press.

Hunt, Lynn. 2007. 'Review of Jean-Clément Martin, "Violence et Révolution: Essai sur la naissance d'un mythe national."' *H-France Forum* 2 (2): 27–9.

Hunt, Lynn. 2013. *The Family Romance of the French Revolution*. London: Routledge.

Kantorowicz, Ernst. 1997. *The King's Two Bodies: A Study in Mediaeval Political Theology*. Princeton: Princeton University Press.

Kates, Gary. 1998. 'Introduction'. In *The French Revolution: Recent Debates and New Controversies*, edited by Gary Kates, 1–15. London: Routledge.

Latour, Bruno. 2004. 'Why has Critique Run Out of Steam? From Matters of Fact to Matters of Concern'. *Critical Inquiry* 30: 225–48.

Linton, Marisa. 2013. 'Robespierre and Revolutionary Authenticity'. *Annales Historiques de la Révolution Française* 1 (371): 153–71.

Martin, Jean-Clément. 2006. *Violence et Révolution: essai sur la naissance d'un mythe national*. Paris: Éditions du Seuil.

Mayer, Arno. 2001. *The Furies: Violence and Terror in French and Russian Revolutions*. Princeton: Princeton University Press.

Migeon, Christophe. 2018. 'La mort du roi, un spectacle codifié'. *Les Cahiers Science et Vie* 175: 42–9.

Murat, Laure. 2014. *The Man Who Thought He Was Napoleon: Towards a Political History of Madness*. Translated by Deke Dusinberre. Chicago: Chicago University Press.

Peretti, Nicholas de. 2012. 'Qu'un sang impur abreuve nos sillons'. *Le Monde*. Accessed 11 March. http://www.lemonde.fr/idees/chronique/2012/03/11/qu-un-sang-impur-abreuve-nos-sillons_1656090_3232.html.

Prendergast, Christopher. 2008. *The Fourteenth of July and the Taking of the Bastille*. London: Profile Books.

Prudhomme, Louis-Marie. 1796. *Histoire Générale et Impartiale des Erreurs, des Fautes et des cimes commis pendant la Révolution Francaise*. Paris: n.p.

Robespierre, Maximilien de. 1958. *Oeuvres de Maximilien Robespierre Volume 9, Discours 1792–3*, edited by Marc Bouloiseau, Georges Lefebvre, Albert Soboul and Jean Dautry. Paris: Société des Études Robespierristes.

Sewell, William. 1996. 'Historical Events as Transformations of Structures: Inventing Revolution at the Bastille'. *Theory and Society* 25 (6): 841–81.

Sonenscher, Michael. 2008. *Sans-Culottes: An Eighteenth-Century Emblem in the French Revolution*. Princeton: Princeton University Press.

Tackett, Timothy. 2000. 'Conspiracy Obsession in a Time of Revolution: French Elites and the Origins of the Terror 1789–1792'. *American Historical Review* 105 (3): 691–713.

Tackett, Timothy. 2001. 'Interpreting the Terror'. *French Historical Studies* 24 (4): 569–78.

Tackett, Timothy. 2015. *The Coming of the Terror in the French Revolution*. Cambridge, MA: Harvard University Press.

Tafarella, Santi. 2012. 'Bruno Latour's Question: Are There Things We Shouldn't Deconstruct?' *Prometheus Unbound*. Accessed 13 June. https://santitafarella.wordpress.com/2012/06/13/bruno-latours-question-are-there-things-we-shouldnt-deconstruct/.

Thomassen, Bjørn. 2012. 'Notes Towards an Anthropology of Political Revolutions'. *Comparative Studies in Society and History* 54 (3): 679–706.

Wahnich, Sophie. 2003. *La Liberté ou la mort: essai sur la Terreur et le terrorisme*. Paris: La Fabrique éditions.

Wahnich, Sophie. 2009. *Les Émotions, la Révolution française et le présent: exercices pratiques de conscience historique*. Paris: CNRS Éditions.

Wahnich, Sophie. 2012. *In Defence of the Terror: Liberty or Death in the French Revolution*. London: Verso.

Zizek, Joseph. 2016. 'Revolutionary Gifts: Sacrifice and the Challenge of Community during the French Revolution'. *Journal of Modern History* 88: 304–41.

2

Rupture and Repair: A Museum of the Red Age Confronts Historical Nihilism

Michael Rowlands, Stephan Feuchtwang and Lisheng Zhang

Introduction

It is difficult to tell the difference between rupture and repair. We shall present a case of rupture as repair, but we must first acknowledge how common such a perception of rupture as repair and repair as rupture must be. When it issues from a new narrative of history, every break with the past (as Benedict Anderson 1991 and 1999 pointed out) that is facing the future rather than repeating a liturgical or ideal historical foundation results in a project that is the formation of a new kind of state, a nation state. But it presents the break as a repair, which is to remove the blocks preventing the realization of the potential of the people, or, in China's case, just as in every decolonizing moment, the removal of humiliation and repression of its people. It is the repair of the human, of a civilization that can realize what is universally human but in and from a local, territorially sovereign, base. Hannah Arendt, both in *The Human Condition* (1959, chapter 6) and *On Revolution* (2006, 216) refers to Greek antiquity for the idea of human action as engagement in politics, the capacity to listen to and be changed by different others, and the contradictory capacity to make a secular world of humanity but not yet to have done so, creating a rupture with whatever knowledge and belief are present with a prospect of promise. This European tradition of emancipation was universalized as modern civilization, imposed as imperialism and in counterviolence used for counter-European, anti-imperialist revolutions of liberation. In all cases the claims to humanity and civilization became the universalizing modes that complement and extend nations in their international relations. In the case of China, emancipating its empire from the English lessons (Hevia 2003) of the Euro-American imperialists and the Manchu emperors involved, as Wang Hui writes (2016), was a movement that like all other nationalisms was both historical and revolutionary, a movement in which the new idea of culture bore the idea of humanity and of a universalizing and renewed civilization. Such emancipatory and universalizing assertions of civilization are a future-oriented temporality through which all the civilizations of the planet are turned into projects of repair and of rupture. Therefore there are different versions of emancipatory rupture besides that of simply achieving nation-state sovereignty. One is liberation from colonial rule. Another is toward a promise of greater social justice, socialist revolution. So we come to the ruptures that bring that promised future into the drama of the modern history of China.

From such a drama of repair follow dramatic turns redefining the authority of state sovereignty commemorated by the year and month in which they began as a repair that was at the same time a rupture. In China these were October 1911, the new Republic of China; 4 May 1919, the launch of the New Culture and New Youth movement; October 1949, the Liberation from the Republic into the People's Republic of China (PRC); and less formally the two renewals of that revolution in the Great Leap Forward of 1958 and the Great Proletarian Cultural Revolution of April 1966, which ended in the repair of Reform and Opening in 1978.

Emancipations are revolutionary, but they are also restorations of humanity. This is both a new thing and ancient, historically and biologically in its ontological justifications. At the same time each revolutionary restoration is a rupture that itself needs either to be restored or renewed or repaired, each repair maintaining itself to be a continuation of selected past lines of revolution and modes of revolutionary government. We will be arguing that revolutionary ruptures are repairs and that they prompt repairs that are themselves further ruptures. What is ruptured and repaired is in all cases a people's sovereignty and its promise. Personal lives are at stake but always as part of a trajectory far greater in scale. We will base this argument upon a case study of a state-sanctioned private museum and its entrepreneurial author, Fan Jianchuan, in China under the market reforms of the Chinese Communist Party (CCP). Most importantly these reforms include the strengthening of an historical restoration that is also a self-proclaimed New Era under the personal leadership of Party leader Xi Jinping. Even while conducting his own historical claims to authority, Xi wields against other such claims the accusation of disloyalty and the denial of the Party's revolutionary accomplishments, a denial that may be named 'historical nihilism'.

'Historical nihilism'

This accusation has precedents in previous phases of the market reform and opening of China that ended the politics of class struggle and mass mobilization but sought to maintain the authority of and from Mao Zedong. This awkward contradiction has made it impossible in China officially and publicly to commemorate the suffering of the Great Leap Forward and the Cultural Revolution alongside the officially proclaimed suffering of the pre-Liberation period without risking accusations of 'historical nihilism'.

In October 2016, in an editorial published by Xinhua, China's official news agency, the author Guo Songmin wrote: 'The vital part of historical nihilism is to radically deny the leading role of Marxism and the historical inevitability of China's socialist path, and to deny the leadership of the Communist Party of China. We should be on guard for the influence of historical nihilism, and ... declare war on it.' The author defines historical nihilism as a systematic denial of the historical achievements of Mao Zedong and the CCP in the Chinese revolution, namely the establishment of the PRC. In party-speak, historical nihilism means denying the 'inevitability' of China's march towards socialism (the country is currently deemed by the CCP only to be in the early stages of it). It is a term that came into vogue among party officials after the crushing of the Tiananmen Square protests in 1989. Jiang Zemin, who was then party chief, declared that historical nihilism was one of several ideological vices that had 'seriously eroded' the party. Other, more obvious ones, included yearnings for freedom and democracy. By reviving Mr Jiang's rhetoric on nihilism, Mr Xi Jinping (the current President) is signalling that the party could again face regime-threatening danger unless it tightens its grip on the way history is told (*The Economist* 2016).

The notion that an evidential history that is objective can also constitute nihilism has a Nietzschean ring to it. A moral nihilism is threatened, a collapse of order being the outcome of a particular delineation of past events. Yet, conversely, it is an accusation that is being used to tell observers and residents of China to 'forget' unfortunate events – in other words those that force themselves into one's consciousness, notwithstanding the pressures to keep them repressed. They should not be remembered because they threaten the current narrative with the possibility of another one, which would replace, indeed negate, it. This is more than some homily about committing the past events to oblivion – more than 'the need to forget to taste the full flavour of the present' (Augé 2004, 3). The political and ideological repression of the past is part of the inevitable process of ensuring not only that what would have an alternative, counter-hegemonic, repressively named, counter-revolutionary narrative is set in the past, but also that the unfinished business of revolt will not constitute an ongoing suppressed ideal that is just waiting for the right occasion to happen again. Yet committing past events to oblivion is unlikely to be totally successful even when it is engineered socially by powerful elites.

Restoration that skirted historical nihilism

Our main focus here is on an instance of rupture and repair in which an alternative historical understanding of the Mao era was encouraged. In 2003, a private museum was created by a retired businessman, Fan Jianchuan, near Chengdu in Sichuan. Clearly with the support of central authorities in Beijing, it manages to embed factual accounts of key events in the Mao era within acceptable heroic and patriotic narratives. Instead of being condemned as nihilistic histories, the installations combine belief and knowledge to domesticate any potential for nihilism. Between the editorial on historical nihilism and the original authorization of the museum, complex salient issues are being worked out in contemporary China at different levels of politics, ideology and everyday life.

The seeking of alternative understandings referred back to the Socialist Education movement (1964–6) and the Cultural Revolution in China (1966–76), attacking the 'four olds' (old customs, old cultures, old habits, old ideas) that could only be replaced with 'four new things' of the same kind. Eventually, in 1977, these were referred to as the Four Modernizations, of agriculture, industry, national defence, and science and technology; and in their turn these were taken up and transformed into the introduction of markets that had Chinese socialist characteristics. Political practices at one stage in this progression were delegitimized during the next, but always they were placed in a teleology of socialist progress. Relegitimizing has meant more or less the contemporary disappearance of the imagery of Mao as well as, since the 1990s, vast sums being spent on copying, restoring and rebuilding many of the images destroyed in the Cultural Revolution. Contemporary attacks on historical nihilism, on the other hand, constitute attacks on the production of knowledge about events of the Mao era, such as on one hand positive reminders of the necessity for class struggle and on the other the magnitude of the 'mistake' of causing the famine in the Great Leap Forward. Wang Hui's history of China's revolutionary twentieth century (2016) comes close to the first reminder without endorsement and totally avoids the second. Accused of attempting to delegitimize the socialist path of the CCP, authors can be imprisoned, sacked from their university posts or silenced in other ways. The irony of such retroactive de- or relegitimization of a socialist path, is that Mao did the same for the previous era; that ended with mainland victory for the CCP over the Guomindang in the civil war. Intellectuals and authors of the Guomindang either fled to Taiwan, disappeared or were converted. Yet current re-legitimizing of the past under Xi Jinping involves new calls for the retroactive reinstalling of a similar Confucian morality and teaching – the spread of Confucian institutes and schools – as a new potentiality that is drawn from a past reality similar to the revised Confucianism that Chiang Kaishek made his own. What we find is a dialectic of knowledge and belief that entails delegitimization is always founded on possibilities of retroactive relegitimization. The ruptures that are produced by both appear very different. But of course they encounter and reproduce each other. Each is at the same time a new rupture and a repair.

When the mainland ruptured from the 'four olds', in Taiwan there was an amplification of Chiang Kaishek's New Life version of Confucianism, itself a modernizing adaption and a break from more conservative ways, into a cultural renaissance (*wenhua fuxing*). Since then the rejection in Taiwan of Chiang Kaishek's military command era on the island and a celebration of new religious organizations, as well as the finding of opportunities for parties to gain votes in local festivals, has coincided with a mainland renewal of admiration of the General and an accompanying plethora of touristic and governmental cultural heritage projects.

Attacks on historical nihilisms are directed against attempts to objectify a different past, the revolutionary past. If the revolution has to be a permanent process, then past failures are both a problem and not so easily empirically denied. An element of belief is essential to portray objective accounts of past events as lacking in patriotism and fundamental misrecognition of the true potential that an appropriate history can provide for the realization of the future of China. New pasts have to be created and retained to repair previous iconoclastic rejections of a past through selective retrieval from what had previously been rejected, creating a certain shape that links the new present to past beliefs or past practices and knowledge. We can see this in images from the opening ceremony of the Beijing Olympics in 2008.

The first image is the percussive effect of 4,000 bronze drums of the Shang Early Bronze Age, followed by iconic images of the major creative innovations of 4,000 years of civilization. Nothing about the twentieth century in China appeared in the opening ceremony. The following year, in Tiananmen Square in Beijing, at the 60th anniversary of the founding of New China in 1949, the intensity of an abstract icon shorn of any reference to particular individuals or events was marked by the fact that the female soldiers in the first row marching past President Hu Jintao were models selected for their beauty, the men were told they could not blink and the whole event was choreographed by the theatrical director of the Beijing Olympics opening ceremony.

Whilst the 'errors' of the Cultural Revolution (and to some extent earlier catastrophes such as the Great Leap Forward and the Anti-Rightist campaigns) have been recognized by the CCP and in turn thrust into a pre-history, this frees the present dialectic of belief and knowledge to create a temporal paradox between rupture and repair. 'Nihilistic' remembering is what is left after the commitment to oblivion. Though it is positively dangerous to remember 'bad pasts', a disciplined amount of facticity is needed, melded with patriotic fervour, to create an acceptable normative understanding. The normative and the forgetting are closely imbricated through these movements of belief and knowledge, and internalized in the reproduction of a strong, populist, everyday sense of the normative.

But if this dialectic of rupture and repair was so successful, then why would there be the lurking subversive questioning about what actually happened? The contemporary Chinese version of post-truth is, after all, played out in an environment relating to the future of the CCP and socialism in China, which is less than secure though it is asserted as normative. Mao's insecurity after the failures of the Great Leap Forward instigated his own turn to the Cultural Revolution and his call for the right of youth as 'Red Guards' to rebel.

In the Maoist era, the Anti-Rightist campaigns depicted the past in the present in two contradictory ways. In films, cartoons, posters and parades of the accused counter-revolutionaries and revisionists seeking to reintroduce capitalism and the past of semi-colonialism and semi-feudalism, victory over them is guaranteed. But Mao had also written and made speeches saying that the revolution had not been secured and its perpetuation required constant class struggle (Meisner 2007, 161–3). Celebration of victory was at the same time also a condemnation of the threat to the revolution, which is why the enemy elements were depicted as monsters (*guai*). The old is a threatening past in the present. Rupture is not secure. The new moment of the Deng Xiaoping reforms is indeed the revision that Maoism so fervently opposed. New norms for this new present have to be established, but without denying a selected and restricted continuity with what went before.

The new norm

It may not be a surprise that since 2003, this necessity for the supplementary factive content of pasts to be kept at a safe distance should coincide with a massive boom in museum-building in China. In 1949 there were only 21 museums in China. By contrast, a survey in 2016 put the number at over 4,000 (State Administration of Cultural Heritage 2016). China is also second, after Italy, in the world ranking for the largest numbers of UNESCO World Heritage-nominated sites. Much of this boom in Chinese heritage has taken place since 2003 as part of the latest top-down development plans that are aimed at transforming the social, economic and cultural life of the country. Within this massive appeal to restoring tradition – in particular intangible cultural heritage – only one museum, a so-called private initiative, has been allowed to develop as a museum of the twentieth-century history of China. Ironically there is no explosion of 'negative heritage' in China (creation of memorials/trauma sites/ recognition of sites of injustice, etc.), unless suffering is embedded in acts perpetrated by foreign invasions and matched by heroic response. In this sense the curation of facticity in a symbolic matrix is valued as a widespread normative patriotic device. A museum embeds norms in the significance of the imagery of its displayed objects. A single museum, now the largest private museum in China, devoted to twentieth-century history was the beginning of something different.

The Jianchuan Museum Cluster

The Jianchuan Museum Cluster is the brainchild of Fan Jianchuan, a former People's Liberation Army officer from Sichuan who turned to business and real estate. The museum is in the famous historic small town (*guzhen*) of Anren, the home of the Land Reform hate figure of landlord Liu Wencai.[1] It is a vast complex of more than 20 exhibition halls and installations devoted to China's twentieth-century history and covers an area of 82 acres (33 hectares), featuring some 8 million pieces, with many of them classified as Class One National Treasures. The largest non-governmental (*minjian*) museum in China, it is upheld as a model for museum privatization in Sichuan, but it is also not infrequently criticized by the central authorities for its 'controversial' narrative of China's twentieth-century history. It should be noted that all the exhibits and their captions are subjected to detailed scrutiny by Beijing's or local officials who periodically demand the removal or revision of some of its potentially unacceptable didactic messaging. For instance, the museum of the Red Age presents dioramas and vast quantities of everyday objects, from enamel washbasins, diaries (5,000 from the Cultural Revolution), 50,000 letters, sewing machines, bicycles, matchboxes, towels and flannels, mirrors, chopsticks, badges and posters, musical instruments and toys, shoes, satchels – all presented in cabinets and displays with captions personally written by Fan Jianchuan. Fan Jianchuan's plans to open an exhibition hall on the Great Famine (1959–61) in 2010 have since then been repeatedly denied. In fact any further 'objective pasts' of the twentieth century by Fan Jianchuan have been refused since 2012. In the meantime, Fan has a Weibo profile (Weibo is a popular social media site in China), with 1.5 million followers, which he updates every day. His posts seem to suggest that everything he does is government-endorsed and transparent.

Here we need to note Mr Fan's personal trajectory and his self-construction as a charismatic maker of history, noting how this project coincides with the history-making charisma being constructed around President Xi Jinping. Both conduct themselves as heroes of repair. For Fan it is the future of the to-be-remembered past; but for Xi it is in order to lead China into what he has defined as a New Era of consolidated Party rule with Xi as its core, material prosperity and the global projection of *Amazing China* (a 2018 film) in China and throughout the world, this definition now being inserted into the PRC's Constitution (Lee Myers 2018).

Fan Jianchuan was born in 1957 to military parents. His father, born in Shanxi, joined the army at the age of 13 and fought in the War of Resistance, the War of Liberation and the Korean War, and was the only survivor of 13 brothers. He gave his son the name 'Jianchuan', meaning Build Sichuan, when he moved south to Sichuan in the early 1950s. He was condemned as a 'capitalist roader' (*zouzhipai*) during the Cultural Revolution and purged (Fan 2013). Jianchuan's interest in collecting, as he came to realize, was motivated by a search for the truth about his father's life. What had happened that meant a man who had devoted his life to the Party was so brutally treated? In 1979, when Jianchuan enrolled to study at university in Xi'an, he started to collect Cultural Revolution artefacts systematically, trawling through rubbish collection depots for badges, sheets, ration tickets, mirrors and much more.

Such personal motivation to collect and display the past is not unusual, and there are certainly hundreds of private museums in China devoted to local history, memorials and ancestral halls. In many cases they respond to the expectations of party officials and others for people to use their wealth to support the CCP. Fan could not have begun this complex in Anren without political support from the Sichuan Provincial party and the central authorities in Beijing. The combination of his filial piety, his personal obligation to his father and the idea of creating a museum to establish a 'truth' came at a good time. The central authorities were willing to promote a fusion of patriotic and heroic remembering with the recognition of 'error' in a brief period from 2003 to 2012.

It was not just the museums of the Red Period that broke new ground. It was also the museums of the war against the Japanese fought jointly by the Nationalists under General Chiang Kai-shek and the Communist-led forces under Mao Zedong that opened a past for the new present. They added impetus to the rehabilitation of Chiang, which started slowly in the 1980s with a publication of analyses of his military campaigns in the war against Japan and accelerated with the promotion of Nanjing as the capital of the Nationalist government in the period of its unificatory prime, and the posting of pictures of his memorial in Taipei on the internet; just a few of many steps toward the unification of Taiwan with the mainland.[2]

Xi Jinping has taken his own route to claim he is representative of China's traditional values, parallel to but distinct from Chiang Kai-shek's nationalist version of Confucianism, the New Life movement. For instance, he has endorsed the commemoration of the innovative Ming Confucian philosopher Wang Yangming and quotes from his works.

Fan Jianchuan is now mainstreaming his capacity to plan museums of military munitions and other patriotic commemorations of the Republican era in PRC cities, at their authorities' requests, because of his fame as founder of his own museum complex. This fame restores his father's reputation, with his own name sharing the stage on which the far bigger figure of Xi Jinping is embodied as the core of the Party, representing the civilization of China and its patriots, and rupturing from the Mao-era iconoclasm.

In 2018, the Jianchuan Museum Complex is building its first branch in the city of Chongqing. Chongqing fits the theme of rupture and repair as a place that has witnessed a rupture that was meant to be repaired. During his tenure as the party secretary of Chongqing from 2007 to 2012, Bo Xilai launched two main political movements that drew nationwide attention, 'to sing red songs and strike against organized crime', commonly known as 'sing red' and 'strike black' (*changhong, dahei*). The campaign against organized crime and corruption, *dahei*, was a large-scale crackdown not only on petty criminals, but also on business people and government officials; it targeted more than 5,000 people between 2009 and 2011 (Wang 2013). The campaign won Bo a nationwide reputation as someone who gets things done and helped to form his personality cult locally. It was propagated as an effort to restore order and safety in a crime-ridden city; but it was also criticized by scholars and legal professionals for eroding due legal procedures, and was regarded as having been implemented chiefly to target Bo's political rivals (He Weifang's 'open letter to Chongqing legal professionals', Bandursky 2011).

'Singing red' was the best-known part of Bo's 'red culture movement', which included 'Singing revolutionary songs, Reading classic books, Telling stories and Spreading mottos'. Public reactions towards the 'red culture movement' were mixed. Some welcomed the revitalization of a Maoist-style revolutionary ethos, which helped to restore a sense of patriotism and national pride that had been broken by the increasing individualism and materialism bred by the economic reforms. Some were concerned by the movement's echoing of the Cultural Revolution (Demick 2011; Richburg 2011; Moore 2012).

The campaign was endorsed by the central party authorities in the beginning. Xi Jinping, who was then serving as vice-president, publicly expressed support for Bo's work in Chongqing. But soon afterwards, in 2012, Bo was overthrown and the already controversial campaign was brought to a halt. Bo's 'Sing Red' campaign was condemned by the then-Premiere Wen Jiabao as 'remnant poison of the Cultural Revolution' and hence a potential threat to the reforms (Lam 2012, 4). On 28 February 2012, the *People's Daily* ran a commentary entitled 'While reform carries risk, abandoning reform will bring jeopardy to the party' (Lam 2012, 5).

The irony is that Xi is now launching a much broader and more comprehensive nationwide campaign to promote 'red culture', and some aspects of it are more alarmingly reminiscent of Mao's era; for instance, setting himself up as the 'core' of the party, constitutionalizing Xi Jinping thought and reintroducing 'comrade' (*tongzhi*) as the official term of address among cadres (Leng 2016) and in public (in subway station announcements, for example). Is this not a re-legitimization of the 'singing red' type of repair work? And it is joined by an even wider and deeper campaign against corruption that rids Xi of Bo and many other potential political rivals.

So, on the national level Xi is resuming the work of rupture and repair that was rehearsed in Chongqing, and on the local level Fan has got himself the job of retelling the city's patriotic history. From early

2016, Fan was in contact with the Chongqing Jiulongpo District Bureau of Housing on a potential collaboration of developing a local block of air-raid shelters. It was agreed that Fan would build eight museums in the block to be managed as the Chongqing branch of the Jianchuan Museum Complex, and the District Bureau of Housing would develop an adjacent commercial street. The eight museums in the Chongqing branch are:

Museum of Chongqing Port Culture
Museum of Vernacular Prayer for Blessing (*qifu*)
Museum of Ration Tickets
Museum of Chinese Matrimonial Culture
Museum of Chinese Medicine
Museum of History of Arms
Museum of the Hanyang Arsenal
Museum of Resistance War

The Museum of Ration Tickets is the only one touching on the Red era. During the preparation, the museum team was advised by Chongqing authorities (propaganda bureau and office of party history) to minimize its content on the Red Age, and avoid 'unnecessary interpretation', both criticism and eulogy. In their feedback to the draft exhibition outlines, the Chongqing propaganda authority urged the museum to be cautious about 'the remnant poison of Bo-Wang' (*Bo-Wang yidu*).[3] The message was clearly that any sort of overt celebration of Red Culture in Chongqing would be seen as political taboo. Fan told the staff in work meetings to do nothing that might be problematic. Fan's local repair work is therefore self-censored to follow the updated logic of Xi's larger scheme.

The emphasis was then placed on wartime history. Perhaps no other city is more symbolically appropriate than Chongqing to be the locale of a resistance war museum. It was not only the wartime provincial capital of the Republic of China, but also marked the union of the CCP and Guomindang against Japan.

The Museum of Hanyang Arsenal celebrates the local military legacy by showing how Chongqing became the military base of the Great Rear (*dahoufang*) after the Hanyang Arsenal was relocated there from Wuhan during the Japanese occupation. The Museum of Resistance War covers the whole period from 1931 to 1945, in response to the official extension of the war history from 8 to 14 years (Zhang 2017). The exhibition consists of five units: the mainstay, the front battlefield, the Sichuan Army, American aid and war prisoners. It repeats all the main themes that Fan Jianchuan had already shown in his Anren museum.

Here the approved retelling of history in a private museum increasingly affirms the official narrative. Nothing is said about the acute violence in Chongqing during the Cultural Revolution. While Chongqing is where the only Cultural Revolution cemetery is located, no attempt to 'heal the scars' seems to be tolerated (Yining 2010; Zhang 2013).

Xi Jinping has taken over Bo Xilai's platform. In addition, he finds in a further past, heroes such as Wang Yangming, who, like Mao, sanctioned the right to rebel. Yet at the same time he clamps down on actual dissidence. Unable to bear the ambivalence of what he presents as a rupture that repairs the mistakes but accepts continuities with the legacy of Mao, he has promoted the slogan 'do not indulge in rash thoughts' (*wang yi*).

The ordinary effects of repair

If we examine the effectiveness of collecting and exhibiting the remains of the past in terms of how the twentieth-century history of China is allowed to be remembered, perhaps the most striking theme is the connection made between recovering the waste of the past and its potential redeployment in repair. Millions of artefacts, posters, diaries, in fact anything that reminded people of the past of the Cultural Revolution, were thrown out from ordinary households all over China. 'Abandoning the past is both a tangible and intangible process. It is about broken knowledge, about what no longer fits, about a mark between old and new' (Martinez 2017). As Martinez goes on to say, waste and obsolescence are categorized and generated within a certain framing of value. Collecting and hoarding the waste of the past implies a very different temporality from the one that encourages obsolescence of all things, buildings and ideas of the person. When the ordering sense of a time with its past is vanishing, acts of retrieval intervene to assert care over the past and restoration of memory. Fan Jianchuan's father, being declared obsolete as were many thousands during the Cultural Revolution, was paralleled afterwards by the wasting of all things that reminded people of being superfluous and dispensable, leaving an uncomfortable sense of disordering. Through an assemblage of person and thing, doubling the effectivity of waste generates the double rupture of a sense of the past, both in terms of the inability to recover the value of those who suffered during the Cultural Revolution and the switch to consumer citizenship that abolishes any value in remembering what ordinary material life was like in the Mao era. To become a curator of discarded things, then, is to give them a new life, on the one hand by restoring the value of ordinary life at the time and, on the other, allowing representations to make allusions to suffering. Repair is therefore a form of re-enactment intended to defeat the consequences of obsolescence.

There are over 8 million artefacts in the storehouses of the Fan Jianchuan Museum Complex, of which probably less than 3 per cent are actually on display. The main purpose of the museum is, in fact, to preserve these artefacts, to make it known that they are there and, if the collection is designated as a national treasure, to ensure their safety. In fact, surplus items are sold in the museum shop and given out on loan or exchanged with other collectors, consistent with the reputation of Fan Jianchuan as the possessor of the largest collection of Cultural Revolution memorabilia. The history that Fan Jianchuan has provided is intensely personal and he opposes interventions by experts, either historians or museologists. He chooses the artefacts and images, writes the captions and decides what images to use. It is basically Fan Jianchuan's twentieth-century history of China, curated by himself and a loyal team of about ten people who have been with him since the time when the first museum, on the Anti-Japanese war, was opened in 2005.

If we concentrate on Fan Jianchuan's representation of the Red Age, it is clear he does not wish to provide a 'factual' account of the Cultural Revolution. Instead, using dioramas (which are no longer fashionable as museum displays), his first aim is to recreate what ordinary life was like during the period.

The attention to detail is remarkable – even down to the way in which newspaper was used to insulate walls against the cold. Whilst the 'Little Red Book' is prominent, it is the detail of a shared reading accompanied by the drinking of tea that dominates attention. In the background are the ordinary everyday farm implements of a peasant household. Another diorama, of the village shop, is strangely adapted to the repetitive display of Mao era artefacts rather than food or domestic goods. Restitution, in fact, depends on repetition to have a maximum effect. This is no more obvious than in the open displays of rows of Mao figurines, making it impossible to forget the image of the 'great helmsman'. Teapots and jars, plates and chopsticks – the everyday articles of eating and drinking,

Figure 2.1 Gongxiaoshe (supply and marketing cooperative) diorama in the Museum of Red Age Everyday Objects. Photo by Lisheng Zhang.

Figure 2.2 Porcelain teapots, Museum of Red Age Porcelain Artwork. Photo by Lisheng Zhang.

washing and cleaning are displayed in repetitive numbers rather than dioramic displays to emphasize the sheer quantity of artefacts produced to occupy every aspect of domestic life. From drinking tea in the morning to bowls for washing in the evening, by replicating daily events, the words and images of Mao stare out at you. Images of striking gestures and optimistic bright colours shine up into the faces of people eating and drinking their modest meals. Restitution, repetition and replication are the key organizing signs of the exhibits in the Museum of the Red Age.

Figure 2.3 Mao effigies, Museum of Red Age Porcelain Artwork. Photo by Lisheng Zhang.

Figure 2.4 Plate and chopsticks decorated with Maoist slogans, Museum of Red Age Everyday Objects. Photo by Lisheng Zhang.

These vignettes merely hint at the effect these images have on visitors. Only to the very old would they now evoke memories. They are rather latent memories. The museum is directed at the young, quite explicitly. It is Fan Jianchuan's worry that the young will remain oblivious to the past and only be concerned with the making of money that occupies him and his negotiations with the officials of the provincial and central committees of the Party. There is an active concern with retaining a legacy of the past, the idea that everyday life had a certain pungency that gave pride and fortitude to people in poor or otherwise adverse circumstances. Regardless of the speed of economic reforms, the idea that personal virtues emanating from revolutionary ardour should still be there and not be obliterated by the appeal of civic consumerism generates the shared morality that brings officials to Fan Jianchuan's door, ostensibly to check on the probity of the stories being told but also to validate the ideals being promulgated by this cultural legacy.

Recasting rupture

Events of massive rupture are the basis of recasting social worlds into new configurations. Events gain cohesion by their assemblage within a longer time frame than is realized in our case study through the forms offered by the museum in the public realm. We may also be dealing with a sequence of ruptures that in the longer term are aiming to achieve a more cohesive narrative. Yet similar sequences of rupture, reaction and repair are frequent and often terrible in their consequences. Normativity is asserted, and is by this very assertion never secure. Rupture as repair conjures ambivalence. Ambivalence becomes intolerable to the normalizing regime when it offers another narrative altogether.

We can see that committing past events to oblivion is rarely if ever completely successful, and maybe is never intended to be. Moreover, historical objectivity, like its counterpart of scientific objectivity, has never implied the suppression of subjectivity. So the current attack on 'historical nihilism' in China could be taken to be an expression of ambivalence and of some possibilities of personal, subjective restoration. Fan Jianchuan may not be so unusual in China at present, in his demands to find a problematizing way of knowing that his father was punished and to have a sense of obligation to achieve this without feelings of guilt. It satisfies a need to find another political narrative with the tolerance of ambivalence about the absurdity of contradictions between a people and the Party that purports to represent it, reinforced by revolution. The personal is raised into the people's trajectory, but it also scales back down to individual initiatives. Rupture and its subsequent repairing of ruptures are probably incipient, certainly repeated in China's trajectory of revolution and reforms. A history is needed that is a more fractured and open coincidence of norms and histories, of nation narratives in which realities can be questioned and alternative futures can be seen enacted and propagated. Yet new pasts have to be created or retained that repair the damage of iconoclastic acts by creating a certain shape for them in the present. The dialectic that ostensibly creates a temporal paradox between rupture and repair can then be resolved by a certain amount of facticity.

Acknowledgments

Thanks to Leverhulme Trust Grant Research Project RPG-2012-726 and the ERC Consolidator Grant on Comparative Anthropologies of Revolutionary Politics (ERC-2013-CoG, 617970, CARP).

Notes

1. A large clay figure model of the Rent Collection Courtyard was copied in all media to promote land reform and collectivization. The original is kept in Anren.
2. There is a Chiang Kai-shek restaurant in Beijing and a Chiang Kai-shek liquor advertised on the web in the PRC with a picture of Taipei's memorial to him.
3. 'Wang' here refers to Wang Lijun, who served as vice-mayor and police chief during Bo Xilai's tenure in Chongqing. His visit to the US consulate in Chengdu on 6 February 2012 led to the downfall of Bo Xilai and himself.

References

Anderson, Benedict. 1991. *Imagined Communities* (revised edition). London: Verso.

Anderson, Benedict. 1999. 'The Goodness of Nations'. In *Nation and Religion: Perspectives on Europe and Asia*, edited by Peter van der Veer and Hartmut Lehmann, 197–204. Princeton: Princeton University Press.

Arendt, Hannah. 1959. *The Human Condition: A Study of the Central Dilemmas Facing Modern Man*. Chicago: Anchor Books.

Arendt, Hannah. 2006. *On Revolution*. London: Penguin Books.

Augé, Marc. 2004. *Oblivion*. Minneapolis: University of Minnesota Press.

Bandursky, David. 2011. 'A Letter to Chongqing Colleagues'. Accessed 12 April. http://chinamediaproject.org/2011/04/12/letter-to-my-chongqing-colleagues/.

Demick, Barbara. 2011. '"Red Song" Campaign in China Strikes Some False Notes'. Accessed 3 June. http://articles.latimes.com/2011/jun/03/world/la-fg-china-red-20110604.

The Economist. 2016. 'China is Struggling to Keep Control over its Version of the Past'. Accessed 29 October. https://www.economist.com/china/2016/10/29/china-is-struggling-to-keep-control-over-its-version-of-the-past.

Fan, Jinchuan. 2013. *Slave to the Great Museum* (大馆奴). Beijing: Sanlian Publishing House.

Guo Songmin. 2016. *Editorial Historical Nihilism*. Beijing: Xinhua News Agency.

Hevia, James. 2003. *English Lessons: The Pedagogy of Imperialism in Nineteenth Century China*. Durham, NC, and London: Duke University Press.

Lam, Willy. 2012. 'Hu Jintao Draws Blood with the Wang Lijun Scandal'. *China Brief* 12 (5): 3–5. Accessed 23 May. https://jamestown.org/program/hu-jintao-draws-blood-with-the-wang-lijun-scandal/.

Lee Myers, Steven. 2018. 'With Xi's Power Grab, China Joins New Era of Strongmen'. *New York Times*. Accessed 26 February. https://www.nytimes.com/2018/02/26/world/asia/china-xi-jinping-authoritarianism.html.

Leng, Sidney. 2016. 'Call Me Comrade … Party Requires Members to Resurrect Maoist Term to Signal Equality'. *South China Morning Post*. Accessed 13 November. http://www.scmp.com/news/china/article/2045455/call-me-comrade-party-requires-members-resurrect-maoist-term-signal.

Martinez, Francisco. 2017. 'The Ordinary Affects of Repair'. *Eurozine*, 16 March. Accessed 16 March. https://www.eurozine.com/the-ordinary-affects-of-repair/.

Meisner, Maurice. 2007. *Mao Zedong: A Political and Intellectual Portrait*. Cambridge: Polity Press.

Moore, Malcolm. 2012. 'Neil Heywood Death in China: Bo Xilai "Drowned Chongqing in a Sea of Red Terror"'. Accessed 17 April. https://www.telegraph.co.uk/news/worldnews/asia/china/9209177/Neil-Heywood-death-in-China-Bo-Xilai-drowned-Chongqing-in-a-sea-of-Red-terror.html.

Richburg, Keith B. 2011. 'China's "Red Culture" Revival Unwelcome Reminder to Some'. *Seattle Times*. Accessed 29 June. http://old.seattletimes.com/text/2015452798.html.

State Administration of Cultural Heritage. 2016. 'The Directory of all Museums in People's Republic of China'. Accessed 4 January. https://commons.wikimedia.org/wiki/File:2016年度全国博物馆名录.pdf.

Wang, Hui. 2016. *China's Twentieth Century: Revolution, Retreat and the Road to Equality*. London: Verso Books.

Wang, Peng. 2013. 'The Rise of the Red Mafia in China: A Case Study of Organised Crime and Corruption in Chongqing'. *Organized Crime* 16 (1): 49–73.

Yining, Peng. 2010. 'Red Guards Cemetery Reveals Scars Yet to Heal'. *China Daily*. Accessed 8 April. http://www.chinadaily.com.cn/china/2010-04/08/content_9699494.html.

Zhang, Congtian. 2017. 'The Significance of Recognising the 14-Year War of Resistance'. *People's Daily (Renmin Ribao)*. Accessed 6 February. http://dangshi.people.com.cn/n1/2017/0206/c85037-29059518.html.

Zhang, E. 2013. 'Grieving at Chongqing's Red Guard Graveyard: In the Name of Life Itself'. *China Journal* 70: 24–47.

3
Times Like the Present: Political Rupture and the Heat of the Moment

Carol J. Greenhouse

Anthropological commentary on the current chasms in the social fields of politics underscores the challenges populism poses for the discipline's classic association of relativism with the expansion of liberal democracy (see, e.g., Edelman 2016; Gusterson 2017; Hartigan 2016; Rosa 2017).[1] The unilateral exclusions of the rightward populist turn point the other way, toward the contraction of democracy around nativist terms of citizenship. A priority on an ethnographic attitude of distance in this context means denying, or at least deferring, that contradiction.

Conventional relativism calls for a specific sort of indifference as a precondition of analysis – a non-relation that demands a 'cool indifference to time' (Harms 2013, 353); however, in a context of political crisis, indifference would seem to compound the contradictions of relativism, more than resolve them. For anthropologists, this may be a conceptual dilemma as well as a personal one – a rupture both revealed and produced in relations rearranged by events. When cool indifference to the times is not tenable, is there another kind of relativity better adapted to heat? Is it possible to reconcile relativity and engagement? I think yes, once these are seen as linked problems of knowledge. The rupture that became visible in Donald Trump's election to the US presidency in November 2016 draws attention to both the necessity and possibility of another relativity – one that renounces personal indifference, and is predicated on a conviction of co-presence to which there is no outside (see Fabian 2014b, 204). In what follows, I argue for a different understanding of relativity better adapted to the forms of political agency revealed and produced in rupture. Roitman's formulation of rupture as a crisis of social judgement (Roitman 2013) is suggestive in this regard, in its call to explore rupture as a destabilization of social knowledge.[2] The kind of rupture I am considering here upturns conventional relativism by its locations close to home, or even at home, where a determinate distance is unsustainable and an everyday 'politics of participation' (Kirsch 2018, 2) is unavoidable. The kind of rupture that is my focus in this chapter precludes any certainty of social distance as well as any steady difference between inclusion and exclusion, and even between past and present (since indeterminate futures proliferate socially). I will call conventional relativity *relativism*, reserving *relativity* for this other formulation that shifts the focus from an optic of distance to a reflexive improvisational relation of nearness.

As Johannes Fabian famously observes in *Time and the Other* (2014a), this other relativity places priority on the question of what time it is that coevals – mutually present to each other – share, when 'social life is no longer posited as existing within the "flow of time", but as *generated in an immanent field*' (Hodges 2014, 47; note omitted, original emphasis). Indeed, rupture does not defy time (by exceeding a flow in an encompassing event), so much as it renders time plural, kaleidoscopic and probabilistic, as the force of doubt teases social fields with a surfeit of times that run in every direction (possible futures running back to reconsidered pasts).

Under such circumstances, ethnographic knowledge is inseparable from self-knowledge, knowledge of others in the world, others in oneself, uncertain knowledge amidst a host of contingent values. Time's arrows suddenly point everywhere, for better or for worse. Again, the kind of situation I am thinking of offers no sure scope for distance (I am not sure what distance I can claim now), since by definition such a rupture unsettles habits of time, place, scale and standpoint. Notwithstanding the hardening of partisanship that has ensued around the Trump presidency, it is still too soon to know what, out of the present chaos, will turn out to have been the history of ... something else; however, the experience of temporal undecidability is instructive in itself. In that state of rupture – that sense of being in transition toward something unknowable from a past that demands reassessment – political agency is a problem of knowledge hinged on many kinds of power, not just in relation to state powers or the strategic instrumentalities of political campaigning. States are not the endpoints of political agency, but rather highly immediate congeries of signs in circulation – diversely constituted in time and space according to the ways people read their own experiences of power and powerlessness and work them through as principles to act on. From that perspective, political agency is highly labile, less immediately attached to policies than to believable powers (whether one's own, the candidate's or something else entirely). For the same reasons, as I shall suggest, democratic states are surprisingly available (ethnographically speaking) to ways of knowing the world not ordinarily associated with the power arrangements of modern politics. These are among the makings of the different kind of relativity I seek for and as ethnography. In search of other thinkable relativities that do not begin a priori in the distance associated with division, throughout this chapter, I draw on a variety of sources, including poetry – all of it published (though not necessarily written) in the ten weeks that yield the main body of this account. I do so not just to lend art to the conundrums of rupture, but to take guidance from poets' instructive formulations of conscious shock as temporal crisis – a rupture felt at once as inescapability, involvement, intrigue and perhaps, too, as a compulsion to authorship. I also draw on current theories of relativity drawn from (lay) literature on physics – finding in that work an understanding of time's fragments as a sustainable source of heat, lending affirmative meaning to *the heat of the moment*. Indeed, the sense of relativity I pursue *is* the heat of the moment, as I shall explain.

'A purple fog descended upon the land'[3]

Can 'ethnographic "revelation" – in which unanticipated, previously inconceivable things become apparent – be taken seriously in anthropological discourse' (Henare et al. 2007, 1)? This question is a trenchant reminder that we are always doing ethnography – always living – in times that we might misrecognize. Hope and dread make ironies of time – a multiplication of meanwhiles, pasts and futures that trump linear time's hegemonic assertion of time as a cascading flume of events. Linear time is the time of the nation as an 'imagined community', sculpting histories and washing over differences (Anderson 1991, 192–9).

But linear time, secular and infinite, puts eternity and extinction on the same path, as much mapping a logic of expedient plunder as animating a vision of human possibility. Among anthropologists of late, the critical convergence of these storylines seems to mark out a rhythm of dread (current anthropological tropes include tragedy, the great wave, the sixth extinction, the end of the world).[4] Linear time singularizes time's origins, rendering agency generic and concealing the precarity, indeterminacy and 'polyphony' of the 'pulses' and 'patterns' in human and other life forms that '[make] life possible' (Tsing 2016, 20–1). An account in linear time can find agency only after the fact, an anachronism that perpetually edits difference into a single storyline that is always passing. Linear time, too, is Other (Greenhouse 1996; see Fabian 2014a).

By contrast, crisis has no defined channel, taking its narratable forms instead from procedures of diagnosis and the reckonings of experts (e.g. priests or pollsters), even as it makes such diagnoses suspect – open ground for opportunism (see Roitman 2013). But crisis also invites poetry – gatherings of 'sense and sense, sense and countersense: a chance meeting at a place in language-time nobody can foresee' (Célan 2017, 405). Ethnography, with its openness to difference, seeks out and anticipates such 'meetings'. Anthropology's 'language-time' (Célan's phrase, again) is a miasma of futures, some of them behind us or beside us. Ethnography – even when it is historical – opens another way of thinking the future of the world, and ourselves (whoever we are) in it. I take this to be the 'revelation' Henare et al. (2007) challenge us to consider when a condition of rupture explodes linear time. Whether as liberation or cataclysm, the question of 'what then' can have no sure answer. Stripping away the veneer of linear time from ethnography means first of all recognizing the other times we ourselves live personally, all at once, as individuals – circular (in search of second chances), branching (in crisis), fragmented (mixtures of beginnings, endings, and uncertain passages), no time at all (absorbed in thought) or unbundled (segments on the evening news, e.g. children caged in a detention centre, followed by an advertisement), among other arrangements. The index of these times is not sequence or output (identifiable as outcomes or measurable as progress), but the immeasurable energy they give or take from us. As anthropologists, once we let go of the idea of time's shape or direction in favour of time's energy for difference from itself, produced by the heat of contest and commitment, myriad times become thinkable – proliferating, uncontainable. The salient aspects of time are the social density of partnership and the ambit of imaginative freedom, not a direction. In this sense, time may be strong or weak, thick or thin, but not forward or backward. Anyone who claims to know time's direction – or even more so, to own it (e.g. 'Make America Great Again') – is aiming to draw others' purposes into their own heat, even at the risk of being burned themselves.

For physicists, time is this transfer of energy. Cooler particles usually draw the heat of warmer ones (Rovelli 2016, 52–3). At a very small scale – say, just two atoms (an example entirely thinkable in today's material sciences; Meier 2014) – energy consumption can be equal to the energy produced by the resistance in the electron transfer itself (this is the basis of nanotechnology; Feynman 1999, 37). Time is kinetic energy – heat – made of connection and resistance. The transfer of energy is what makes the future different from the past – or rather, it is the difference that literally makes the future (Rovelli 2016, 53). Kinetic energy as heat results from the velocity of particles in a given distribution, not their direction of movement as such (Reichenbach 1971, 65). Indeed, physicists tell us that the 'direction of time' is not a dimension of space, but 'a grab bag' of other problems of a probabilistic sort (Earman 2002, 261; Rovelli 2016, 53).

To the extent that rupture calls into question the hegemonic temporalities of offices and industries and brings credence to our own discipline's uneasy relation to linear time (e.g. Bear 2014; Fabian 2014a; 2014b; Greenhouse 1996; 2014; Holbraad et al. 2014; Miyazaki 2004; Pandian 2012; Scott 2013; Tsing 2016; Yvinec 2014), such discussions among physicists are suggestive. For ethnographers, too, it is useful to consider that past and future are not locations on a settled timeline, but social effects of convergence and divergence – belonging or excluding, acting or waiting, being one among yeas or nays or refusing to take part.[5] I am drawn to the idea that time accumulates and dissipates with the shifting conditions of connection and resistance, circulating and distributing the heat that will differentiate futures from each other along with their pasts and presents.

Heat as energy distributed by contact will be my key image for the personal and social times entailed in the rest of this chapter. In the temporal explosion of ruptures, I find the metaphor of heat useful where the more orderly notion of *event* falters. Events may drive a recognition of rupture, but rupture is not in itself reducible to an event, since in the process of probing revealed contingencies the future may turn out to be behind us, even without us, as in Mary Ruefle's poetic image of the photograph that reveals a country with no people (Ruefle 2017). Erin Manning writes of 'memory for the future' (Manning 2015, 44–50), but memory *of* the future is also generative.[6]

For ethnographers, the heat of time – in Nemirovsky's phrase, 'writ[ing] on burning lava' (quoted in Muhlstein 2016, 42) – widens the critical space around routine contradictions: contradictions that promote austerity as the condition of increase (Davis 2015), carbon as the externality of value (Dalsgaard 2013, 82), war as the condition of peace (De Lauri 2013, 7–8), killing as the essence of civic order (Bonilla and Rosa 2015), expulsions as infrastructures of growth (Sassen 2014) – among other examples from current anthropology. Registering the time that gathers around such contradictions is ethnography's distinctive algorithm. The heat of imagined 'worldings' (Pina-Cabral 2014; Mackenzie 2010) gives time multiple futures, presents and pasts. In the co-present relationality of heat, another relativity is immanent, forging solidarities not as structures but as people's agentive experience as they live the times, as they know them.

But I am getting ahead of myself.

Let us shift to a different ethnographic present, to the season between the US presidential election in November 2016, and the inauguration in January 2017.

Ten weeks of winter: remixed notes from the field

Donald Trump campaigned on promises of repeal and reversal currently being seen to by his political strategists, cabinet secretaries in their own departments and the Republican-majority Congress.[7] In its first days, the Trump administration reversed legislation and even long-standing doctrines in an explicit effort to erase the legacy of President Obama and much else, including constitutional and customary checks on presidential power – as is now plain in the executive orders affecting immigration and national security, social security and environmental safety (among other domains).[8] The pace of events has been at lightning speed.[9] The current havoc (a neutral term in this circumstance) is the projection of power that – in this concentrated and highly public form – is both wholly unfamiliar in US politics, and deeply consequential.

The morning after Mr Trump won the US presidential election, I started a log – snippets of conversation, poetry, published commentary, passages from anthropologists' writings and other artefacts. Partly, I will admit, this was for personal reasons. But it was also to track whatever might later turn out to be relevant knowledge – an answering "there!" to an as yet unasked question. In what follows, I draw on that log, among other sources, to explore three questions that have dominated the private and public conversations as I know them from my own social and media horizons. I phrase them in the first-person plural – an actual but indeterminate (i.e. not rhetorical) 'we': Why didn't we see this coming? Is the public a social reality? Does democracy have a future? These are heated questions – heated in the dual sense of their controversial substance and their probabilistic potential for generating renewal. They are pressing personal questions for many people, but they are also impersonal questions corresponding respectively to themes of relativity, solidarity and agency. The ease of movement between the personal and the impersonal may seem confounding at first; later, I will suggest that this very impasse might actually clarify something of what these times reveal about the challenges of understanding high elected office as a human relation.

Why didn't we see this coming?

Even on the eve of the election, most pollsters calculated the odds of a Trump victory as very low, even as low as 1 per cent.[10] But on 8 November 2016, as the polls rolled to a close across the key battleground states (as the political pundits call them), most of these being in the eastern time zone, the likelihood of his win jumped to near certainty shortly after supper. For some people, this was a dream fulfilled; for others, a nightmare. I was with friends at a small gathering. People stopped eating, speaking and drinking, in that order, and began to drift away. I take this sort of break in intimate sociability seriously, as an experience of time thinning out, cooling down. Mary Ruefle again: 'The roots of trees curled up' (2017).

The outcome all but certain later that night, television pundits had to provide analysis without a playbook. The first assessment I heard on the air was that the Democrats lost because they lost touch with the problems of working people in the middle class. The same argument held that Trump – while seeming to be inept – had been a political genius, tapping into people's unspoken anger, fears and hopes. By Day Two, these same pundits were calling on the American public to heal and work towards unity. Many people I know stopped watching the television news at that point, in frustration – turning to print instead, as a way of recalibrating the ratio of fact to opinion alone, in silence. They were not alone; nationally, subscriptions to the *New York Times* soared in the days after the vote.[11] Meanwhile, my local newspaper, serving a college town and rural county, seemed to take advantage of the proximity of the Thanksgiving holiday, and Christmas, to feature community events that might transcend division (and not only there; see Hampson 2017).

But in the broader political space, divisions were not going away.[12] Throughout the transition between the election and Inauguration Day, there was mounting debate over the legitimacy of the election in light of intelligence briefings confirming a Russian influence campaign and (at that time) unconfirmed suspicions of the Trump campaign's involvement (see, e.g., Blow 2017). In his first days in office, Trump hit back hard with policy positions communicated as executive orders – volleys that were in turn immediately rejoined with court-ordered stays and public protests, and again answered with new executive orders – and on and on. A contest thus joined in a way that fused the debates over policies to the debates over the legitimacy of the new president, conciliation was bound to be elusive.

Meanwhile, closer to the policy front, the 'lost touch' analysis became standard. An anthropologist readily recognizes in it the template of cultural relativism: red states and blue states, two cultures, two identities, in need of mutual translation and tolerance. The class stereotypes that populate this imagery are elaborate but they rapidly fail in light of the campaign itself. I do not mean that people's needs are not real or urgent. Moreover, it is true that Trump campaigned hard in rural areas among people who had never voted, and channelled the frustrations of white working people facing the challenges of precarity – some of them former Democrats whose jobs the Obama administration had saved in 2009. Clinton, meanwhile, spoke to the working poor and middle class in a different language, with proposals to improve the minimum wage, health care and free college tuition, among other things. On some points, she took up proposals Bernie Sanders had made first, and that was a serious complication. But the larger political context was already shaped – emptied out, in some respects – by years of elite Republican obstruction to Obama initiatives and decades of resistance to 'big government'. Democratic talk of 'programs' registered for Trump voters across the socioeconomic spectrum mainly as tax increases and more government control – paradoxically making income inequality and precarity into wedge issues that put business tycoons and trailer dwellers on the same side.

The image of the 'Trump base' as gun-toting rednecks or tattooed bikers is supremely inaccurate; nor were Clinton supporters mainly coastal urban elites or women of a certain age, as the press and pundits might have had us believe. Trump was elected by a preponderance of white men, men and women over the age of 65, and, among men, mostly college educated (Tyson and Maniam 2016). Among whites who voted for Trump, many previously voted for Barack Obama (Hartigan 2016). Clinton voters were younger, more female, racially more diverse and in general better educated than Trump voters (Tyson and Maniam 2016). Still, the fictions remain embedded in media talking points that reiterate class and regional stereotypes – perhaps finding in this improvised moral economy of taste a new 'geontology' for the United States (Elizabeth Povinelli's term for a formation of power built on the distinction between life and non-life; see Povinelli 2016, 4–5). Be that as it may, what we have come to think of as Trump's core base was statistically small, not large enough to elect him or, even at the very end, enough to win him the popular vote.

The implicit relativism in such accountings relies on the translatability of each candidate's appeal to the other side, as if the electoral field were normally flat and equally open to both candidates.[13] But this was not the case. The reasons behind Trump's victory cannot simply be flipped to explain Clinton's loss. For one thing, she did not lose the popular vote (she won by almost three million ballots, and lost the Electoral College by only about 80,000 votes distributed across three states). A related point is the fallacy that either candidate's supporters were available for conversion to the other side.[14]

Many people prepared to vote for Trump were *never* available to Clinton, and vice versa. Throughout the campaign, it was said of Trump that he was willing to give voice to the positions people held but were afraid to acknowledge, id to their ego. This was no doubt true to some extent in some quarters, particularly at the beginning – when the polite response (often heard on television and in conversation) to Trump's pledges to build a wall along the southern US border, unleash massive deportations, and institute a ban on Muslim immigration, among other things, took the form of welcoming open discussion of tough issues. But for many other people, these were repugnant non-starters. Trump's promises had (and continue to have) multiple versions, reversals and revisions as the political winds shift – including winds interior to the Republican Party, where the leadership, unable to rein him in, finally decided to chance the ride and hold on. This widened a second front against Clinton, bringing into the mainstream what had been Congressional Republicans' efforts over many years to disqualify her pre-emptively, long before her candidacy, including but not limited to Congressional hearings on the attack on the US consulate in Benghazi (Libya) while she was secretary of state.[15] It was those hearings that revealed her private server and use of unofficial e-mail accounts while in office – unleashing the persistent sense of scandal that dogged her candidacy.

Given the long involvement of Congress and the FBI in the investigation of Clinton while she was a candidate (and even before, in her public service and as First Lady), the campaign of vilification against her was not organic in the same way that expressions of xenophobia and Islamophobia apparently were for some Trump supporters. But it became that. As Trump's epithets of 'lying Hillary' and 'crooked Hillary' gained traction at rallies, the group chants ('lock her up!', 'traitor!') morphed into an argot of misogyny that even cable networks did not allow their reporters to quote verbatim (see Solnit 2017). Meanwhile, pulling in his allies (including former federal prosecutors), Trump declared himself 'the law and order candidate', positioning himself with the Fraternal Order of Police against the Black Lives Matter movement – among other moves calculated to reinforce the image of Clinton as outside the law. Constant reference to 'the e-mails' positioned Clinton herself as a virtualism. The high-ranking Republicans in Congress and in the party who had criticized Trump's excesses during the campaign ultimately supported him, and – as of this writing – for the most part continue to do so.

In sum, those of us who did not see this coming were perhaps blinded by the fact that the two cultures argument was there from before the beginning, baked into the candidates' strategic design. A conventional relativism in this context would cabin ethnographic understanding within a reiteration of one or the other of those partisan commitments.

Is the public a social reality?

A few more pages from my log – still winter:

The state where I vote went massively for Trump (though not the college town where I live). At restaurants and cafés that first week, election talk was sotto voce. The tear in the social fabric was palpable. The day after the election, one friend said, 'I look around and I can't believe half of my neighbours probably voted for him.' My log notes a few messages from friends as their sense of social time unspooled from the gap: 'I just can't believe it'; 'I feel like I'm sleepwalking'; 'I'm still mourning'. Some academics I know said at the time that they don't know any Trump supporters, but I know for a fact they are mistaken. The rallies, among other things, left some of Trump's 'secret admirers' (Sanneh 2017, 24) reluctant to admit to their support. The evasive small-talk in public places on the morning of 9 November might not have been indifference or despair, but self-preserving tact for all concerned.

To be fair, the visceral distaste between the two candidates' camps was apparently mutual, if asymmetrical.[16] The campaigns, run on an infrastructure of market shares, instantiated a politics of affect that left little room for intersubjectivity – *appeal* trumped *engagement* (see Martin 2013). By this I mean that both campaigns ran on the other side's unfavourability, apparently leaving people not just with a sense of alienation from the other side, but also with the sense that to vote the other way would mean *becoming another person* – in the most negative sense. That impasse – the rending of *the public* as a warrant for legitimate power – corresponds to a restructuring of power wholly in terms of the majority's control. This aspect of the state of rupture is palpable, highly visible in the Congressional session coinciding with Trump's first year in office – the minority counting for the most part only as a zero, even though they were shy of a Senate majority by only three seats.

That zero-ing is not limited to the government of the day. The Trump administration has made long strides in reversing Obama-era law, erasing the Democratic majority of *that* time. The response of this administration to its control of both the White House and the Congress, in effect, is to abjure any obligation of the majority party to the minority – swallowing up the democratic possibility of a political minority *being represented* within political institutions, or by them. Reserving representation as the majority's privilege in this way is a striking departure from the idea of the public as a collectivity – an idea relating civic life to social life that is foundational to social science. Minority politics have moved to the streets and other public sites of protest – evidence that understanding 'politics' as a plural noun is important to an accurate description of the state of affairs.

Even before the waves of demonstrations that followed almost daily after the inauguration while executive orders rolled out effecting a travel ban from seven Muslim-majority countries, the symbolic rending of the public was evident in substantive ways in the cabinet choices and policy positions emerging from the administration. During the campaign, Trump surrounded himself with theorists of the white nationalist movement, participating knowingly in their coding of 'worker' and 'middle class' as white. Steve Bannon, his chief political strategist, was brought into the White House as a senior adviser, briefly holding a seat with the principals on the National Security Council. The original cabinet (turnover has been rapid) was stocked with billionaires and retired generals. Social security, voting rights, and the government agencies responsible for the social safety net are all under review for dismantling in the name of the taxpayers. Trump's positions on trade, immigration and domestic job creation varied in substance during the campaign but never wavered in their zero-sum formula with respect to foreign workers, whether as immigrants or in their own homelands. The sharpest lines of alienation follow the border, dividing citizens from immigrants and workers from workers.

The day after the election, a friend – a woman in her 60s – wrote in a group e-mail that she felt as if she was 'giving birth to a baby that already died'. Her grief, expressed in that harrowing image out of time, left me thinking about rupture as at once a mystery, an irreparable tear in the temporal fabric, and a social disturbance that reshapes who or what anyone might become. Jameson Fitzpatrick's poem, 'I Woke Up' (2017), speaks of awakening to the perfusion of the political field as he once lived it without seeing – those retrospective insights culminating in a discovery:

I thought I was not a political poet and still
my imagination was political.
It had been, this whole time I was asleep.

As with the first question ('Why didn't we see this coming?'), the question regarding the social reality of the public quickly doubles back on itself, since it is itself in contention under the populist agenda of erasure, repeal, refusal and repatriation. The representational void at the end of the idea of the public puts politics everywhere and nowhere, as Fitzpatrick's lines suggest. This brings us to the question of agency in relation to the dark matter of democracy's future.

Does democracy have a future?

More from the log: In the days and weeks after the election, when Trump supporters are asked why they voted for him by journalists and pollsters, the keynote response is *change*. One word, one man; perhaps this is the rejoinder to Barack Obama's *hope* in the 2008 election. But where 'hope' was an invitation to spark time's heat (e.g., the Obama campaign's slogan 'Yes, we can'), 'change' claims ownership of time – the promise of a strong man to use his power. And now that we know more – his disregard for norms across a wide spectrum of public and private domains – the strong man looms large in public performances designed for his 'base'. Among his critics, since the early days of the transition, pundits, political opponents and ordinary people have wondered aloud if he is a threat to democracy. I hear this as a question they are asking about their own political agency.

I have referred to the dualism produced by the campaign – the two camps of supporters yielding a sense of the public as composed of two kinds of person, neither (by their own accounts) translatable or transformable to the other. The absence of a middle ground has strategic value, as suggested by Eduardo Kohn in a superficially different context: 'One might say that dualism, wherever it is found, is a way of seeing emergent novelty as if it were severed from that from which it emerged' (Kohn 2013, 57). That '*as if*' is consistent with Kohn's notion of iconicity: 'Icons involve not noticing' (Kohn 2013, 32) – an observation wholly apt in the case of this election cycle's divisions, in which the candidates' alleged excesses and deficits were apparently matters of indifference to their supporters. In televised focus group discussions, supporters described Trump's appeal as his readiness to 'shake things up' – the bombast being (in their view) a show of his energy and earnestness, but not necessarily his intentions. Clinton's supporters emphasized her long career, but this made it difficult to see her as an independent 'change' candidate, except for her status as the first woman to gain the presidential nomination of either of the main political parties.

Even for Trump supporters, his personal comportment, the wall, deportations, the Muslim ban and the rest were not so much specific objects of their endorsement as they were the poetics of a power they deemed desirable, transforming in itself. Such poetics cannot be explained wholly in relation to Trump (notwithstanding its benefits to his candidacy); rather, they draw on forms of relation that gather heat to themselves well away from the capital (an image I draw from Essy Stone's 'Among the Prophets' (Stone 2016): 'Yes, he is a good king, how the K.K.K. chopped my daddy's wood for him, winter, 1968 … '). Indeed, Trump does not actually claim to speak *for* his supporters – rather, he claims to speak *as* them, their iconic 'us'. The issue of public or political consensus does not arise, then, since the stereotypical 'base' – and here, I am not referring to his major donors or party elite – was brought into being by an act of self-description before the event, not by a groundswell of support for a particular set of policies.

As for Trump's extreme statements and prevarications, it seems that some part of his success actually depended on his inconsistencies, and not just because they kept him in the news. By varying his positions on any given point, he could assert his ownership of meaning while continuing to tailor his message for voters and give queasy establishment Republicans momentary room to breathe. Furthermore, perhaps more fundamentally, as his own language floated on the winds of the moment, his positions became unanswerable in conversational form or standard news formats – on issues as disparate as Barack Obama's birthplace, the human role in climate change, the Intelligence Community's assessment of Russia's role in the election, the relevance of ethics in government, and Brexit and the future of Europe. (By now the list is too long to attempt.) The campaign and transition gave early signs of the frailty of critical discourse in this regard. Quotation stood in for commentary; debate gave way to repetition and reinterpretation. In this way, Trump's staging of his personal power became unanswerable in its own terms (and so it has remained, even as his business and campaign associates come under federal indictment).

In the immediate aftermath of the 2016 election, political commentator Mark Danner wrote: 'Trump is an improviser, a performer, a creator of new worlds' (2016, 14). As Essy Stone's poem about the rural American

King Saul helps us see, he invites his supporters to remake themselves in him, to be change agents through him. He offers himself as their double negative, redeeming their alienation (whatever their class position) from a privileged position all his own. Stone's imagery reaches into rural America, but, again, Trump's iconic power should not be imagined as reserved for the poor and uneducated. It is there for anyone's borrowing or lending, a highly bankable charisma.

As with Stone's analysis, Trump's impunity – 'Saul – domineering, cunning, powerful' – is misread if one takes his statements as reflections of his supporters alone; rather, they remix powers familiar to any of us from our own relations and experiences. The question of democracy's future thus cannot be answered only in reference to 'them'; if democracy is a social fact, it must include 'us', too, and what we know or could or should know about inequality. This (at last) returns us to the matter of what rupture reveals of relativity – not the hackneyed antagonism of red and blue cultures, but rather, the diverse ways in which people understand state power in relation to powers of other kinds, including their own.

Prey are hunters, too: January 2017

In *How Forests Think*, Eduardo Kohn urges readers to consider how people know themselves and the world, including their relations to the non-humans around them. In his monograph, this means (among other things) the jaguars prowling the forest. To a jaguar, he points out, the world is divided between prey and non-prey. For the people Kohn writes about, alert to the jaguar's habits and appetite, the jaguar is a sign, emblematic of their own everyday canniness, valour and vulnerability, lending meaning to language. The jaguar does not symbolize humans' power; it is itself subject to a human master (the white shopkeeper in town). Rather, it materializes the very significance of power from the perspective of potential prey who elude its bite and, in the meantime, also hunt jaguars.

Kohn's analysis of the hunter/prey relation to the jaguar is suggestive of an approach to understanding modern state power that merits exploration. I mean this seriously, not as an analogy but as an ethnographic prompt to consider what it is that is usually left out of discussions of high elective office. This new president seems to belong more to the worlds of appetite and charisma than to bureaucratic protocols and norms. In his own words, Trump sees a binary world of 'terrific people' who are 'nice' to him, and on the other side 'enemies' or 'haters' – categories that are meaningful wholly and only as they relate to himself. The binary structure of his personal myth is easily lent to the nationalist discourse he promotes, itself a binary discourse hinged on the fold where his self-vaunted deal-making skills conjoin his personal wealth to a vision of the national interest. His self-aggrandizement is essential to this convergence, appreciated and even enjoyed by his supporters and apparently worth the risk of exposure by his critics, since in his 'nationalist ontology', 'the reinvention of experiential reality in the terms of the mythical realities' (Kapferer 2012, 99) potentially works to his benefit either way.[17]

In Trump's binary world of terrific people and enemies, terrific people are as prone to being prey as are enemies (perhaps even more so, since their loyalty makes them sweeter to his purposes).[18] The sense of rupture is clarified by this image, since it highlights the difficulty of knowing the difference between safety and danger, yet also the inescapability of a mortal need to know the risks of miscalculation. Not surprisingly, by the first day after the inauguration, millions of people – not centrally organized as a group – moved to the freezing streets. Demonstrations continue. Those disinclined to be potential prey are warming themselves elsewhere, making their own heat as they seek out like-minded others, together gathering different futures around their fires both figurative and literal (staying warm on the street). No doubt there is fire for Trump supporters, too; the televised rallies are a performance of heat. In a related vein, the rallies and demonstrations are also expressions of a diffuse but intense politicization of the body – standing up and turning up extend key tropes of race, gender, war, work, abortion, immigration, and demanding removals (among others) into contingencies of person-state relations, and, for some, adjoining physical selves to partisanship. Proper bodies – living or dead – seem to be the confirming vital sign of Trump's truth for his strategists, but there is a visceral quality of intense emotion that slips in and out of language, for supporters and critics alike (at least those who are following the news). The jaguar is not just hunter and prey, it is also everywhere in people's speech, seeping into our idioms, shaping our stories, our narrative relish ('Did you hear … '), our testimonies of fear, close calls, or bravado. The jaguar reminds us to think of power before we think of partisanship, and to follow power where it leads ethnographically, uncomfortable though this may be.

In anthropologists' recent work on forms of life beyond the human, there are suggestive resources for thinking about power unchecked and the agency that thickens around indeterminacy. We have much to learn from people who know the world not first as consumers, but as jaguars' potential prey, or as stewards of their families' dreamings. Their alertness – or ours, whoever we are – is honed at home, and the relevant signs, whatever they may be, prickle the skin, anything but remote or abstract.[19] Clinton supporters wondered aloud how Trump supporters could tolerate his personal behaviour, failing to see how very pervasively familiar his behaviour actually is in terms of what passes for everyday normal in other settings in the asymmetric powers and vulnerabilities of relations between bosses, employees, partners and spouses; in situations of precarity, security and deceit; in efforts to hold others to account or evade accountability oneself; in their expectations of safety or danger at home or in the street – and so forth. This is not partisan knowledge. These are domains of knowledge anyone might have, as they are widely distributed among the population at large – familiar and 'familiarized' (Brown 2018, 18). Experiencing the campaign from home, perhaps Clinton supporters felt they were looking *at* a president, drawn to her special qualifications, while Trump supporters were looking *for* a president, seeking familiar attributes. The closing lines from Elizabeth Willis's 'Plot' (2016) evoke the potential for alienation in the non-relation of imposed choices:

What would you choose, a sandwich or a phone call.
What did you expect, a question or an answer.
A piano or a clock.
Take all the time you want.

These reflections suggest that our understanding of political agency would benefit from uncoupling the bureaucratic fact of elected incumbency from the charismatic power of office, since elements of that same charisma circulate in private life, as people rehearse their own agentive powers, calibrating their own experiences of acceptance and refusal in relation to known partners, opportunities and perils. With regard to electoral campaigns, this means that the means and ends of political agency as imagined instrumentally by strategists might be only ambiguously aligned for voters and potential voters, especially with regard to what are conventionally referred to as *interests*. I am not for a moment suggesting that people vote in a misguided or mystified way, only that our situations as hunters and prey are fundamentally problems of knowledge about the world as we know it or wish it to be – uncommon knowledge of a world we share.

One implication of these reflections is that presidential powers – which is to say, powers as they circulate from different parts of the forest through high elective office (not just for Trump), and perhaps the powers of other high offices – break the bounds of democratic discourse, notwithstanding their centrality to the institutions of democratic government. Their escape is by reference, away from representation and individual liberty, toward realized and unrealized experiences of hunters who are also prey: inequality, manipulation, vulnerability, pride and vindication, are among the relations that may be elided as partisan attitudes.

Now: visible heat

Let us return to the present.

We seem now to be in an open moment of preoccupation shared across disciplines with the significance of temporality and difference as means and ends not only of human understanding, but humanity itself.[20] Time is gathering heat in multiple senses – material, conceptual, political, cross-disciplinary.[21] Once we think of living in time not just as an ethnographic topic, but also as ethnography's ethic (see Mauss 1967, 35, on the contract as 'uniting two moments in time')[22], then subject and object, means and ends, fieldwork and authorship, subject disciplines and self-discipline, students and teachers, thinkably fold together, potentiating what Durkheim – introducing his idea of organic solidarity – refers to as the 'warmth' of 'a form of life sui generis' (Durkheim 1984, lii).[23] This is not a cosy image. On the contrary, it is a challenging one, Durkheim prodding his readers with the heat that is gained or forfeited when people find value or lose it in their engagements with others. If we are searching for sources of a future politics beyond the fantasy of market shares and consumer choice ('a piano or a clock' as Stone puts it), the eloquent explorations of *non*-human worlds currently enlivening anthropology are full of implication. The registers of state power – quasi-occult, impersonal, inhuman – gain legibility in the immediacy of close personal experience. We are used to thinking of a president as an elected individual, but far less so about how the presidency comes to life (if indeed it does), with the president giving it human form and a locus of responsibility. This aspect of the presidency (its coming to life) is not accomplished by an election alone. It comes to life – if it does – diversely, in actual encounters, skin-side out, amongst ourselves, as already discussed.

I reiterate the point to explain my interest in the question of how people know and live their own agency in relation to the *in*human aspects of state power in their everyday experiences.[24] Agency is not something an individual does or does not have; rather, it circulates, lent and borrowed, waxing and waning, changing the scope and scale of the human vis-à-vis the inhuman, as they discover their own thinkable relevance. The intimate registers of agency and their creative movement away from inevitability deliver heat to time. In this sense, agency is not *in* time; it *is* time, indeterminate and potentiating heat. Lifting the brackets from other forms of life and non-life offers fresh possibilities for understanding contemporary state powers amidst powers of other kinds, including the powers of ordinary people unexpectedly gathered together. Those connections 'gather sense' in a world in which we are also present, anything but indifferent or apart.

Hence my hopes for anthropology as a source of timely renewal not just within the discipline, but also beyond it. Explaining the electoral outcome that brought Donald Trump to office or prognosticating about how Democrats will respond in 2020 – or before then, given the widening gyres of criminal investigations – are issues that will continue to occupy political strategists and activists in the United States. For anthropologists here and elsewhere, an explanation of the lines of antagonism in 2016 or their shifting horizons in the midterm elections of 2018 is likely less urgent than understanding the connections between all forms of political energy and the diversity of people's practical experience of democracy (or lack of it) in their own lives. It would seem that Americans who voted this way or that, or not at all, had different experiences, tolerances and expectations in the moment – experiences and attitudes not in themselves subject to red/blue binaries. Acknowledging those experiences and attitudes as 'ours' as well as 'theirs' (the division suspended in the jaguar's appetite) restores the co-presence that relativity requires. In contrast to the conventional construction of the present moment as a battle between 'red' and 'blue' cultures, this other relativity offers no 'outside' – that is its ethnographic advantage, the heart of its realism.

To be clear: to argue for ethnographic relativity is not an argument for either personal neutrality or absolute difference. I am not looking away from the sharp edges of political division, the tactics of political power, or the vastly moneyed interests on this same terrain. Rather, my effort is to look through them, to the complexities and possibilities they reveal and conceal regarding anyone's agency, solidarities and sense of democratic possibility – the three questions posed earlier. Once one recognizes (like Fitzpatrick's political poet) that there is no place apart, relativity widens the space for personal conviction and action as mutually necessary prompts for knowledge, discipline and engagement. If there is a methodological point to this discussion, it is to suggest that a relativism that frames ethnography with lines of red and blue is unsustainable, as it can only totalize and essentialize social life in partisan political terms. That move is already established in the populist playbook. Ethnography drives in the other direction, drawn by discipline and need into the midst of social times 'when any heat at all rises and becomes a visible thing' (Burleson 2017).

Acknowledgements

My reference to 'rupture' throughout this chapter is indebted to Martin Holbraad, Bruce Kapferer, Michael Rowlands and Julia Sauma, organizers of the conference 'Ruptures', held in London in February 2017, as well as to discussions with colleagues at the conference. I am grateful to the editors of this volume – Martin Holbraad, Bruce Kapferer and Julia Sauma – for their detailed comments on previous versions, as well as to the anonymous reader from the publisher. In the course of developing the chapter, I accumulated happy debts to Paul Frymer and colleagues in the Program on Law and Public Affairs at Princeton University, Eileen Julien and colleagues at the Institute for Advanced Study, Indiana University-Bloomington, and Anne Cheng and colleagues in the Program on American Studies, Princeton University. I am particularly grateful to Kessie Alexandre, James Boon, Anne Cheng, Eileen Julien, Rachel deLue, Judith Hamera, Suzanne Godby Ingalsbe, Rita Kesselring, John Logan and Sarah Malone. As always, my deepest debt is to Fred Aman.

Notes

1. Accounts of the populist turn in Europe and the United States now abound. For one influential analysis see Müller (2016).
2. I am indebted to Janet Roitman for her discussion of *crisis* at the London conference.
3. Ruefle 2017.
4. 'Tragedy' (Scott 2013); 'the great wave' (Povinelli 2016); 'the sixth extinction' (Kolbert 2014); 'the end of the world' (Tsing 2016) – all tropes from current anthropology.
5. For physicists, convergence becomes more likely as the entropy of systems increases with isolation or containment, and divergence becomes more likely as entropy decreases with openness (see Earman 2002, 261–2). The direction of time has no opposite (see Reichenbach 1971, 207–11).
6. Cf. 'Tragedy is irreparable' (Steiner 1979, 8); 'possible redemption from the predicament of irreversibility' (Scott 2013, 165). In this sense, 'historicity' is fundamentally different from 'temporality', the experience of living in time (Scott 2013, 12, 21). Rupture is irreparable but not necessarily irredeemable; its temporality is irreversible but renewal is not necessarily foreclosed.
7. The 2016 election yielded Republican majorities in both chambers of Congress; after the 2018 elections, the House of Representatives was retaken by Democrats.
8. Legislative steps toward repeal of ACA (Reuters 2017; United States House of Representatives 2017).
9. One day's front-page headlines give some sense of this: 'Trump sets off backlash with attack on civil rights icon'; 'The assault on health and safety begins'; 'Pick for Labor Department has long

history of fighting labor laws'; 'Trump calls NATO "obsolete" and floats Russia nuclear deal' (*New York Times*, 15 January 2017: 1). The pace accelerated, and reached deeper, after the inauguration on 20 January.

10. On 6 November, Sam Wang's assessment put the probability of a Clinton win at 99 per cent (Wang 2016).

11. In the week following the election, the *New York Times* added 41,000 new digital and print subscriptions – 'a drastic uptick' (Spayd and Gershkovich 2016; *New York Times* 2016).

12. Almost a month later, on 4 December, a local Indiana newspaper ran a front-page story with a full two pages inside about the recent development of an encampment by the Traditional Worker Party – a white nationalist movement that has found a congenial home nearby (Bavis 2016).

13. For anthropological accounts of the campaign and election, see *Political and Legal Anthropology Review*'s online 'Emergent Conversations Part 5' (Edelman 2016 and Hartigan 2016).

14. I say 'fallacy,' since once they became their parties' respective nominees, the two leading candidates essentially ran against themselves. By this I mean that for potential supporters on either side, 'no' – for the most part – would have meant not voting at all. Over the past 60 years in US presidential elections, but never more than in 2016, high 'unfavourables' correspond to very low voter crossover (Wang 2017).

15. On pre-emption as 'a new dominant' see Brian Massumi's analysis of the George W. Bush administration's unilateralist doctrine and the campaign to mobilize public perception in the run-up to the war in Iraq (Massumi 2015, loc. 55).

16. In any case, the antagonisms went far beyond the reach of any accommodation of divergent interests – even beyond discussion. 'Talking heads' from the two sides adopted a strategy of talking over each other when they appeared on the same televised panels (as did the candidates at the vice-presidential debate).

17. Bruce Kapferer's assessment of the ethnographic value of ontology in his study of nationalism in Sri Lanka applies here: '[C]ertain dynamics connected with the re-formation of the person in ritual contexts were, through the mediation of a nationalist discourse, expanded into a populist ideological discourse of nation and identity' (Kapferer 2012, 443).

18. Along the way to his inauguration, pundits and members of both parties assured themselves that when he became the nominee, or when he was elected, or when he began to govern, Trump would change his behaviour to become *presidential* (the term commonly used). This has not happened; it seems he cannot, or will not, alter from himself (to borrow a phrase from Holbraad and Pedersen, quoted in Holbraad et al., 2014).

19. The reference to 'prickling the skin' is indebted to Pearson 2015.

20. Recent discussions (in anthropology and philosophy) of ontology – construed as 'the material and conceptual structures' of 'emergence' (Grosz 2008, 1) – have contributed new formulations of social life to anthropology, and new formulations of anthropology itself (although not entirely or necessarily from within the 'ontological turn'; Hodges 2014, 46).

21. Anthropologists and sociologists 'have reopened the question of capitalist time' and 'global time' (Bear 2014, 3). Lawyers have turned to temporality as a feature and function of legal pluralism (von Benda-Beckmann 2014). Environmentalists and community activists find in 'temporal belonging' a conceptual and practical counterweight to the fracturing effects of a public sphere conceived in liberal terms as separate from nature (see Bastian 2012, 2; Bastian 2014).

22. My thanks to James Boon for the reference to Mauss in this context.

23. In her published lectures on chaos, territory and art, philosopher Elizabeth Grosz evokes 'cosmological imponderables – among the most obvious, the forces of temporality, gravity, magnetism' as 'among the invisible, unheard, imperceptible forces of the earth, forces beyond the control of life that animate and extend life beyond itself ... in which life folds over itself to embrace its contact with materiality...' (2008, 23). I appreciate this image since, as I understand these words now, they suggest sustainability, indeterminacy, and energy as each other's conditions of possibility.

24. My usage of *non-human* differs from that of philosophers and literary scholars who associate themselves with 'the nonhuman turn' (see Grusin 2015), in that those discussions are grounded primarily in Western philosophical traditions. My own interest derives primarily from ethnographic accounts that dwell with people's relations with non-humans (as in Kohn's analysis) and the non-living (which turn out to be alive; see, e.g., Povinelli 2016).

References

Anderson, Benedict. 1991. *Imagined Communities*. London: Verso.

Bastian, Michelle. 2012. 'Fatally Confused: Telling the Time in the Midst of Ecological Crises'. *Journal of Environmental Philosophy* 9 (1): 23–48.

Bastian, Michelle. 2014. 'Time and Community: A Scoping Study'. *Time & Society* 23 (2): 137–66.

Bavis, Lauren. 2016. 'White Nationalist Group Seeks to Form Separate Community in Paoli'. *Bloomington Herald-Times*, 4 December: A1, A6–7.

Bear, Laura. 2014. 'Doubt, Conflict, Mediation: The Anthropology of Modern Time'. *Journal of the Royal Anthropological Institute* n.s. 20: 3–30.

Benedict, Ruth. 1934. *Patterns of Culture*. New York: Houghton and Mifflin.

Blow, Charles. 2017. 'John's Gospel of Trump's Illegitimacy'. *New York Times*. Accessed 16 January. https://www.nytimes.com/2017/01/16/opinion/johns-gospel-of-trumps-illegitimacy.html?action=click&pgtype=Homepage&clickSource=story-heading&module=opinion-c-col-left-region&region=opinion-c-col-left-region&WT.nav=opinion-c-col-left-region.

Bonilla, Y., and J. Rosa. 2015. '#Ferguson: Digital Protest, Hashtag Ethnography, and the Racial Politics of Social Media in the United States'. *American Ethnologist* 42: 4–17.

Brown, Wendy. 2018. 'Neoliberalism's Frankenstein: Authoritarian Freedom in Twenty-First Century "Democracies"'. In *Authoritianism: Three Inquiries in Critical Theory*, edited by Wendy Brown, Peter E. Gordon and Max Pensky, 7–44. Chicago: University of Chicago Press.

Burleson, Derick. 2017. 'Untitled'. *Poetry* 209 (6): frontispiece.

Célan, Paul. 2017. 'From "Microliths"'. Translated by Pierre Joris. *Poetry* 209 (4): 405–10.

Dalsgaard, Steffen. 2013. 'The Commensurability of Carbon: Making Money and Value of Climate Change'. *HAU: Journal of Ethnographic Theory* 3 (1): 99–115.

Danner, Mark. 2016. 'The Real Trump'. *New York Review of Books* 63 (2): 8–14.

Davis, Elizabeth. 2015. '"We've Toiled Without End": Publicity, Crisis, and the Suicide "Epidemic" in Greece'. *Comparative Studies in Society and History* 57 (4): 1007–36.

De Lauri, Antonio. 2013. 'Introduction'. In *War*. Antropologia: *Annuario* 13 (16): 7–23.

Durkheim, Emile. 1984. *The Division of Labor in Society*. New York: The Free Press.

Earman, John. 2002. 'What Time Reversal Invariance Is and Why It Matters'. *International Studies in the Philosophy of Science* 16 (3): 245–64.

Edelman, Marc. 2016. 'Emergent Conversations Part 5: The Nastiest Candidate Won. Now What?'. *Political and Legal Anthropology Review*. Last edited 16 November. https://polarjournal.org/the-nastiest-candidate-won-now-what/.

Fabian, Johannes. 2014a. *Time and the Other: How Anthropology Makes Its Object*. New York: Columbia University Press.

Fabian, Johannes. 2014b. 'Ethnography and Intersubjectivity: Loose Ends'. *HAU: Journal of Ethnographic Theory* 4 (1): 199–209.

Fandos, Nicholas. 2017. 'Politics – White House Pushes "Alternative Facts." Here are the Real Ones.' *New York Times*. Accessed 22 January. https://www.nytimes.com/2017/01/22/us/politics/president-trump-inauguration-crowd-white-house.html.

Feynman, Richard P. 1999. *The Pleasure of Finding Things Out*. London: Penguin.

Fitzpatrick, Jameson. 2017. 'I Woke Up'. *Poetry* 209 (4): 370.

Graham, Jorie. 2016. 'The Mask Now'. *Poetry* 209 (3): 256–7.

Greenhouse, Carol. 1996. *A Moment's Notice: Time Politics across Cultures*. Ithaca, NY: Cornell University Press.

Greenhouse, Carol. 2014. 'Time's Up, Timed Out: Reflections on Social Time and Legal Pluralism'. *Journal of Legal Pluralism and Unofficial Law* 46 (1): 141–53.

Greenhouse, Carol. 2017. 'Aftershocks of Relativism'. *Anthropological Quarterly* 90 (4): 1053–84.

Grosz, Elizabeth. 2008. *Chaos, Territory, Art: Deleuze and the Framing of Truth*. New York: Columbia University Press.

Grusin, Richard, ed. 2015. *The Nonhuman Turn*. Minneapolis: University of Minnesota Press.

Gusterson, Hugh. 2017. 'From Brexit to Trump: Anthropology and the Rise of Nationalist Populism'. *American Ethnologist*. Accessed 27 April. https://anthrosource.onlinelibrary.wiley.com/doi/full/10.1111/amet.12469.

Guynn, Jessica. 2016. 'Zuckerberg: Facebook "Fake News" Didn't Sway Election'. *USA Today*. Accessed 10 November. http://www.usatoday.com/story/tech/news/2016/11/10/mark-zuckerberg-facebook-fake-news-didnt-sway-election/93622620/.

Guynn, Jessica, and Kevin McCoy. 2016. 'Zuckerberg Vows to Weed Out Fake News'. *USA Today*. Accessed 13 November. http://www.usatoday.com/story/tech/2016/11/13/zuckerberg-vows-weed-out-facebook-fake-news/93770512/.

Hampson, Rick. 2017. 'In Trump Nation, Healing is Overrated'. *The Herald-Times/USA Today*, 18 January, Section B: 1.

Harms, Erik. 2013. 'Eviction Time in the New Saigon'. *Cultural Anthropology* 28 (2): 344–68.

Hartigan, John, Jr. 2016. 'Emergent Conversations Part 5: Race and the 2016 Election'. *Political and Legal Anthropology Review*. Accessed 14 November. https://polarjournal.org/2016/11/14/emergent-conversations-part-5.

Henare, Amiria, Martin Holbraad and Sari Wastell. 2007. 'Introduction: Thinking Through Things'. In *Thinking Through Things: Theorising Artefacts Ethnographically*, edited by Henare, Holbraad and Wastell, 1–31. New York and Oxford: Routledge.

Hodges, Matt. 2014. 'Immanent Anthropology: A Comparative Study of "Process" in Contemporary France'. In *Doubt, Conflict, Mediation: The Anthropology of Modern Time*, edited by Laura Bear, 33–51. Oxford: Wiley Blackwell.

Holbraad, Martin, Morten Axel Pedersen and Eduardo Viveiros de Castro. 2014. 'The Politics of Ontology: Anthropological Positions'. *Cultural Anthropology*. Accessed 13 January. https://culanth.org/fieldsights/462-the-politics-of-ontology-anthropological-positions.

Kapferer, Bruce. 2012. *Legends of People, Myths of State: Violence, Intolerance, and Political Culture in Sri Lanka and Australia*. Oxford: Berghahn Books.

Kirsch, Stuart. 2018. *Engaged Anthropology: Politics Beyond the Text*. Berkeley: University of California Press.

Kohn, Eduardo. 2013. *How Forests Think: Toward an Anthropology Beyond the Human*. Berkeley: University of California Press.

Kolbert, Elizabeth. 2014. *The Sixth Extinction: An Unnatural History*. New York: Henry Holt.

Mackenzie, Adrian. 2010. *Wirelessness: Radical Empiricism in Network Cultures*. Cambridge, MA: MIT Press.

Manning, Erin. 2015. 'Artfulness'. In *The Nonhuman Turn*, edited by Richard Grusin, 44–50. Minneapolis: University of Minnesota Press.

Martin, Emily. 2013. 'The Potentiality of Ethnography and the Limits of Affect Theory'. *Current Anthropology* 54 (s7): S149–S158.

Massumi, Brian. 2015. *Ontopower: War, Powers, and the State of Perception*. Durham, NC: Duke University Press.

Mauss, Marcel. 1967. *The Gift: Forms and Functions of Exchange in Archaic Societies*. Translated by Ian Cunnison. New York: The Norton Library.

Meier, Christian J. 2014. 'Chips from a Sheet'. In *Max Planck Research*, 1/2014: 34–41.

Miyazaki, Hirokazu. 2004. *The Method of Hope*. Stanford, CA: Stanford University Press.

Muhlstein, Anka. 2016. 'A Marvelous Writer in a Hopeless Situation'. *New York Review of Books* 63 (20): 8–14.

Müller, Jan-Werner. 2016. *What is Populism?* Philadelphia: University of Pennsylvania Press.

New York Times. 2016. 'The New York Times Adds 41,000 New Subscriptions Since Election Day'. Accessed 17 November. http://investors.nytco.com/press/press-releases/press-release-details/2016/The-New-York-Times-Adds-41000-New-Subscriptions-Since-Election-Day/default.aspx.

New York Times. 2017. 'Politics – Donald Trump's News Conference: Full Transcript and Video'. Accessed 11 January. https://www.nytimes.com/2017/01/11/us/politics/trump-press-conference-transcript.html?_r=0.

Pandian, Anand. 2012. 'The Time of Anthropology'. *Cultural Anthropology* 27 (4): 547–71.

Pearson, Heath. 2015. 'The Prickly Skin of White Supremacy: Race in the "Real America"'. *Transforming Anthropology* 23 (1): 43–58.

de Pina-Cabral, João. 2014. 'World: An Anthropological Examination (Part 1)'. *HAU. Journal of Ethnographic Theory* 4 (1): 49–73.

Povinelli, Elizabeth A. 2016. *Geontologies: A Requiem to Late Liberalism*. Durham, NC: Duke University Press.

Reichenbach, Hans. 1971. *The Direction of Time*. Berkeley: University of California Press.

Reuters. 2017. 'U.S. Republicans Start Framework for Obamacare Replacement'. *New York Times*. Accessed 13 January. http://www.nytimes.com/reuters/2017/01/13/us/13reuters-usa-obamacare-changes.html?_r=0.

Roitman, Janet. 2013. *Anti-Crisis*. Durham, NC: Duke University Press.

Rosa, Jonathan, and Yarimar Bonilla. 2017. 'Deprovincializing Trump, Decolonizing Diversity, and Unsettling Anthropology'. *American Ethnologist*. Accessed 27 April. https://anthrosource.onlinelibrary.wiley.com/doi/full/10.1111/amet.12468.

Rovelli, Carlo. 2016. *Seven Brief Lessons on Physics*. Translated by Simon Carnell and Erica Segre. New York: Riverhead Books.

Ruefle, Mary. 2017. 'Genesis'. *Poetry* 209 (4): 371.

Sanneh, Kelefa. 2017 'The Political Scene – Secret Admirers: The Conservative Intellectuals Smitten with Trump'. *The New Yorker* 92 (44): 24–30.

Sassen, Saskia. 2014. *Expulsions*. Cambridge, MA: Harvard University Press.

Scientific American. 2014. *Secrets of the Universe: Past, Present, Future*. 23 (3).

Scott, David L. 2013. *Omens of Adversity: Tragedy, Time, Memory, Justice*. Durham, NC: Duke University Press.

Shear, Michael D., and Emmarie Huetteman. 2017. 'Trump Repeats an Election Life to Top Lawmakers'. *New York Times*. Accessed 12 February. https://www.nytimes.com/2017/01/23/us/politics/donald-trump-congress-democrats.html?hp&action=click&pgtype=Homepage&clickSource=story-heading&module=first-column-region&region=top-news&WT.nav=top-news

Skow, Bradord. 2010. 'What Makes Time Different from Space?' Accessed 12 February. http://web.mit.edu/bskow/www/research/temporality.pdf.

Smolin, Lee. 2013. *Time Reborn: From the Crisis in Physics to the Future of the Universe*. London: Penguin.

Solnit, Rebecca. 2017. 'From Lying to Leering: Donald Trump's Fear of Women'. *London Review of Books* 39 (2): 3–7.

Spayd, Liz, and Evan Gershkovich. 2016. 'Public Editor – Friday Mailbag: No More Politics. Just Kidding'. *New York Times*. Accessed 18 November. https://www.nytimes.com/2016/11/18/public-editor/friday-mailbag-no-more-politics-just-kidding.html.

Steiner, George. 1979. *The Death of Tragedy*. New York: Oxford University Press.

Stone, Essy. 2016. 'Among the Prophets'. *The New Yorker* 92 (38): 81.

Strathern, Marilyn. 2014. 'Reading Relations Backwards'. *Journal of the Royal Anthropological Institute* 20 (1): 3–19.

Tsing, Anna Lowenhaupt. 2016. *The Mushroom at the End of the World: On the Possibility of Life in Capitalist Ruins*. Princeton: Princeton University Press.

Tyson, Alec, and Shiva Maniam. 2016. 'Behind Trump's Victory: Divisions by Race, Gender, Education'. *Pew Research Centre – Fact Tank*. Accessed 9 November. http://www.pewresearch.org/fact-tank/2016/11/09/behind-trumps-victory-divisions-by-race-gender-education/.

United States House of Representatives. 2017. 'HR 5. Regulatory Accountability Act of 2017. ("To reform the process by which Federal agencies analyze and formulate new regulations and guidance documents, to clarify the nature of judicial review of agency interpretations, to ensure complete analysis of potential impacts on small entities of rules, and for other purposes.")' 115th Congress, 1st session.

Von Benda-Beckmann, Keebet. 2014. 'Trust and the Temporalities of Law'. *Journal of Legal Pluralism and Unofficial Law* 46 (1): 1–17.

Wang, Sam. 2016. 'Is 99% a Reasonable Probability?'. *Princeton Election Consortium*. Accessed 6 November. http://election.princeton.edu/2016/11/06/is-99-a-reasonable-probability/.

Wang, Sam. 2017. 'Polarization Removes the Ability to Make Distinctions. Princeton Election Consortium'. Accessed 3 January. http://election.princeton.edu/2017/01/03/polarization-removes-the-ability-to-make-distinctions/

Willis, Elizabeth. 2016. 'Plot'. *The New Yorker* 92 (37): 72–3.

Yvinec, Cedric. 2014. 'Temporal Dimensions of Selfhood: Theories of Person among the Surui of Rondonia (Brazilian Amazon)'. *Journal of the Royal Anthropological Institute* 20 (1): 20–37.

4

Inner Revolution: Reaction and Rupture in a Danish Lutheran Movement

Morten Axel Pedersen

> In the world of faith and the gospel, leaping has to be done! But in the world of earthly reality, which politics for instance is, leaping is an impossibility ... so when political system-creators or ideological politicians nevertheless seek to leap via revolutions, then they destroy the natural development and effectively molest and tyrannize the humans. (Krarup 1987, 14; translated by the author)

So goes a telling citation from *Conservative Essays*, one among a number of books published over the last 30 years by Søren Krarup, a former Lutheran priest and a retired MP for the Danish People's Party, who is widely considered to be the leading intellectual and political figure of Denmark's national-conservative right. What Krarup is suggesting in the citation, with explicit reference to the nineteenth-century Danish theologian and philosopher Søren Kierkegaard's notion of 'leaps of faith',[1] is that in Christianity there can be only one kind of rupture, namely the 'inner revolution' needed to re-enter the kingdom of God of which Man was originally an inseparable part, but from which he has since been evicted and detached. Any attempt to change or improve this primordial fall or rupture in the form of progressive reforms, let alone political revolutions, are not just utopian and totalitarian but evil and ungodly. For the same reason, as Krarup argues in the chapter 'The Anti-Totalitarian Kierkegaard' (1987), there is a direct relationship between existential leaping and reactionary politics:

[T]he conservative rejection of leaping within a temporal duration is a consequence of the necessity of leaping in the religious or eternal world, where God cannot be known but only be an object of faith, and where no human has direct or natural access to the divine and truth. Since God is not of this world, you are in this world *not* supposed to relate to society and politics in a god-like and absolute way. Or with reference to [Kierkegaard's] expression, it is just because the relationship to eternity demands leaping that leaps do not belong to the dimension of time. (1987, 14; translated by the author)

This chapter is based on fieldwork within the small but highly influential Danish Lutheran movement Tidehverv (in which Krarup and others from his family have for several generations played a central role), as well as a historical genealogy of Danish concepts of freedom (*frihed*) in nineteenth-century theological and cultural political discourse. By combining ethnographical and historical perspectives, I show what it means to subscribe to and practise a doggedly Lutheran and explicitly Kierkegaardian form of Christian faith, which celebrates the existential 'leaps' (*spring*) that are induced from sudden and always unexpected encounters with God. Crucially, these ruptures must take a strictly interior and existential, and not exterior and political, form. Thus, from the perspective of my interlocutors it is not just immoral but downright sacrilegious to try to bring about any human progress and societal development in the world, especially change couched in and executed in the name of political revolution (i.e. of the sort discussed by Humphrey and Rowlands et al., this volume). My ambition in what follows is to unpack some of the historical processes and cultural dynamics that undergird this peculiar combination between a theology that celebrates inner rupture and a politics, which is all about resisting outer revolution. Precisely how and why is it that 'Christian leaping' becomes anathema to societal progress and a precondition for 'genuine conservatism'? And what are the wider lessons gained from the case of Tidehverv not just for influential anthropological work on Christianity and ethics/freedom (Robbins 2004; Keane 2007; Laidlaw 2014), but also the burgeoning literature on ethno-nationalism and conservative identity politics in Denmark and elsewhere in Europe (Gullestad 2006; Hervik 2011; Gingrich and Banks 2006; Thorleifsson 2016; 2017; 2018; Kublitz, this volume)

'What is old, is good'

In spite of its explicitly anti-revolutionary and self-proclaimed reactionary discourse, Tidehverv is an apposite choice of study for the anthropology of rupture. Indeed, rupture features in the name of this Lutheran movement. Thus, the Danish word *tidehverv* is derived from a *fin de siècle* German journal called *Zeitwende*, a term that denotes a 'rupture between two eras' (Larsen 2006). Established in 1926 by four male theology students in reaction to a time they lamented to be 'too modern to respect the elementary human', Tidehverv for the first decades of its existence fought its battles with other branches of the Danish Protestant church. Its original arch-enemy and *raison d'être* was thus the ascetic Inner Mission that had risen to prominence in various parts of rural Denmark and deprived inner-city Copenhagen areas as part of the pietistic awakening that had swept across Protestant Europe in the late nineteenth century (Bramming 1993). Indeed, the fathers and families of several founders were devoted followers of the pietistic lifeways portrayed in Danish novels and films such as *Babette's Feast* or *Breaking the Waves*. In that sense, it could be argued, the bigger societal rupture lamented by Tidehverv's founders was ironically replicated on the smaller level of family via their separation from their Inner Mission background. But crucially (also for understanding the role of fathers and their offspring in Tidehverv today), this cut was done in a way that was intended to be respectful to these fathers and to continue the patriarchal social, cultural and moral order more generally. This notion of a benign, productive and necessary 'interior' rupture can also be detected, as I shall now demonstrate, on a more theological and existential level.

Conservatism is a word that one hears all the time in relation to Tidehverv. Its many theological critics as well as left-wing politicians and commentators frequently accuse the Krarup family for being 'old-fashioned' and 'reactionary'. What these critics seem to fail to understand is that, among Tidehverv adherents, being old-fashioned is a badge of honour. Søren Krarup and other Tidehverv figures like to call themselves 'genuinely' (*ægte*) conservative as opposed to what other national-conservatives like to sarcastically dismiss as the 'so-called Conservative Party'. As he rhetorically asks in *Conservative Essays*,

> But progress must happen, mustn't it? We need to develop and move ahead … The only thing that is given for time and development surely is that they take care of themselves … Rather than saying, along with 1968 ideology, that everything that is old is wrong, we need to say, in tune with people's experience [*den folkelige erfaring*]: what is old, is good! (Krarup 1987, 126–7)

As I will show, this arch-conservative injunction is taken quite literally by certain participants in the annual Tidehverv summer meeting, a week-long event of theological and cultural political talks, debate and gossip that is held at a *folkehøjskole* ('people's high school' for adult learning) located in Southern Jutland close to the German border.

The obligatory after-dinner psalm-singing session was over, and groups of attendants were clustered around the dozen sofa tables scattered around the open fireplace that occupied the centre of the *højskole* study. Steaming hot black coffee and lavish servings of old-school Danish pastries were being consumed as the conversation slowly reached its usual menacing level, interspersed as it was with frequent outbursts of loud laughter and occasional swearing. At one table, an MP from the Danish People's Party was engaged in a heated theological discussion with a female pastor from a rural parish; at another, two prominent members of the Society for Freedom of Speech (*Trykkefrihedsselskabet*) were bantering and gossiping with a young nurse, a retired professional musician and a civil servant from a major provincial town. As for myself, I was still at this early point still trying to figure out which table, and conversation, I should try to join for the rest of the evening. Judging from my experiences from the two previous evenings, there was every reason to assume that it was going to be a long night. But above all, I realized, I was in urgent need of a drink and, perhaps, a cigarette; for although I had stopped smoking years before, there were still certain rare moments that I experienced with such intensity that they compelled me to make an exception. This was one such moment. After all, I had reached (and 'survived') the third day of my first Tidehverv summer meeting, an event that over recent years has been widely hailed (or feared, depending on how one sees things) as the intellectual heart of Denmark's ascending national-conservative right, and which for several decades has exercised an extraordinary influence among not just Danish theologians but also on Danish national politics (Grosbøll 2007; Pedersen 2017). There was too much new ethnography, and too many epistemological and ethical quandaries, for me to process.

So (heeding the lesson I had picked up the previous evening from watching other, mostly male meeting participants), I grabbed the Tuborg beer that I had already purchased before the psalm-singing began from the impromptu kiosk selling beers, cheap wine and other necessities, and went outside. As is usually the case at Tidehverv gatherings, several groups of smokers were huddled under the thin overhanging roof that was providing at least a measure of cover from the summer drizzle. Most of these groups of men and women were engulfed in heated discussions, so I went up to three young gentlemen who were occupying a corner for themselves, with shy and somewhat quizzical expressions on their stern-looking faces. I had already noticed them the previous day; indeed, they were hard not to take notice of. They seemed to be constantly keeping together in tightly knit groups of almost identically looking young men, dressed in what might be described as the standard uniform of Danish national-conservative intellectuals: sharply pressed suits or neat tweed jackets accompanied with ties or bow ties, as well as freshly polished and shining formal leather shoes. All them were smoking, two of them cigarettes, the last one what looked like an expensive pipe. 'Excuse me, do you have a light? (*undskyld, har du ild*)', I asked as I walked up to the group with a polite smile. The tallest and most dapper of the three young men looked straight at me and shot back, with a friendly but nevertheless serious tone, 'Do you mean the tinderbox (*fyrtøjet*)?' Here, I could not help laughing (indeed, I thought he was making a joke), enquiring: 'The tinderbox? That's a rare word to use!' At which point the man pulled out a Ronson lighter, lighting my cigarette while lecturing me (accompanied by nods from the two others): 'Well, no reason to use a new word when there is an old one that works perfectly fine, is there?'

Not all men at the annual summer meeting are dressed in suit and tie (although a fair number of the younger male theology students are), and I have never experienced anyone else making an issue out of the fact that smokers in Denmark and elsewhere in the world tend to use disposable plastic lighters instead of more old-school technologies for making fire. Nevertheless, while the above example can be described as an extreme outlier and therefore not representative of Tidehverv as such, it does, I think, capture the very explicit manner in which 'being conservative' is something that is celebrated in formal and informal discussion and is also practised at Tidehverv events. In many situations, this constant highlighting of 'conservative' ideas and deeds takes the form of criticism and ridicule of norms and values associated with the so-called 'cultural radicals' (left-wing progressive artists and intellectuals, more on whom below). Preferences for ecological and organic food, for example, are referred to as 'ridiculous' (*latterlige*), as are all references to 'climate-friendly' and 'green' products and solutions more generally. As a female priest told me during an interview, giggling as she recalled what was clearly a fond memory:

> Do you remember last year when a [recently employed] staff member from the kitchen introduced the menu for the final dinner, making a big thing out of the fact that all the vegetables were ecological? [Indeed, I did remember the situation all too clearly – it was

in fact one of the things I had jotted down in my notebook before crashing to bed that same night following another whisky and theology binge.] He [the staff member] was so surprised, I will never forget the confused look on his face when the entire room burst into laughter once he started bragging about ecological food. He just could not understand what was going on. I actually felt quite sorry for him, but it was also *so* funny!

Another issue around which the practice of 'being conservative' revolves is drinking and, perhaps to an even higher extent, smoking. While many other Danish Christians also drink (and smoke) when meeting for social and/or theological purposes, Tidehverv stands out for the sheer quantity of alcohol consumed and the proportion of people who at a given time of the day may be observed outside puffing on their cigarettes and/or pipes. As Agnete Raahauge, current editor in chief of the Tidehverv journal and de facto leader of this movement, concluded her traditional welcome address at the 2017 summer meeting:

> One more thing: I have been again this year been instructed by our hosts that it is strictly forbidden to drink your own alcohol on the premises [laughter, of the knowing sort that indicates everyone knows that people won't obey]. However, and in keeping with the procedure of previous meetings, our hosts have also on my request promised to procure large amounts of cheap wine, so that we shall be able to meet our often substantial needs for alcohol without going bankrupt [more giggling]. And finally, I have promised to make sure to remind you that smoking is *strictly* forbidden inside, so please remember to go to designated outside areas equipped with ashtrays when the need arises! [here Raahauge made a rhetorical pause, directing her gaze at the people occupying the front rows with a mock-stern expression]: I know that, until a few years ago, especially certain older members chose to ignore this smoking ban during especially late-night whisky-drinking sessions. But, seriously, we cannot have that any more! [grumbling sounds and reluctant nods].

As it happened, several middle-aged men did turn out to have brought their own single malt whisky to the gathering, which was revealed with much bluster and beaming expressions at every night at some point after midnight, which was also when a few daring individuals started lighting up cigarettes inside in defiance of the rules.

Elsewhere (Pedersen forthcoming), I have discussed how this 'obligation' to drink and smoke is part of a wider 'ethics of anti-piety' undergirding Tidehverv's theological project, and how this ethics can be traced back to the pietistic theology professors (as well as in several cases, fathers) against whom the four Tidehverv founders had revolted. For present purposes, however, let me point to the two most significant and political 'others' in opposition to whom my interlocutors worked so hard to define themselves, namely Islam and 'cultural radicals'. From a Tidehverv vantage, as I have also described elsewhere (Pedersen 2017), Islam and left-wing green progressives have more in common than what separates them. Notwithstanding the fact that Muslims believe in a God whereas cultural radicals proclaim not to do so, what unites them is the shared notion that it is possible for human beings to better themselves by adhering to explicit and normative rules or rights. And precisely for this reason – because Islam is a 'law-religion' (*lov-religion*) and because progressives have 'elevated human rights to their religion' – both are ideological abstractions that disobey God by infringing on his territory by either (in the left-wing atheist project) announcing His death and replacing Him with 'totalitarian human rights' and other 'abstract humanist universals', or – in what some would see as the opposite thing but from the Tidehverv vantage amounts to just the same sacrilegious moralism – by formulating religious laws for how to believe in Allah and to be a pious Muslim, as if one, anyone, could second-guess God's intentions.

Yet, as my interlocutors keep telling themselves in publications and seminars, as well as over coffee and lunch and not least those intense late-night drinking sessions, God's will cannot be known by man, for He is forever removed from and eternally distant from the sinners He created, and later manifested himself through an act of unfathomable divine grace and love, so it is only by succumbing to the irresolvable paradoxes of a human, all too human, existence full of impossible choices and endless suffering that one can obey God and be a slave of His will, without ever fully knowing how, when or indeed whether one succeeds in doing so. This, then, is why seemingly pedestrian and profane issues such as ecological good and anti-smoking campaigns take on such an inordinate importance. Along with pursuing a wealth of other 'genuinely conservative' practices, things and ideas, which taken together constitute a distinct and fine-masked system of signification that Tidehverv members learn to master, every element of their personal and theological being is invested 24/7 in the fight against cultural radicals, Islamists (well, all Muslims really) and other forces of political revolution and social rupture.

A genealogy of Danish freedom

But how did political revolution and societal progress become anathema to Tidehverv, and why is it that 'Christian leaping' and other forms of inward-oriented ruptures are not just permitted but required for the Christian subject, according to so many adherents of this Lutheran theological movement? To address these questions, we need to go back into history. Accordingly, in what follows, I shall make a foray into the genealogy of the modern Danish nation state, with particular focus on concepts of individual agency and more specifically freedom (*frihed*). This will involve a discussion of how three concepts of *frihed* map onto three different Danish cultural-cum-theological/political movements, whose origins are frequently traced back to three prominent nineteenth-century intellectuals, but are still vibrant and influential in contemporary Denmark. I am referring to the movements Grundtvigianismen, Tidehverv and Cultural Radicalism. These are associated, respectively, with the priest, poet and politician N.F.S. Grundtvig (1783–1872), who, among other things, is celebrated for his psalms and is credited for sowing the seeds for the Danish co-operative movement and pedagogic tradition; the philosopher and theologian Søren Kierkegaard (1813–55), who (alongside his part-contemporary, Grundtvig) had lasting influence on the Danish Protestant church, including Tidehverv itself; and literary critic and public intellectual Georg Brandes (1842–1927), father of the Modern Breakthrough and so-called cultural radical movement, which (to the regrets of conservatives, and in productive tension with some Grundtvigians) has dominated Danish arts, culture and education ever since (as illustrated, for example, by the contribution from Stine Krøijer on Danish left-radical politics in this volume). Since literally hundreds of books have been written on Grundtvig, Kierkegaard and Brandes, and given that all three were extremely prolific writers, I have neither the space nor the expertise to engage with their authorships and specific influence in any comprehensive manner. Instead, I shall attempt to provide a more general overview of the broader nineteenth-century intellectual, political and theological landscape from which first Grundtvig, then Kierkegaard and finally Brandes arose to fame, by homing in on the specific ideas about agency, subjectivity and freedom that more or less implicitly may be said to undergird their thinking.

According to Webb Keane (2007, 49–50), a key theme within the Protestant Reformation 'was the idea of restoring agency to its proper subjects. To reveal more directly the ultimate divine agent meant liberating individuals from the domination of illegitimate clerics and their rituals, and restoring people to their own principled agency.' However, as Keane also stresses,

> the point here is not that Protestantism introduces agency, or even individualism, into a world that had formerly lacked them … But … Protestantism … foster[s] particular kinds of self-consciousness about agency and the possibilities for human action – for instance, what may or may not be accomplished by human agents, what by divine ones. (2007, 52–3)

This observation captures a central preoccupation of nineteenth-century Danish theological and political-philosophical discourse as well as my Tidehverv interlocutors, namely how 'principled agency', to use Keane's term, is optimally fostered. Still, there are subtle as well as not so subtle differences between the specific ways in which these 'particular kinds of self-consciousness about agency and the possibilities for human action' have been promulgated and played out in different Protestant ethnographic contexts. Denmark is a case in point. Here, I suggest, competing vernacular politico-theological theories of virtuous agency rub off against each other in the three freedom-notions of *frisind, frimodighed* and *frigjorthed*, which may be described as partly overlapping, part conflicting ideals about what it means to think, speak and act independently and virtuously as an individual and group/people/nation (cf. Laidlaw 2014). None of these three Danish concepts of freedom corresponds fully to standard Western ideas of political liberty, economic choice and political-economic security of the sort widely associated with the French, Scottish and American enlightenments (Rothschild 2011; Rose 1999; Pedersen and Holbraad 2013). Rather, *frisind, frimodighed* and *frigjorthed* are each imbued with distinct theological-cum-political moral inflections, which can be traced back to the nineteenth century, when a middle-sized Northern European empire in the course of a few decades was reduced to a monolinguistic and monocultural nation state; a process that led to the collapse of the alliance between conservatives and national-liberals and the birth of a more inward-oriented but no less muscular and romanticist identity politics (Østergaard 2004). Nowhere is this more clear than in the oeuvres of Grundtvig, Kierkegaard and Brandes, as we shall now see.

As Denmark's folk hero number one, the poet, priest and politician N.F.S. Grundtvig is today celebrated for his lasting contribution to Danish arts and culture (he was, among other things, the author of many of Denmark's most popular Christian psalms), and for the broader theological, cultural, nationalist and indeed pedagogical movement (*Grundtvigianismen*) that he spurred (Allchin 1997; Buckser 1996). Thus, Grundtvig is celebrated for having planted the seeds for two lasting institutions emerging from the national awakening and quest for self-organization among Denmark's farmers in the late nineteenth and early twentieth centuries; namely, on the one hand the cooperative movement (*andelsbevægelsen*) and on the other the high school (*højskoler*; vocational schools especially for young adults of the same kind where the annual Tidehverv meeting takes place) with a unique pedagogic tradition (Michelson 1969). But Grundtvig also had a profound impact on Danish Christianity as a whole (Allchin 1997, 80–3). Indeed, faith and nation are inseparable for Grundtvig, for whom a full love of God and trust in God requires a full love of and trust in the people (Backhouse 2011, 81; see also Vind 1999). In keeping with the Lutheran celebration of emotions as a vital source of spiritual rapport with God, this is precisely what Grundtvig's emphasis on collective singing during sermons and in the community more generally is all about: a fusion between the Holy Spirit and the spirit (*ånd*) of the people: 'The spirit of the people is the necessary presupposition for living Christianity … Only when Christians everywhere make common cause with the natural person [*Natur-Menneskene*] in this respect, only then will Christianity and Popular Culture [*folkelighed*] generally, *and especially in Denmark*, come into their original, free and only proper natural relationship' (cited in Backhouse 2011, 81). Thus, according to Grundtvig, '*man*, apart from the nation to which he belongs, is an abstraction', and the Danish *folk* is imbued with a unique capacity but therefore also unique responsibility in this respect. For '[w]here the German gift to history was an awareness of the need to preach Christianity, it now falls to the Danes to give life to the Word by fusing the historical-cultural with the spiritual … Denmark is the place where the "Christian" and the "Human" will be united' (2011, 88).

So, Denmark, as Grundtvig summarized his fatherland's predicament in characteristic florid language, is nothing but 'history's Palestine'. From this national-theological perspective, the Nordic peoples, and especially the Danes, had emerged as not just the vanguard of humanity but as the second incarnation of God's chosen people, only now in the landscapes of Scandia inhabited by noble savages with Viking blood and vibrant warrior lore. In the words of Steven Backhouse, '[h]istory, says Grundtvig, ha[d] now developed to a point where there [was] a need for "a people" whose task it is to demonstrate to the world authentic

Christianity. It was to the Northern peoples [and] to Denmark, Queen of the Northern races, that the Divine mission to the world falls' (2011, 69). 'It is for this reason', as Backhouse goes on to explain, 'that Grundtvig was thankful for the 1848 war with Prussian Germany and the Slesvig-Holsten crisis, for it helped to awaken a sense of hitherto dormant Danishness' (2011, 83, 85). This was a notion that really struck a chord in war-fatigued nineteenth-century Denmark, as evidenced from the fact that a saying with the same message, *hvad udadtil tabes skal indad vindes*, is now part of the general historical knowledge and cultural repertoire of most adult Danes.

Let us now turn to Søren Kierkegaard, the famous Danish philosopher and theologian, who, along with his part-contemporary Grundtvig, was to have a lasting influence on the Danish Protestant church and theology, including Tidehverv. Now Kierkegaard respected and was well acquainted with Grundtvig's work, but he was also a vocal critic of his cultural-cum-political project. In fact, Kierkegaard's entire theological oeuvre was arguably a reaction, if not to Grundtvig in particular, then to the peculiar Hegel-inspired amalgamation of Protestant pietism and muscular national-liberalism, which occupied a dominant position at Copenhagen University and the city's intellectual salons in the mid-nineteenth century. At issue was not just what Kierkegaard dismissed as the self-righteous and hypocritical pompousness of the clergy, or the moralism and self-pity to which the well-trodden path to piety could lead. More than anything else, Kierkegaard's problem with Grundtvig revolved around his ideas about Christian faith and subjectivity. For whereas 'Grundtvig prioritizes a person's "culture-relation" over their "God-relation", and thinks that "man", apart from his nation, is an abstraction … Kierkegaard forcefully maintains that the abstraction occurs when one defines the individual as a mere component of a transgenerational cultural herd – which is the vision Grundtvig seems to hold' (Backhouse 2011, 90). Indeed, from a Kierkegaardian perspective, Christian faith can only be located at one scale, namely that of the individual, whose relationship to God is autonomous from and bypasses whichever social and cultural group, community or nation to which he or she may happen to be part.

We recognize here Kierkegaard's existentialism, which has been the subject of so much philosophical and theological (and, of late, anthropological) work. This is a project that could be characterized as radically individualist, in that the single human (*hin enkelte*) is posited as the ultimate ground and arbiter of not just moral judgement but also faith. For Kierkegaard, unless moral and religious thinking, actions and feelings are not based on individual acts of daring decisions, then such thoughts and deeds do not qualify as truly ethical let alone Christian. For the same reason, 'Christian faith … requires a terrifying inward struggle' (Evans 1989, 348). Or as Nigel Rapport summarizes Kierkegaard's project:

> human truth, Kierkegaard felt, the truth of the individual human situation, possessed a moral quality. To submit to majority opinion, to what was merely conventional, was an act of cowardice, and a consequence of a lack of respect for one's own integrity. Similarly, positing abstract entities such as 'humanity' or 'the public' was a means merely of eschewing and absolving individual responsibility for what was done, thought or said. At all costs one ought to resist the comforting temptation of according abstractions a separate reality … It was morally incumbent on one to draw forth notions of the individual and the subjective. (2002, 171)

In my discussion of Tidehverv's micro-history below, I shall explore certain concrete ramifications of this radical individualism, especially with respect to the question of what constitutes true Christian ethical and moral action. For the time being, I wish to conclude my genealogy of Danish freedom by considering the so-called 'Modern Breakthrough' which reached its peak in the *fin de siècle* years around 1900, and its relations to the post-First World War period, which saw not only the rise of increasingly polarized social and political movements, but also significant turmoil within the Danish Church (*Folkekirken*) itself, including the birth of Tidehverv.

The origin of cultural radicalism can probably be traced back to the Danish literary scholar and public intellectual Georg Brandes as well as other figures associated with Denmark's 'Modern Breakthrough' (which might just well be translated as the 'Modern Rupture'), as it was instigated by an influential group of writers and intellectuals who explicitly revolted against what they dismissed as Copenhagen's inward-looking and conservative cultural establishment. But to an even higher degree, cultural radicalism is associated with an influential constellation of left-leaning scholars, intellectuals and artists which reached its zenith of influence in the interwar and post-war period, but which has remained very present in intellectual, political and public debate ever since (Bay 2003; Jensen 1976; Seidenfaden 2005). According to Bredsdorff, post-war Denmark, with its rising anti-Soviet sentiment and its cold war paranoia, at this historical juncture was in dire need of an alert and brave cultural radicalism; a mind-set built on respect for humanity, which is international in outlook and which is infested with [*belastet med*] a social conscience. There is a need, too, for a spiritual heresy [*åndeligt kætteri*] that exposes convention, hypocrisy, and all jargon and clichés; a spiritual openness that does not just restrict itself to the surface of things [*ser på etiketterne*] but adopts a firm stance towards the underlying realities. There is a need for an ethics set free from [*frigjort*; here meaning 'liberated from'] the Church and from conservative convention. There is a need for an impatience, which does not wish to postpone progress until it has become a given or a regression. (1955, 57)

It is in formulations like these – in their unapologetically modernist and almost nihilist insistence on a violent break with tradition and (especially) with all religion, and in their radically humanist if not vitalist celebration of the autonomy and limitless potentiality of all human beings in their unique mental and bodily capacities – that the influence from Brandes and other figures associated with the Modern Breakthrough shows most clearly. It certainly is telling that one of Brandes's most famous essays (an introduction to Nietzsche, which the latter praised as one of the best accounts of his work that he had come across) was entitled 'Aristocratic Radicalism' (2014 [1897]). As Brandes bombastically summarized the Nietzschean project (2014 [1887], 35), 'without the ability to feel ahistorical, there can be no happiness'. Reminiscences of this 'aristocratic radicalism' can also be recognized in Denmark's 1968 'youth rebellion' and its aftermath, including the systematic critique of authorities, including university professors and the wider intellectual, artistic, literary and societal establishment. Just consider the following long passage, which is Brandes's attempt to summarize Nietzsche's problem with *Bildung*, one of the most central concepts of nineteenth-century German romanticist humanism (Bruford 1975) and closely related to its Danish sister concept of *dannelse*:

> The culture-philistine regards his own impersonal education as the real culture; if he has been told that culture presupposes a homogenous stamp of mind, he is confirmed in his good opinion of himself, since everywhere he meets with educated people of his own sort, and since all schools, universities, and academies are adapted to his requirements and fashioned on the model corresponding to his cultivation. Since he finds almost everywhere the same tacit conventions about religion, morality and literature, and with respect

to marriage, the family, the community and the State, he finds it demonstrated that this imposing homogeneity is culture … [Yet this] is not even bad culture, says Nietzsche; it is barbarism fortified to the best of its ability, but entirely lacking in the freshness and savage force of original barbarism; and he has many graphic expressions to describe Culture-Philistinism as the morass in which all weariness is stuck fast, and in the poisonous mists of which all endeavour languishes. (2014 [1897])

While Brandes and most of the other figures associated with the Modern Breakthrough were explicitly critical of religion in general and of Christianity in particular (Allen 2012), secular modernity has itself been described as a 'species of hedonism shot through with Christian ambitions for humanity' (Gray 2011, 25). For the same reason, I suggest we can conceive of cultural radicalism as a secular-humanist subspecies within Denmark's wider vernacular political theological landscape. As was found to be the case with the two explicitly Lutheran political theologies of Grundtvig and Kierkegaard, cultural radicalism is thus closely tied up with deep-rooted but largely tacit and undertheorized eighteenth- and nineteenth-century idea(l)s and assumptions about what makes someone a virtuous subject and a truly free and proper citizen in the Danish body politic. For as Brandes put it in his Nietzsche essay, with explicit reference to Kierkegaard (of whom he wrote another influential book), the key question with which the Modern Breakthrough was concerned was 'how to find oneself; how to dig oneself out from oneself' (2014 [1887], 21; emphasis added).

I have now completed my genealogy of modern Danish subjectivity. One key finding to emerge from this account is the three distinct concepts of freedom, which in crude terms can be mapped on to the key nineteenth- and twentieth-century politico-theological movements (Grundtvigianismen, kulturradikalismen and Tidehverv) and associated cultural heroes (Grundtvig, Kierkegaard and Brandes). Thus *frisind* ('open-mindedness'), following Grundtvig's peculiar combination of nineteenth-century romanticism with ideals from the Enlightenment and liberalism, denotes a liberal openness towards the perspectives of other people, but also (and this is of utmost importance to many right-wing contemporary adherents of Grundtvig) a right and obligation to defend one's own perspectives and to stand one's ground. Like cultural radicalism, *frigjorthed* ('uninhibitedness') may be traced back to Brandes and the Modern Breakthrough. Owing to its close ties with the ideal of a cosmopolitan individual freed from the shackles of tradition, religion and small-mindedness (*småborgerlighed*), it denotes generic tolerance and openness towards everything different, including the right and again the obligation to perpetually seek out and experience such new horizons in one's own life with regard to literature, art, sexuality, pedagogics, food and so on. As for the concept of *frimodighed* (lit. 'free daring'), it shares with the two other concepts of *frihed* the injunction to be true to one-self, but differs in the absolute and unforgiving way it is attainable only via continual struggle with various adversaries (*modstandere*) via which the freely daring person can fully become who he or she is. Indeed, *fri-modighed* is celebrated by Tidehverv adherents, who associate it only with heroes (*hædersmænd*) with the integrity and guts to stand their ground and speak their mind, be that in the context of heated theological controversies (about gay marriage, for example) or pressing political matters (such as the current refugee crisis) that spark controversy in both private and public contexts (see Pedersen 2017; 2018).

Inner revolution 1.0

With these points about past and present Danish concepts of freedom and faith in mind, we can now turn more specifically to the question of rupture, and particularly the tension between outer political revolution and existential/spiritual 'leaping'. To repeat the central question of this chapter: why is it that, according to my Tidehverv interlocutors, any notion of social progress and political revolution is not just utopian but sacrilegious? One answer, I suggest, can be found in the fact that Kierkegaard's (and by implication Tidehverv's) 'fundamentally existentialist' theological project can be understood as a radicalized form of pietism that takes its world-renouncing asceticism to its logical and necessary conclusion. To make this argument, I draw on the work of one of few anthropologists who have dared to pose big questions about what, for lack of a better word, might be referred to as modern European civilization. I am referring to Louis Dumont, who in *German Ideology* boldly suggested that:

> German culture had already adopted individualism in … its first or 'former' advance … the Lutheran Reformation. The Reformation applied individualism to the religious level, while it left out the socio-political level. In eighteenth-century Germany, Lutheran individualism had developed and spread into what is called pietism, a purely internal individualism which left untouched the sentiment of belonging to the global cultural community. In the second half of

the century, pietism is confronted with what I would call the second wave of individualism, that of the Enlightenment, and later on of the French Revolution … [T]he Reformation 'immunized' Germany against the Revolution, and Herder's [work] may be seen as a counteroffensive of the German community, supported by Luther's individualism, against the latter form of individualism. (1994, 10)

What Dumont suggests is that the French Revolution assumed a peculiarly *involuted* form in Germany; a process set in train both by the fact that its condition of possibility had already been established with the Reformation, and by the fact that the authoritarian political climate of late eighteenth-century and early nineteenth-century Prussia was not conducive to explicit political discontent or overt revolutionary agitation and action. The result was the emergence of a counter- or perhaps alter-revolutionary subjectivity infused with both Protestant technologies of the self (introspection, guilt, etc.) and humanist ethical ideals (*Bildung* and other nineteenth-century German notions of self-cultivation and spiritual development) – or what Dumont aptly calls 'a jealous interiority devotedly attended to' (1994, 20). Thus, Dumont goes on to explain:

the German Enlightenment differed from its Western counterpart in that it was religious. The Enlightenment in the West, and, topping it all, the French Revolution, took a path from which Germany gradually distanced itself … [I]n retrospect, it looks as if German culture, being outdistanced, had wanted to reassert itself and in so doing had produced in its turn an unheard-of development of the human mind … [This] allowed the Germans to react in their own way to the secular Enlightenment of the West … The Revolution was received *in the mind*, in the pattern set by the Reformation. (1994, 19–20; original emphasis)

In the spirit of Dumont's macro-comparisons, and with a nod to scholars such as Kapferer (2010), Iteanu (Iteanu and Moya 2015) and Robbins (Robbins and Siikala 2014), who have spurred a renewed anthropological interest in his work, I propose that, sufficiently adjusted, Dumont's analysis of the German case might be extended to the Danish one too. In fact, I shall go far as suggesting that both Grundtvig and (especially) Kierkegaard can be understood as extreme versions of the so-called 'purely internal individualism' that Dumont identified as a unique feature of Germany's 'religious enlightenment'. Beginning with Grundtvig, the analogy between the German and the Danish case is straightforward; after all, as

I described above, Grundtvig's ethno-nationalist and romanticist cultural-theological project in many ways calls to mind similar philosophical and intellectual developments in Germany in the nineteenth century.

As for Kierkegaard, the comparison at first glance seems more difficult, for how to reconcile his radical individualism and anti-authoritarianism with what Dumont calls the dominant 'community holism' and spontaneous subordination to political and social authorities in the context of post-Reformation and post-Enlightenment Germany? One solution lies in the realization, already hinted at in these discussions, that Kierkegaard's project *itself* was a reaction to the Enlightenment; only in his case it was a reaction to Grundtvig's Hegelian (and thus German) Enlightenment. Thus understood, Kierkegaard's theological and philosophical project emerges as a *reaction to a reaction*, which takes the form of what might be described as a *double involution*, namely not just the 'inner revolution' that Dumont identified in the German context, but also the inner rupture associated with Kierkegaard's notion of the angst-ridden introspective self.

In that sense, then, Kierkegaard's theological and philosophical project emerges as an extreme version of what Dumont called the German Enlightenment. At issue is a distinct subject-position, namely what might be described as a doubly involuted post-Christian subject, who has not just undergone the 'inner revolution' Dumont associated with German post-Enlightenment philosophy and cultural politics, but has been subject to a further inner revolution in the Danish context that has given birth to a radically introspective or, if you like, 'fundamentally existentialist' self.

Inner revolution 2.0

We can now answer the question posed at the beginning of this chapter, namely why all notions of political revolution and societal rupture are anathema to Tidehverv, and why existential leaps or ruptures are not just permitted but *required* of the genuine Christian believer. As should be clear by now, one plausible answer to this question can be found in the deeply Kierkegaardian underpinnings of Tidehverv; for it is precisely this double-involuted and radically introspective self that can be identified in Tidehverv's theological, ethical and political project. What seems to be at issue is an (irreversible?) transformation from a dimension of extensive or 'social' relationships between different people and their spirits/gods to a realm of intensive relations between different perspectives or 'voices' within a self-relational subject. Much as with Christian conversion in Mongolia, Melanesia and elsewhere (Holbraad and Pedersen 2017, 246–63; cf. Robbins 2007), in the context of certain Danish Christians there is a strong emphasis on ongoing self-rupture. Indeed, as we saw, faith in Tidehverv is conceived as a sort of 'inner leaping'; a mode of belief that must never cease to question itself lest it becomes sacrilegious. Counter-revolution, then, but as an involution of revolution, or to coin a term, inrevolution!

Tidehverv's 'truly Christian' (and thus also 'genuinely conservative') subject thus emerges as someone who is obliged to be radically introspective and make himself subject to perpetual inner rupture; not only because this is his duty and only path to salvation, but also because it helps to roll back, via *frimodige* existentialist actions, all evil-cum-utopian attempts by socialist revolutionaries, liberal progressives and Islamist fundamentalists to institute rupture and leaping within the realm of political life. This does not imply that one should seek to refrain from being involved in politics, or societal affairs more generally. On the contrary, one is welcome – meant even – to partake in political infighting on several levels ranking from the local and the national to the international and global. The stakes, after all, could not be higher, for this is a struggle over not just our right and obligation to remain only human, all too human, but also over God's sole right and responsibility to be our god. Accordingly, the purpose of politics is to ensure that it remains just that – concrete politics as opposed to abstract dream work by keeping us away from committing the ultimate sin of confusing ourselves with God, confusing the immanent plane of human politics, earthly life and natural law with the transcendental realm of eternal truth, ubiquitous love and divine grace.

To substantiate this point, let us delve a little deeper into the way in which certain late nineteenth- and early twentieth-century theological and philosophical problems have continued to inform the Tidehverv project. Consider again Krarup's chapter on 'The Anti-Totalitarian Kierkegaard' (1987). The reason why Kierkegaard, according to Krarup, was 'pre-eminently anti-totalitarian' is that his life:

> from its beginning to its end revolved around maintaining the totality of God's reign and possibility, with Man as a sinner facing God relegated to be a single individual given by his vocation and background [*hin enkelte i kald og stand*] … whose existence is framed by earth and temporality, and who is incapable of creating a totalitarian paradise in which perfection, truth and classless human happiness shall rule inhibited and eternally. (1987, 27)

This is why refusing to accept humanist conventions of political discourse shows *superior* faith and personal integrity. For only the 'knight of faith' has the ability, guts and character needed to pursue the socially and existentially challenging quest of 'sinning boldly', as the title of another of Krarup's books goes (citing Luther). Or as Torben Bramming explains in his book about Olesen-Larsen (one of the Tidehverv founders and a noted Kierkegaard authority in the theological establishment):

> During decisive moments of life even the greatest human is empty-handed facing God, who requires us to decide. This is a decision that is made by the single individual ... It [involves] thinking in contradictions, but this thinking in contradictions does not merely have a rhetorical purpose; on the contrary it reflects the ambivalence of existence; indeed, one might say that it is the essential condition of the existing human which it lives out on a daily basis. (1999, 88–90; translated by the author)

Here, the Christian believers can never be certain (that would be too easy), but must face the paradoxes of being suspended between eternity and time, between the concrete immanence of mankind and the abstract transcendence of God. Only via constant leaps of faith is 'the knight of faith' able to momentarily straddle (but never overcome) the absolute ontological divide between God and man, between transcendence and immanence, eternity and time.

Existentialist effervescence

The question remains, of course, how is all this done in practice? What can humans do to ensure that they keep on 'thinking in contradictions'? How does one go about embracing, with all the gusto expected from the 'knight of faith', the human, all too human, predicament of 'bold sinning'? Elsewhere, I have explored this via ethnographic analyses of selected sociological, political and theological tensions surfacing in the annual Tidehverv summer meeting and in the individual biographies and political lives of key figures from this movement (Pedersen 2017; 2018; forthcoming). Let me, therefore, for present purposes and by way of conclusion, home in on one specific dimension of Tidehverv sociality that encapsulates what has been a central concern in this chapter. I am referring to the prominent role played by alcohol, drinking and drunkenness during the summer meetings as well as (judging from what has repeatedly been emphasized to me) other and more private social gatherings amongst Tidehverv (and national-conservative) circles. Evidently, as we saw, drinking occupied a central place in the Tidehverv self-imaginary, including in the identity work that is constantly performed by my interlocutors in order to distance and differentiate themselves from 'boring' (*kedelige*) and 'pious' (*fromme*) religious groups, whether Christian or Muslim. To be sure, many other Danish Christian and/or political groups also drink when they meet, 'but that's different. Their discussions are boring and they are not serious like we are', lectured a senior Tidehverv priest when I raised this objection. As one of the aforementioned young conservatives told me with a grin on his clean-shaven face during the 2017 summer meeting (which coincided with Roskilde Festival, the biggest, oldest and most famous Danish rock/pop music festival with up to 100,000 participants), 'This place is the national-conservative Roskilde!'

But that is not all. In addition, I would suggest, there is also another and a deeper dimension to this emphasis on drinking and drunkenness in Tidehverv contexts. As I have already tried to convey in my introductory ethnographic vignettes, something more serious and, if you like, existential or even transcendental is at stake during these sessions of late-night boozing. More precisely, I propose, one reason why people find it to be so important to indulge in these five-, six- or seven-hour-long binges is that it makes them 'become who they are', to borrow an expression from one of my interlocutors (Pedersen 2018). Certainly, one is left with a clear sense (speaking here from personal experiences gained from what Fiskesjö aptly coins participant-intoxication (Fiskesjö 2010) that the participants of these intense micro-gatherings are working hard at being a particular kind of person. That is, they are striving towards being *frimodige* individuals, who are not afraid (in fact, find solace and a happiness in) disagreeing with and being contrary to others, including peers with whom they might have been in perfect agreement just before. While this obligation to disagree entails the risk that people may end up being more permanent adversaries (of which there have been several examples over the years), the ideal (and often the reality) is that, at some point well into the night or in some cases the early morning, all matters of concern (*anliggender*) that needed to be discussed and disagreed about (as well as all the wine and whisky bottles) have been depleted. At this point, and at this point only, the table of drinkers can break up and return to their individual quarters, having once again been lucky enough to experience a degree of freedom and self-completion, which according to many meeting participants is not surpassed in any other domain of their lives.

Might there be some kind of connection between this culture of collective drinking at the summer meetings and Tidehverv's more general celebration of existential leaping and inner rupture discussed above? Embarking on a train of thought that shall here remain sketchy but that I hope to develop in future work, I would tentatively suggest that we are faced with a sort of extended or distorted 'collective effervescence'. According to established wisdom, this arch-Durkheimian concept is used to denote social events characterized by an usually intense sense of unity and connectedness, which for the same reason is often associated with sacred and transcendental domains of human existence. Now on the face of it, the recurrent and ritualized after-dinner boozing sessions described above would fit this definition well. Also during these memorable summer nights, people seem to experience a beefed-up version of several social relations and social norms that they cherish the most. As such, perceived from the vantage of the ethnographic fieldworker, these events are marked by a dense social atmosphere where the most sociologically sacred Tidehverv values are made temporarily visible.

But we can take the analysis one step further. For is there not a sense to which a different, more introspective transcendence is also brought about during these bouts of collective effervescence? I would tentatively infer that, simultaneously with the intensification of social relations that is perceived to take place between participants at the intersubjective level, a concurrent intensification is also experienced to occur *within* each (or at least some) of them in form of what might be called 'existentialist effervescence'. And that, I would further venture, is the ultimate and deeper, or dare one say 'sacred', purpose of all that drinking and debating during the summer meetings and other Tidehverv gatherings: the enactment, in the realm that could be referred to as self-relational or intra-subjective, of an almost spiritual and mystical 'leaping into' a complete version of the person that I 'really am' (that is, of the person that I would like to be). And, crucially, it is exactly this experience of 'a jealous interiority devotedly attended to' (Dumont 1994, 20) that can only be ascertained via repeated inner ruptures, but never any outer revolution.

Acknowledgements

Research for this article was supported through my participation in an ERC Consolidator Grant on comparative anthropologies of revolutionary politics (ERC-2013-CoG, 617970, CARP). I thank Martin Holbraad and the other members of the CARP team for great discussions and good company during my visit to UCL during the spring of 2017.

Note

1. While this term is commonly associated with Kierkegaard, it has been disputed whether he ever used it himself. He did, however, discuss 'leaps' (*spring*) on many occasions, including the 'qualitative transition' involved in becoming a Christian believer (McKinnon 1993).

References

Allchin, A.M. 1997. *Grundtvig: An Introduction to his Life and Work*. Aarhus: Aarhus University Press.

Allen, Julie K. 2012. 'Georg Brandes: Kierkegaard's Most Influential Mis-Representative'. In *Kierkegaard's Influence on Literature, Criticism and Art: Denmark*, edited by Jon Stewart, 17–41. London: Ashgate.

Backhouse, Stephen. 2011. *Kierkegaard's Critique of Christian Nationalism*. Oxford: Oxford University Press.

Bay, Carl E. ed. 2003. *Kulturradikale Kapitler fra Georg Brandes til Otto Gelsted*. Copenhagen: C.A. Reitzel.

Bramming, Torben, 1993. *Tidehvervs Historie*. Copenhagen: ANIS.

Bramming, Torben. 1999. *Livsmod på Guds Ord. Studier i Kristoffer Olesen Larsens eksistensteologi og tid*. Frederiksberg: Anis.

Brandes, Georg. 2014 [1887]. *Aristokratisk Radikalisme*. Copenhagen: Informations Forlag.

Bredsdorff. 1955. 'Om at fodre sine karusser'. *Politiken* 11. Accessed 31 December 2014. http://modkraft.dk/node/25363.

Bruford, W.H. 1975. *The German Tradition of Self-Cultivation: 'Bildung' from Humboldt to Thomas Mann*. Cambridge: Cambridge University Press.

Buckser, Andrew S. 1996. *Communities of Faith: Sectarianism, Identity, and Social Change on a Danish Island*. Oxford: Berghahn.

Dumont, Louis. 1994. *German Ideology: From France to Germany and Back*. Chicago: University of Chicago Press.

Evans, C. S. 1989. 'Is Kierkegaard an Irrationalist? Reason, Paradox, and Faith'. *Religious Studies* 25 (3): 347–62.

Fiskesjö, Magnus. 2010. 'Participant Intoxication and Self–Other Dynamics in the Wa Context'. *The Asia Pacific Journal of Anthropology* 11 (2): 111–27.

Gingrich, A., and M. Banks. 2006. *Neo-Nationalism in Europe and Beyond: Perspectives from Social Anthropology*. Oxford: Berghahn Books.

Gray, J. 2011. *Voltaire and Enlightenment*. London: Phoenix Books.

Grosbøll, Mette Kathrine. 2007. *Teologisme – Om Tidehvervs vej til Christiansborg*. Copenhagen: Anis.

Gullestad, Marianna. 2006. *Plausible Prejudice, Everyday Experiences and Social Images of Nation, Culture and Race*. Oslo: Universitetsforlaget.

Hervik, Peter. 2011. *The Annoying Difference: The Emergence of Danish Neonationalism, Neoracism, and Populism in the Post-1989 World*. Oxford: Berghahn Books.

Holbraad, Martin, and Morten Axel Pedersen. 2017. *The Ontological Turn: An Anthropological Exposition*. Cambridge: Cambridge University Press.

Iteanu, André, and Ismael Moya. 2015. 'Introduction: Mister D.: Radical Comparison, Values, and Ethnographic Theory'. *HAU: Journal of Ethnographic Theory* 5 (1): 113–36.

Jensen, E.B. 1976. *Kulturradikal litteraturkritik, litteratur og samfund i mellemkrigstidens kulturradikale debat*. Odense: Odense Universitet.

Kapferer, Bruce. 2010. 'Louis Dumont and a Holist Anthropology'. In *Experiments in Holism*, edited by Ton Otto and Nils Bubandt, 187–208. Oxford: Wiley-Blackwell.

Keane, Webb. 2007. *Christian Moderns: Freedom and Fetish in the Mission Encounter*. Berkeley: California University Press.

Krarup, S. 1987. *Det Tavse Flertal: Konservative Essays*. Tønder: Tidehvervs Forlag.

Laidlaw, James. 2014. *The Subject of Virtue: An Anthropology of Ethics and Freedom*. Cambridge: Cambridge University Press.

Larsen, Knud E. 2006. 'Hvad betyder Tidehverv?'. Accessed 22 August. https://www.kristendom. dk/spørg-om-kirkehistorie/hvad-betyder-tidehverv.

McKinnon, Alistair. 1993. 'Kierkegaard and "The Leap of Faith"'. *Kierkegaardiana* 16: 107–25.

Michelson, Wilhelm. 1969. 'From Religious Movement to Economic Change: The Grundtvigian Case in Denmark'. *Journal of Social History* 2 (4): 283–301.

Østergaard, Uffe. 2004. 'The Danish Path to Modernity'. *Thesis Eleven* 77 (1): 25–43.

Pedersen, Morton Axel. 2017. 'The Politics of Paradox: Kierkegaardian Theology and National-Conservatism in Denmark'. In *Distortion: Social Processes beyond the Structured and Systemic*, edited by Nigel Rapport, 84–106. London: Routledge.

Pedersen, Morten Axel. 2018. 'Becoming What You Are: Faith and Freedom in a Danish Lutheran Movement'. *Social Anthropology* 26 (2): 182–96.

Pedersen, Morton Axel. Forthcoming. 'Existentialist Fundamentalists: The Ethics of Anti-Piety in a Danish Protestant Movement'. *Journal of the Royal Anthropological Institute*.

Pedersen, Morten Axel, and Martin Holbraad. 2013. 'Introduction: Times of Security'. In *Times of Security: Ethnographies of Fear, Protest and the Future*, edited by Martin Holbraad and Morten Axel Pedersen, 1– 27. London: Routledge.

Rapport, Nigel. 2002. '"The Truth is Alive'. Kierkegaard's Anthropology of Dualism, Subjectivity and Somatic Knowledge". *Anthropological Theory* 2(2): 165–83.

Robbins, Joel. 2004. *Becoming Sinners: Christianity and Moral Torment in a Papua New Guinea Society*. Berkeley: University of California Press.

Robbins, Joel. 2007. 'Continuity Thinking and the Problem of Christian Culture: Belief, Time, and the Anthropology of Christianity'. *Current Anthropology* 48 (1): 5–17.

Robbins, Joel, and Jukka Siikala. 2014. 'Hierarchy and Hybridity: Toward a Dumontian Approach to Contemporary Cultural Change'. *Anthropological Theory* 14 (2): 121–32.

Rose, N. 1999. *Governing the Soul: The Shaping of the Private Self*. London: Free Association Books.

Rothschild, E. 2011. *Economic Sentiments: Adam Smith, Condorcet, and the Enlightenment*. Cambridge, MA: Harvard University Press.

Seidenfaden, Tøger. ed. 2005. *Den Kulturradikale Udfordring. Kulturradikalismen Gennem 130 år*. Copenhagen: Tiderne Skifter.

Thorleifsson, Cathrine. 2016. 'From Coal to UKIP: The Struggle over Identity in Postindustrial Doncaster'. *History and Anthropology* 27 (5): 555–68.

Thorleifsson, Cathrine. 2017. 'Disposable Strangers: Far Right Securitisation of Forced Migration in Hungary'. *Social Anthropology* 5 (3): 318–34.

Thorleifsson, Cathrine. 2018. *Nationalist Responses to the Crises in Europe: Old and New Hatreds*. Research in Migration and Ethnic Relations Series. London and New York: Routledge.

Vind, Ole. 1999. *Grundtvigs Historiefilosofi*. Copenhagen: Gyldendal.

5

Blurring Rupture: Frames of Conversion in Japanese Catholicism

Tobia Farnetti

This chapter explores the struggles with rupture of a small Catholic community in the east of Tokyo. Rupture is here conceptualized in two ways. On the one hand, following Robbins (2007), it is a temporal break: a radical interruption of previous modes of existence in favour of new ones. On the other hand, rupture is also here understood as a spatial relationship, as the radical division of a minority religion and the wider society surrounding it. In Tokyo the two go together as conversion into the Christian life entails significantly breaking with urban Japanese society and its rhythms. The community of the Church of the Holy Family struggles with both forms of rupture, imposed on them by both the priest himself and the general understanding of religiosity and its place in society outside the church. What follows focuses on the ways in which people deal with these imposed ruptures in the face of their own feeling and desire for continuity.

The work of Joel Robbins especially (e.g. 2007, 2010) has identified the importance of temporal ruptures for the Christian world view and imagination. Conversion is identified as the breaking point with the past, a divine invasion into the self that leaves everything changed – a radical juncture that spurs people to cut with the old traditions and replace them with new virtuous ways of life (e.g. Meyer 1999; Engelke 2004; Keller 2005; Keane 2007; Vilaça 2014). The scholar of religion Lewis Rambo (1993) had already come up with a similar framework with its identification of seven stages of religious conversion. While the *process* of conversion involves the totality of seven stages, this pivots on a 'crisis', which he defines as a rupture in world view that precipitates change. The rest is dealing with the world post-rupture through the processes of readjustment, reconciliation and reinterpretation that many anthropologists have studied in converted groups (e.g. Lienhardt 1982; also Kan 1991; Scott 2005; Vaté 2009; Chua 2012).

These processes of reinterpretation and reframing of the past are engaged both by the individual, in their understanding of their own life history, and by communities at large, usually as a consequence of missionary activity. Rupture needs not only to be an existential transformation of the self but it is often a collective transformation, and hence signifies a breach with many things that fall under the rubric of 'tradition': rituals, institutions, rhythms that gave meaning to the community's life before conversion. Indeed, Robbins's own concern with rupture emerges from his previous work with the Urapmin of Papua New Guinea (Robbins 2004). Here Robbins focuses on the existential impact of conversion on the Urapmin, whom he understands as locked in an incomplete transition between the 'traditional' value system and the Christian one they recently adopted. In other words, the question of conversion and rupture here becomes one with the question of culture change and its implications. The Urapmin, Robbins argues, have indeed adopted Christianity but they are yet to fully integrate it in their own way of life. They still live between two cultural systems that are in the process of being synthesized and yet are still distinct, and this disjuncture manifests itself in moral contradictions. The Urapmin, that is, still possess two distinct frames for understanding their behaviour and these often clash without resolution, leaving people trapped between conflicting values.

When the Christian mission encounters non-Christian cultures, sometimes pre-existing cultural meanings are altered and yet the wider cultural categories remain untouched, a process that Robbins calls 'assimilation'.[1] Here the indigenous cosmos adapts itself to incorporate foreign elements and yet it remains structurally unchanged, and hence able to propagate itself. The difficulties experienced by Portuguese missionaries working on the evangelization of the Tupi in sixteenth-century Amazonia provide a vivid example of this process (see Viveiros de Castro 2011). To the missionaries' frustration, the Tupi appeared to appropriate only those aspects of Christianity that validated their own cosmology and allowed the continuation of their culture. Similarly, Robbins understands the Urapmin engagement with Christianity to have been initially a form of assimilation – a 'utilitarian conversion' motivated by traditional non-Christian values (2004, 115).

Conversely, a successful mission fostered a situation where people cease to try to reproduce 'traditional' systems and embrace the new culture as a 'whole', as a self-conscious effort accompanied by the eradication of old values (cf. Ortiz 1995, 102–3). Robbins calls it 'adoption' and defines it as the moment in which people take on the new cultural system 'on its own terms' (2004, 115), when the old culture stops providing the frame for action and Christianity takes its place. If assimilation implied the rejection of full conversion in favour of continuity with the past – those attempts to protect cultural boundaries that Shaw and Stewart (1994) branded 'anti-syncretism' – adoption spells the full embracing of that radical temporal rupture demanded by Christian conversion.

In the 1990s the Urapmin were on the road to adoption; that is, they had incorporated Christian values but not fully completed the transition to the new culture. People had indeed radically turned away from their traditional way of life, yet their social and economic structure remained the same as it was before (see also Robbins, this volume). This fracture engendered moments where ideas about social structure came into conflict with Christian ideas of the moral person, leaving the Urapmin with intense moral conundrums (Robbins 2004, 35). They were living with 'two cultures', or rather in the difficult space between them.

Robbins's model has been criticized for treating 'Urapmin traditional culture' and 'Christianity' as two 'wholes' (e.g. Rumsey 2004; cf. Hirsch 2008) and not recognizing the hybridity that already preceded Urapmin conversion. In the Japanese context, treating Christianity and indigenous culture as bounded wholes is, however, somehow fitting, given that people themselves – priest, congregation and the average urban dweller – seem to treat the two systems, despite the indubitable presence of hybridity, as clearly distinct homogeneous wholes and hence the transition between one and the other as a radical shift. In the Church of the Holy Family, whose community this chapter focuses on, people struggle with this transition and try to maintain their own sense of continuity with people, institutions and social forms of Japanese society despite the pressures from both inside and outside. Unlike the Urapmin, however, people here are not afflicted by moral anguish and often fail to conform to Christian precepts in order to participate in the 'old culture' unperturbed, deliberately keeping these deeds away from the priest's eyes and ears. Taking as an ethnographic fulcrum the community's experiences of drunkenness and intoxication, which are explicitly banned by Catholic dogma as conveyed by the priest and yet engaged in by the community on a weekly basis, the chapter investigates the way in which people try to find continuity in the face of rupture. Looking at the ways in which people at times let the Christian frame of meaning encompass social and cultural forms belonging to Japanese mainstream society while at other times allowing mainstream society to encompass Christian elements, the chapter argues that something peculiar happens in those secret drunken nights. In the blur of drunkenness, it is impossible to discern which culture is providing a frame for action: frames become images until one cannot tell which side is encompassing which, which is figure and which is frame. In this haze rupture and continuity are blurred, and activities branded as sin by the church can become themselves fundamental parts of the Christian life.

The picture: the Church of the Holy Family and its community

The Church of the Holy Family is a small Catholic church in one of Tokyo's poorer eastern neighbourhoods in the part of the city known as *shitamachi*, 'down town'. The building is simple and unadorned and stands in a yard that is shared with the Christian school next door, which also comprises a small community centre and the church offices. A single cherry tree stands in the middle of the car park. The inside is unadorned in a way that, although uncommon for the usually ostentatious style of Catholic sacred design, is perhaps more in line with Japanese aesthetic sensibilities. Upon entering one is met, on the two sides of the main door, by two stoups for the holy water mounted respectively by a statue of St Francis Xavier, the missionary who brought Catholicism to Japan in the sixteenth century, and the Virgin Mary. Small stained-glass windows follow the aisles on the two sides, separated by wooden carvings of the Stations of the Cross, and the nave is in shadow even during a bright day. The pews are wooden and so is the simple crucifix behind the altar. Overall, a sober atmosphere of simplicity pervades the building, which remains mostly empty during the week. In the afternoon, when all the cars and bikes have left and the churchyard has returned to its usual stillness, the church runs a Sunday school for the children. A few people, mainly self-appointed 'aunties' (*obachan*), help with the running of the school where the children learn Christian songs, stories from the scriptures and play together for the rest of the afternoon.

The upkeep of the church is taken care of by volunteers, a core of about ten retired people who clean, cook and are responsible for administration. The liturgical activities, on the other hand, are run entirely by the priest, whom everyone simply calls 'the priest' (*shimpu-sama*). His sermons are simple and relatable – they talk about keeping faith in hard times of loss and grief, to trust in the Lord (*kami-sama*) when things don't go the way you desire, of the love of God being reflected in the family and between co-workers. When he preaches from the pulpit he becomes agitated and talks too fast, stutters, turns red and waves his hands in the air. Waiting outside the door after Mass, calm and composed, he greets people leaving the building, inquiring about their health and families.

The priest is very much the moral beacon of the community. Although the prescriptions of Catholicism are laid out in the holy books, the relationship with the scriptures is not always an easy one for the community. The Bible is not a central object of devotion as in other Christian communities around the world (cf. Robbins 2012) – rather it is engaged with only in Bible class once a week and through the hard-to-follow sermons of the priest on Sunday. The strong emphasis on the importance of the scriptures one finds in many ethnographies of Christianity is here eclipsed in favour of other activities.

In the Church of the Holy Family the language of the scriptures is obfuscated and, above all, difficult. The unintelligibility of the scriptures does not trigger processes of intense engagement with the Bible as is often found in narratives of American Protestantism. Carapanzano's (2000) account of Evangelical literalism, Bielo's (2008; 2009) portrayal of the intense processes of Biblical exegesis and knowledge production in Bible studies classes and Malley's (2004) description of the way people link Biblical readings with their own life circumstances are all examples of the ways in which people place the word of God at the very heart of what it means to believe. For the community of the Church of the Holy Family the scriptures do not have such aliveness and do not demand such vehemence. Instead they become inert, a chore, something that is not part of the vibrant life of the community but a duty that simply has to be done (cf. Whitehouse 2000) – sometimes easily, when one can be carried by the lull of the ritual of Mass, and other times more onerously, when one tries to decipher them at Bible study class.

It is instead through participation in church activities that identification with Christianity is felt most strongly by the community. The ritual of Mass is felt to be important and everyone enjoys participating in it. However, when asked for details about the ritual itself or the readings of the day, people claim ignorance and defer to the priest. This self-proclaimed ignorance is never met with frustration but with a placid acceptance – people do try to listen to the Gospels but they are not moved, do try to go to Bible study class but it's too difficult to understand. People do not seem to be motivated to spend more time studying and asking questions about the meaning of the scriptures; what seems to be important instead is *being there* – being at Mass and participating in it. Saito-san, for example, felt strongly moved when she was asked to do the first reading from the pulpit at Mass and she spent hours rehearsing the few lines of the book of Isaiah. 'T: "Was it interesting?" S: "Yes very interesting." T: "What do you think it means?" S: "Oh I do not know … it's difficult … I don't understand it".'

While modesty undoubtedly plays a part in the answer, the point of the rehearsal was never to let the meaning sink in but rather a purely formal concern with getting the reading right in its delivery. Of course, a rehearsal is about performance, and yet the engagement with the scriptures through the repetitive reading of a few lines of the Old Testament was never for Saito-san a spiritual or meditative act. In the same way, the most moving parts of Mass are singing together (especially when one is leading the choir), participating in bringing the offerings to the altar, and simply being there and being seen. Communion is not only a moment of recollection but also an occasion to dart one's gaze around and see who is there, bow slightly to greet people and smile at friends. For the same reasons the informal reception in the community hall after Mass and the time spent in the churchyard outside are extremely important, and people often head off afterwards to spend time together in a café or at a sushi restaurant. Time spent together is, for the community, where the Christian life truly 'happens', where the self-determination as Catholic believers is performed, embodied and most acutely felt.

However, this does not mean that people would rather see the church abandon those activities. Even though the Bible is hard to understand and the rituals are sometimes tedious, people cherish them and they wouldn't want them to be any 'friendlier'. Indeed, many people assert that they chose Catholicism *because* of its rigid structure, because it felt old and legitimate (cf. Brown 2017). People like the formality of Mass, and someone went so far as to propose that Latin hymns be introduced in the choir's repertoire. There is indeed a certain anxiety about authenticity: people are concerned with how their church, their rituals and even the aesthetics of their leisure time resonate with their original source, Catholicism in Europe and the USA. The rituals, meetings and classes' strict adherence to the Italian and American model is what makes people feel connected to a transnational Catholic community. It is not a loose feeling of an international *communitas*, a spiritual community united in the love of God, that holds the church together in people's minds but instead a formal resemblance. 'When I went to Mass in Italy', says Fukuzawa-san, dreamily showing a picture of herself posing in front of the Coliseum, 'it was just like in our church!' The rigid formalism of the Catholic spiritual life is also what distinguishes the community from the Protestant churches in the neighbourhood – 'see … our church looks like a real church … the other churches just look like normal houses'.

The point here is that the community's understanding of Christianity as extremely social, as something to do with the collectivity, is not opposed to the dogmatic form of which the priest is understood to be the keeper. The dogma and formalism are for the community fundamental to their identity as Catholics, even though they do not need to fully understand it. Form is here precisely what it is meant to be – form – and it does not demand the grasping of meaning. However, this more 'communitarian' form of religiosity is not entirely part of the Catholicism the priest is painstakingly teaching the community. In church these religious forms seem almost an emergent phenomenon, something that the community does in order to sit more comfortably in partial foreignness of Roman Catholicism. The priest values the commitment to community, yet he still wishes people would engage with scriptures and dogma in the ways that he is trying to teach them.

The community's engagement with the church is however genuine and marked by a deep commitment. In fact, one could say that the community is doing extra work in engaging the church beyond the bounds of what is expected of them. The faith as promulgated by the priest is highly dogmatic and does not give the community the tools to build and strengthen community: it provides a centre of gravity around which to build such community but not enough occasions and means to do so. Life at church satisfies a certain craving for form and exerts a strong centripetal force that allows people to come together.

However, how to perform and foster community is another matter. Time in church is always too short and too sporadic, and people are constantly creating spaces of sociality outside it where they can *live* the Christian life *together*, as a community. Church only lasts a few hours on a Sunday and on Thursdays at Bible study class. People need more, and thus create occasions to be together meaningfully as Christians. It is in these spaces, this chapter argues, that the struggle with rupture is most strongly felt.

The frame: rupture in a minority religion

Christianity in Tokyo today is very much in a minority. On a national scale the number of Japanese people partaking in any Christian denomination amounts to less than 0.9 per cent, of which only 0.4 per cent is Catholic. In the Archdiocese of Tokyo, the number of Catholics amounts to about 0.5 per cent and similar numbers are seen in the surrounding diocese of Saitama and Yokohama. The demographics tend to be largely constituted by the middle class of the main urban agglomerates with the exception, albeit dwindling, of the countryside in the Nagasaki area. The numbers of Japanese Catholics have been steadily decreasing since shortly after the post-war boom (Mullins 2011), and it is mostly the influx of migrants, mainly from the Philippines and Korea, that allows the percentage to stay the same. Most churches provide services in Tagalog, Korean and other languages along with the Japanese Mass, and church membership – the church studied here being an exception – tends to be ethnically quite mixed.

While Shinto shrines are ever-present features of the urban landscape, the statistical imperceptibility of Christianity is visually reflected in the scenery of the city, where churches are few and often tucked away in back streets. This invisibility is partially reinforced from within: one's faith is rarely mentioned, public displays are not encouraged apart from rare occasions such as the first part of the Mass on Palm Sunday, held in the churchyard. Christianity, and even more Catholicism, is truly a

Figure 5.1 Outdoor service under the cherry tree on Palm Sunday. Photo by the author.

minority religion – small, scarcely visible, unassuming. Discourses of rupture, coming both from within and without the bounds of the community, keep it separate and circumscribed.

In its minority status, the perception of Christianity in Japan today is a complex matter. It is grouped under the category of *shūkyō* – a word translatable as 'religion', but that does not comprise the amalgam of Buddhist and Shinto practices in which virtually everyone partakes. Buddhist and Shinto weddings, funerals, shrine visits, ancestor worship, local festivals – all of these fall under the wider notion of *dentō* – 'tradition' – together with tourist vistas, kimonos, local delicacies, common architectural elements, imperial regalia, and the blend of syncretic elements and secular daily practices that people simply define as 'part of their culture'. In other words, the Shinto and Buddhist elements that pervade the lifestyle of a Japanese person are not necessarily a religious expression, but parts of a wider life-world of signifiers that constitutes – in the collective imaginary – *being Japanese*. Foreign religions on the other hand are, in a real sense, 'religions' – and they imply a certain break with that horizon of signifiers that grounds one in the culturally specific being-in-the-world of Japan.

When one says *shūkyō* the image that generally forms in people's minds is, inevitably, one of the numerous 'new religions' (*shin-shūkyō*) that cropped up just after the Meiji reformation and more intensely after the Second World War (e.g. Clarke 2000). 'New religions' are viewed negatively or with suspicion, especially after the Tokyo subway sarin attacks by the group Aum Shinrikyo (*Oumu Shinrikyō*) in 1995. Most people today see members of new religions as dangerous and, fundamentally, as outsiders. Catholicism is not a *shin-shūkyō* itself, although many groups such as Jehovah's Witnesses and other modern denominations are considered Christianity-based new religions. Yet the word *shūkyō* recalls, if not the extremism of new religions, a certain dissonance with Japanese society and its structures; with the family, its rhythms of inheritance, marriage, burial and so on. For the non-religious person being affiliated with religiosity is difficult, potentially dangerous (*abunai*) and embarrassing.

Because of this perceived distance between 'religions' and majority culture the post-Meiji history of Christianity is not an easy one. Christians in Japan have gone through many challenges, from discrimination to outright violence (see Ghanbarpour 2015). The Church of the Holy Family was established as part of a missionary effort from the Tsukiji parish to spread Catholicism in the east of Tokyo. During the riots that followed the signing of the Treaty of Portsmouth in 1905, churches, representing 'the West', were a prime target for the rioting masses, and the Church of the Holy Family was burned to ashes. Today there are no tensions between church and neighbourhood, and the community does not like to talk about the difficulties that they encountered in the past.

One can find a strong parallel in the story of Ishigawa-san who, together with his wife, runs a non-denominational Protestant church in the same neighbourhood. The church is hosted in the remains of American Second World War army barracks, and when they took over from a foreign pastor, about 30 years ago, the community was hostile and diffident. 'It was horrible', Ishigawa-san says before a candle-lit service, 'people would break our windows at night. I was so scared.' Their attempts to spread the word of God were met with silence, hostility and threats. While things are different today, some of these sentiments linger in a muted interiorized way and, despite all the politeness and kindness that suffuses relations between neighbours, Christians are still seen with a measure of suspicion.

The gulf between Christians and mainstream urban society is, however, not only asserted from the outside, but also from within. While things such as festivals, visiting shrines and keeping a household shrine (*kamidana*) are perceived in the mainstream as 'tradition', the priest himself marks them as religious activities. In so doing, participation in these activities, which are by most people perceived as important moments of bonding with family or the local community, is equated with taking part in rituals from other religions and worshipping false idols. For the priest, *kami* worship, together with Buddhist worship, is incompatible with the doctrine of Catholicism and its one and true God.

This creates considerable problems if one has close family members who are not themselves Christian. Important rituals such as *bon* or the New Year celebrations are incompatible with the Christian life, leaving Japanese Christians in an awkward situation that creates, in practical terms, a real chasm between believers and non-believers. The same can be said of important rituals of passage, such as *shichi-go-san*, in which children from the church cannot participate. In other words – given that both kinship and community life are largely mediated through Buddhist and Shinto institutions such as Shinto weddings, Buddhist funerals, Buddhist remembrance rituals – conversion to Catholicism does engender the sense of rupture that Robbins has identified as being at the heart of the Christian experience. In line with Robbins, this sense of rupture has a strong temporal dimension – activities that characterized one's former life are now part of a prohibited and amoral alien world. However, the rupture is, as we have seen, also markedly spatial insofar as Christians are bound to spaces that are separate from the surrounding world, spaces where different rituals

Figure 5.2 A Christian cemetery at the edges of Tokyo. Photo by the author.

and activities happen in parallel with the world outside. This is reflected in the positioning of family graves, which are usually placed in Christian cemeteries outside Tokyo or, if sharing land with the non-Christian dead, in out-of-the-way parts of bigger existing graveyards. The families of a part of the community, for example, are buried at one extremity of the famous Yanaka cemetery in Ueno, out of the way on a downward slope next to the fence that overlooks the railway lines.

The Christian ban on cultural forms considered part of everyday life outside the church effectively maps, from conversion onwards, an alternative life-course: one that inhabits different spaces, that demands different rituals and that eventually enforces this separation even after its ending. In the face of these strong discourses of rupture – with one's former self, non-Christian kin and the city around them – people in the community have to live with their own strong sense of a continuity between themselves and the urban world that surrounds them.

Conversion and continuity

The temporal rupture elicited by conversion, as we have seen, has been understood by scholars studying Christian communities to be the defining existential experience at the heart of the Christian life. This seems to resonate in the way both the priest and the mainstream discourse of Japanese urban society understand the place and meaning of the Christian life. Yet the community at the Church of the Holy Family has very different stories of conversion that seem to emphasize not a rupture but rather an unproblematic continuity that sees entering into the faith as a chapter in a continuous life-narrative.

For the vast majority of people in the community, their personal Catholic legacy does not stretch backwards for more than one generation. Many inherited their faith from their parents or older siblings, who had themselves converted sometime after the war. In that period, I was often told, Christianity promoted itself as a religion of pacifism and love in a country traumatized by decades of aggressive nationalism and the atomic bombs that ravaged Hiroshima and Nagasaki in 1945. Christianity resonated with the new national pacifist consciousness as well as asserting its presence by investing heavily in volunteering and welfare activities. People who converted had in most cases been at a Christian school at some point during their education. Christian schools were, and are, a middle-class aspiration, and the vast majority of parents who sent their children to these schools simply wanted the perceived benefits of a Western education without considering the Christian teachings that came with it. Many times conversion had been simply a by-product of such education. Yoshida-san, for example, was sent to a Catholic kindergarten and then to Christian schools for most of his primary and secondary education:

> At that time people wanted Western life; the clothes, food, houses, movies. My mother sent me to Christian school and asked me to not believe in Jesus, only learn love and Western culture from the Christian teachers. In senior high school (*kōkō*) I did not follow her advice and when she finally allowed me, I was baptized.

Others, such as Sasaki-san, did not convert until much later. He was baptized in his fifties when, nostalgic about his youth, he remembered fondly the times at Catholic school and developed an interest in Christianity that, within a few years, led him to become an active part of the church's community. Maeda-san's story is a bit different. Now in his seventies, he was first exposed to Christianity when his wife started to frequent church more assiduously after the birth of their first child. Her mother was Christian but she had not paid much attention to it in her youth. Later in life, when she stopped working to be a stay-at-home wife (*shufu*), she started to visit the local church en route to shopping for groceries. Her interest in Christianity grew and she soon started to fill her time with the church's activities.

Shortly afterwards her husband started to attend as well, and both are today part of what constitutes the core of the church's community.[2]

'I developed an interest' (*kyōmi wo mochimashita*) is a phrase I heard often when I asked about conversion. No intense religious experiences, hierophanies or moral epiphanies. No conversions in time of illness, loneliness and despair. The way people talked about their conversion was astonishingly mundane and lacked the radical temporal and existential quality that much anthropology on Christianity has understood as the core of conversion. The gradual and casual nature of the community's experiences of conversion tell a very different story – one where conversion is only a chapter in the longer and continuous trajectory of one's personal history.

For people at the church of the Holy Family, conversion came as a slow process and deliberate decision. Christianity came as a flavour or an afterthought, something that was investigated in one's spare time, at the edges of the everyday. While stories of gradual conversion are not unique, the point here is that baptism and conversion do not leave the person and the world any different. Although people do gain a new social circle and new routines, there is a sense that things are, at a fundamental level, the same as they have ever been. Everyone I spoke to, for example, has very fond memories of their hometown (*furusato*), of its (Shinto) festivals,

Figure 5.3 Fukuzawa and her friends, holding a picture of themselves on holiday a few decades ago. Photo by the author.

its shrines and their experiences as young women and men. The strong bonds developed in secondary education are for many Christians still the most important relationships in their lives; not parts of a previous life but core building blocks of an enduring sense of identity and continuity.

Fukuzawa-san, for example, meets every two months for dinner with two of her oldest friends. Throughout their youth they periodically travelled together in both Japan and Europe. They are somehow extraordinary people for the place and time they grew up in, three women cherishing their bond, travelling without men and having successful working lives. At every meeting they drink and look at pictures of their travels – of them smiling in front of a rural shrine in Kumamoto or in a restaurant in Florence. Her friends are not Christian (and, as we shall see later on, their activities in the restaurant are not that Christian either), but for Fukuzawa-san these meetings are extremely important – they punctuate her time, infuse a sense of belonging and nostalgia in her life and create a sense of continuity. The timeline existing in and through those meetings and pictures has nothing to do with the timeline of her conversion; her life is not a two-part narrative of before and after, but a snaking continuous one of growth, adventure and friendship in which her conversion only provides a background element.

'Don't tell the priest'

Bans on such things as festivals and shrine worship are not perceived by the community as coming from the dogmas of the church, but rather from the priest himself. This does not mean that people believe these restrictions to be his arbitrary whim. Rather the priest is, in this small community, the only real connection with the wider church and the very source of moral and spiritual authority. This section focuses on one of these banned activities – drinking – a moment where the community's sense of continuity comes into direct friction with the rupture that the priest's prescriptions demand. This friction, as we shall see, does not leave people suffering moral torment and guilt as in the case of the Urapmin, but rather to unproblematically act behind the priest's back. Days of celebration, for example the one described next, exacerbate this tendency and bring the very core members of the community to act, in secret, in direct conflict with the priest's prohibition.

After a day trip with the community, the coach parks in front of the church and people pour into the yard. Saitō-san, a lady in her seventies gives people knowing looks while the community slowly starts to disperse. A few days back Saitō-san invited some of the community's members to a drinking party (*nomikai*) after the trip and, upon inviting me, emphatically whispered: 'Don't tell the priest!' When the crowds disperse, she walks over to some of the people who purposefully stayed behind, among them Kimura-san, a younger member known for his sombreness. She asks: 'Are you coming with us?' Kimura brings his hand to the back of his head, sucks air through his teeth and says: 'I have to wake up at 5 a.m. for work, I want to come but … it's a bit … ' As Donald Keene beautifully pointed out, 'Japanese sentences are apt to trail off into thin smoke' (1955, 26) – and Camille Paglia has added: 'a vapour of hanging participles' (1990, 174). 'It's a bit … ' – the silence hangs in the air for only a second before Saitō-san's hand falls heavily on his arm: 'Just come for one drink, won't you?'

Drinking is an important part of Japanese urban social life. Brian Moeran (1986) suggestively painted the cities of Japanese industrial capitalism as comprising two worlds: a world of light, populated by salarymen and housewives moving between office buildings and department stores, and the world of darkness, belonging to the entertainment districts: the *mizu-shōbai*, the 'water trade', made of *izakaya*,[3] bars, hostess clubs and snack-bars. Even thirty years after Moeran was writing, before the bubble burst and the 'Japanese miracle' gave way to enduring economic crisis, the world of darkness is in full force and entertainment districts cluster around many rail and underground stations.

From the industrial surroundings of the church we enter the neon-lit alleys full of *izakaya*, bars and *karaoke* parlours. When we arrive at our destination one of the elders of the community stands up and gives a short speech thanking everyone for the good day and encouraging all to have fun and drink plenty. Drinking starts and the atmosphere gets raucous, glasses are filled and speech soon starts to get slurred. The conversation moves between recent church activities and members of the community. 'Have you seen such and such recently? Is the baby born yet? I heard she went down to Fukuoka to stay with her mother.' There is no elephant in the room, no acknowledgement of sin through omission. All conversations rotate around the church, around its activities and its members. The priest is frequently mentioned, always with respect and affection, and yet we are doing something that the priest has explicitly banned the community from doing.

On a Friday night around the entertainment districts of Tokyo one is likely to see scenes of extreme loss of control: 'throwing up, urinating in public, dancing on train platforms, falling asleep stretched out on the seats of a train, making passes at or otherwise insulting someone normally shown respect, speaking openly about things that usually go unsaid' (Allison 1994, 45) are common behaviours at these times and places. Such scenes dramatically clash not only with the demeanour one expects in the 'world of light', but with the usual personality of one's acquaintances as well. In Tokyo there is an extreme leniency towards inappropriate drunken behaviours, and what is said while drunk is often quickly forgotten the day after.[4] In my experience one can go so far as to say that drinking and drunkenness are positively valued if the social occasion is appropriate – being drunk (*yotte iru*) is a desirable condition and drinking to get drunk is explicitly many people's intent when going out.

Catholic morality works explicitly against this tendency. The loss of control, the breaking of boundaries, the spectre of addiction are all hurled at the community from the pulpit as examples of sinful behaviour and spiritual loss. Around the end of December – when most workplaces, voluntary groups and associations hold their end-of-the-year drinks (*bōnenkai*) – warnings about the spiritual and physical dangers of alcohol intensify. True community, says the priest, is not the one you reach through intoxication but the one you reach through love and care. The priest here is targeting the age-old Japanese trope that intoxication provides a 'frame' for egalitarian relationships (see Nakane 1970); that in the *communitas* of drunkenness one can express one's true self and let go of the façades that one has to wear navigating the hierarchies of everyday life. 'That is not real community; real community is in the heart.'

Yet that night people leave the restaurant drunk, and this is not an exception but one of many such occasions. Suddenly people are out on the streets again; it is dark now and the cold evening air wakes everyone up. A few people bow goodbye, but someone pulls my sleeve gently and asks 'Won't you come for another drink?' A few others nod, more sleeves are pulled and the group sets off into the chilly air of the night, where insistent touts insist on showing their menus and try to pull people into their restaurants. Kimura-san, who was reticent from the beginning, tries to leave but finds himself agreeing to another drink. 'Just one … then I really have to go.' Eventually another restaurant is chosen and the same ritual starts.

Clapping, more food and drinks come to the table, more laughing. Kimura-san finally manages to slip out. Then everyone is outside again, a few people disappear in the night and four of us wander drunkenly to another *izakaya*. That night I have to carry one of them all the way home: she quietly sings songs of her childhood and tries to make me sing along; she mumbles apologies and praises my kindness while I pull her weight on my shoulders. I leave her at her door after helping her find her keys.

People in the community often furtively organized dinners at their houses with the explicit intention of getting drunk – planning ahead what we would be drinking and who should bring what. Inevitably the alcohol would not be enough, and from drinking good French wine one would end up drinking whatever they could find in their cupboard, or making a trip to the corner shop to buy cheap liquor. While the main topic of conversation throughout all the drunken evenings I have participated in is always the church, there is no hint of moral torment, of guilt. Asking about the prohibitions over dinner one gets joking replies such as 'ah it's bad, isn't it' or an upward glance at the sky, the joining of hands as if in prayer and, with a smile and childish voice, 'I am sorry, Lord' (*gomenne kami-sama*).

Dual encompassment and the blurring of rupture

People's engagement with the church suggests that what we are seeing is neither a form of assimilation nor a form of resistance. One could be tempted to see the community on a similar trajectory as the Urapmin were in the 1990s, moving from traditional to Christian culture – their efforts to foster community outside the church still locked in the old framework, into old behaviours that clash with their new culture. What is fundamentally different, however, is that the Urapmin were haunted by this friction, while here people seem to pay it no heed.

In Robbins's analysis, assimilation and adoption are understood as processes whereby one culture comes to frame another (cf. Bateson 1972; Goffman 1974), where one of the two cultures gives meaning and motivation for engaging in elements of the other. A good way to understand this process is Dumont's (1980) notion of 'encompassment', which he saw as the ground for his theory of hierarchy: encompassment is a part/whole relationship in which contraries can coexist. Dumont calls this relationship 'the encompassing of the contrary' (1980, 239) and gives, fittingly here, a Biblical example. Sexual differentiation in the Garden of Eden is predicated on a double relation – Adam and Eve are, as members of the human species of opposite sexes, in a binary opposition. However, given that Eve was created from Adam's rib, that he is the original member of the species from which she was created, he encompasses her; a relationship of identity is established between the two.

'Encompassment' provides a useful lens through which to understand the assimilation/adoption paradigm. The assimilation of Christianity in other cultures is a situation where the traditional culture encompasses

Christian elements. The relationship is hierarchical: only the categories change and not the relationship between them – the image changes but the frame remains. The Urapmin were going through the opposite process: they were slowly encompassing elements of their traditional culture (e.g. notions of big-manship) within the Catholic framework. Robbins's point is that this encompassment is incomplete and the hierarchy has not yet been properly established. Given that the two 'cultures' were at times equally important, not hierarchically encompassed, their friction generated torment and guilt.

When turning to the church's practices in Tokyo, however, it is hard to determine which direction this encompassment is working in. When people are out drinking, they are encompassing Christianity with the wider norms of Japanese society. They are asserting continuity by acting like any other non-Christian person, but within this frame understanding themselves as Christians. In other words, this can be understood as a form of assimilation where Christianity has been encompassed into the wider framework of Japanese society: the content has changed, now a Christian community instead of a group of friends, but not the framework – everything is understood through the categories of urban Japanese modernity.

On the other hand, the opposite is also true. People are encompassing elements of their old life into their Catholic one. Their understanding of Christianity is precisely what is giving meaning to their meetings and the drinking is encompassed within that understanding. People are first and foremost Christians engaging in what they understand as the Christian life – drinking is not antithetical because it is encompassed into Christianity, hierarchically subordinated to the wider framework that gives meaning to people's lives as Catholics. In the same way, people's engagement with the church was deeply motivated by their desire to lead a Christian life, a desire that brings them to explore territories uncharted by the sparse schedules and activities provided by the church. In other words, it is hard to determine if the process is one of assimilation or adoption – which of the two cultures is encompassing the other.

When zooming out to a wider canvas, to the wider scale of urban Japanese modernity, one finds the same difficulties. Since the Second Vatican Council (1962–5) 'inculturation' has been part of the Catholic Church's strategies to make the faith resonate with non-Western cultures. Christian dogma, for instance, condemns ancestral worship as it runs contrary to its ideas of afterlife, and yet many Christians in Japan today have an ancestral altar in their house and honour the spirits of their ancestors (see, e.g., Reid 1981; 1989). While before Vatican II the orthodox line was to encourage people to dispose of them, with the publishing of a pamphlet called 'Guidelines for Catholics with Regards to the Ancestors and the Dead' (*sosen to shisha ni tsuite no katorikku shinja no tebiki*; 1985) people were allowed to pay respect to ancestral altars as long as all Buddhist iconography and devotion be replaced with Christian forms (see Swyngedouw 1984; 1985; also Mullins 2011). The same is true of many other activities, such as the maintenance of Christianized family graves, virtually indistinguishable from traditional ones if not for a small crucifix carved next to the family name.[5]

When one looks away from Christian spaces and to the surrounding urban culture of modern Tokyo, a similar logic is at work. Within the products of mass culture, especially manga, anime and video games, Christian – and overwhelmingly Catholic – symbolism and themes crop up everywhere (e.g. Suter 2015). These imaginary spaces are inhabited by people on a daily basis and bleed into the 'real' world through advertising, messaging applications, corporate branding, fashion and gadgets. Appadurai (1996) has argued that imaginative spaces acquire a new power with modernity, and indeed modernity and Christianity do seem to share a special relationship in Tokyo (cf. Doak 2011). Christmas, white weddings, churches and crosses; all these are appropriated and fused into the wider fresco of Japanese modernity.

For example, while the nation-building of the past has cast Shinto weddings as one of the necessary rites of passage of the Japanese person, today two-thirds of weddings celebrated in the Tokyo metropolis are Western-style ceremonies. 'Western style' here means Christian, even though the vast majority of the ceremonies are Christian only in appearance. These wedding chapels are usually in expensive hotels in the centre of town, modern halls with neon crosses, off-white walls and futuristic interior design in transparent plastics and glass. The pastor performing the ritual is a Western actor reading a script and the ceremony is a short affair that follows the ritual steps immortalized in the last scene of nearly every romantic comedy (Fisch 2001; LeFebvre 2015). In the light of this insistent presence of Christian signifiers in the landscape of urban modernity, one needs to consider whether Christianity really is only a minority culture, a figure in the background, or perhaps a much more prominent figure in the scene. There is, in other words, an ambiguity as to the place of Christianity within its encompassing frame.

One finds, both on the community scale and on a wider societal one, an ambiguity as to exactly what is encompassing what. When the community partakes in Shinto festivals and rituals or gets drunk with non-Christian friends, one could indeed say that Christianity is encompassed into the old culture that surrounds it. However, when people move their grave to a Christian graveyard, or change their ancestral altar for a Christian one, they are performing an act of adoption; it is Christianity which is successfully encompassing the old culture. We find in the life of the community an oscillation, to borrow Edmund Leach's famous term (1954; 1972), where people successfully manage to sometimes let one system encompass the other, while at times the opposite is true. People manage to let Christianity encompass the social forms of majority culture – in their dealing with the altars, with life and death rituals – and, at other times, let the social habits of majority culture encompass their Christian identity.[6]

Drinking, however, seems to achieve both simultaneously. When people transgress the priest's restrictions they are not, in their minds, acting against Christian values but they are precisely living the Christian life. As we have seen in those drunken hours the conversation is dominated by topics to do with the church, and one cannot possibly argue that what people are doing is actually simply taking the formal elements of Christianity and encompassing them within the wider framework. The opposite is obviously not true either – Christianity is not encompassing Japanese social modes of interaction because both the priest and social perceptions of their faith are vocally telling people that this is not possible. Those meetings seem to contain, simultaneously, both kinds of encompassing acts.

Evenings of drinking exist in a continuum with the life of the church; they are just another facet of it (cf. Pedersen, this volume). Yet they also exist in a continuum with people's life outside it, with the other meetings they have with their friends and family. In those nights there is no difference at all between the Christian life and wider Japanese society, between intoxication and piousness, between the world inside the church and the world outside it. The two blur and become one, and thus people feel no moral afflictions. Instead of clashing, the two systems blur, and in that hazy space rupture disappears, if only for a few hours. In those moments people are indeed breaking the rules of Christianity, framing their Christian endeavours within the framework of urban Japanese sociality, interpreting their actions through the latter. However, the drinking itself is understood through their Catholic life, as a means to be a group, to build bonds and a strong Christian community. Being Christian is never hidden, it is never ignored – it is indeed the whole point of drinking, of breaking the priest's restrictions. Through a series of figure ground-reversals, through a dual encompassment where inside encompasses outside and vice versa, the two 'cultures' blur and become indistinguishable. In these moments sinning can be the very Christian life and being Christian can mean its opposite: participating in heathen rites, intoxication and so on. It is impossible to point out which of the two frames is encompassing the other – which system is giving meaning to people's actions: by partaking in activities constitutive of life 'outside' they come closer to the 'inside', and by converting and coming 'inside' they find a community to be built through the 'outside'.[7]

Conclusion

This chapter has investigated the ways in which people try to achieve moments of continuity in the face of intense discourses of rupture. The chapter has worked with two big 'wholes' – Christianity on the one hand and 'urban Japanese modernity' on the other. It has tried to show how people oscillate between the two, letting one encompass the other, bridging the gulf of rupture every time they go into and out of church. In the haze of drunkenness, a double encompassment is achieved – the two cultures overlap and blur, sinful activities become virtuous, transgression becomes the performance of the Christian life.

Given the Christian insistence on rupture, it is not surprising that this chapter has worked, like Robbins, with two extreme outcomes of culture contact and change: rupture, with a new Christian cosmos, or continuity, with the continuation of the old culture. There is of course a middle way, one where the two 'cultures' come to a sort of Hegelian synthesis. This is close to what much anthropological literature has called syncretism (e.g. Shaw and Stewart 1994) or creolization (e.g. Hannerz 1987; Stewart 2007). What we find here is, however, not one of those cases. Rupture is a daily reality for the community, one that they struggle with and that they cannot ultimately overcome. The fleeting blurring and identification of the two cultures only lasts for a few hours, and rupture is imposed on them as soon as they walk around town or into church. At the same time, what we are seeing here is most likely not a process with a definite direction and outcome as it was for the Urapmin but, as is testament in the absence of friction between the two, this does not seem to be the case in Tokyo.

People have no intention of giving up many of the things the priest wants them to give up. 'Giving up' is not something the community does lightly: even giving up chocolate at Lent usually lasts only a few days (and, in recounting their failure to abstain, people do so with the same levity with which they talk about their drinking). They are not striving towards total conversion and stumbling on the way. They are, however, not trying to assert their sense of continuity either, for their activities are hidden from the eyes of the priest. One might comment that, if the community had its way, the Catholicism of its members would develop into a syncretic form. This might be the truth, but it might also be overlooking the community's craving for form and dogma. The affectionate transgressions of the priest's dogma might not mark a desire to be rid of them, but a particular affective way of engaging rupture. People are not challenging rupture, but creating spaces so that continuity can coexist with it.

Notes

1. Robbins is here relying on Sahlins's model (1985; 1992); 'assimilation' here also encompasses what for the latter is a third process – 'transformation'.
2. Even the story of conversion of one of the key figures of Japanese Christianity – Uchimura Kanzō, the founder of the Non-Church Movement (*mukyōkai*) – is underwhelming and gradual (Ch. 1 in Uchimura 1985; also Mullins 1998).
3. A drinking establishment that also serves small dishes of food such as skewers, fried chicken, pickles and fried noodles.
4. Cf. Moeran (1997) for an important counterpoint.
5. Note that the only activities that are encompassed are Buddhist, never Shinto. Shinto, with its perceived polytheism, seems to be much more threatening to the Church than Buddhism. Altars and graves are reinterpreted and encompassed, but never household shrines or amulets.
6. Cf. Daswani (2011) and Werbner (2011) for the use of an oscillatory model in non-Western Christian contexts.
7. Here saliently morality has not been part of the picture, and the notion of encompassment tried to capture the same process without its moral dimension. However, morality has, albeit briefly, surfaced in the ethnography. In Robbins's analysis the Urapmin experienced what Bateson (1972, 201–27, 271–8) has called a 'double-bind': an emotionally distressing dilemma where one receives two conflicting and mutually negating messages. Kimura-san, whom we have seen unsuccessfully trying to avoid drinking with the community, is the closest example I have seen to a moral double-bind. As in the notion of encompassment, for Bateson there is a hierarchical element to the double-bind: a verbal message is framed by non-verbal ones that directly contradict the first. Kimura-san was stuck between the priest's dogma – thou shall not drink – and a situation where drinking was encouraged if not required. While he would have never stated this publicly on the night, when asked on different occasions he confirmed that his reticence and discomfort were explicitly to do with the awareness of the 'wrongness' (*warui*) of the act. Kimura-san is, one could say, only encompassing one way – he is the kind of Christian the priest wants the community to be and is hence, paradoxically, struggling to be part of it.

References

Allison, Anne 1994. *Nightwork: Sexuality, Pleasure, and Corporate Masculinity in a Tokyo Hostess Club*. Chicago: Chicago University Press.
Appadurai, Arjun. 1996. *Modernity at Large: Cultural Dimensions of Globalization*. Minneapolis: University of Minnesota Press.
Bateson, Gregory. 1972. *Steps to an Ecology of Mind: Collected Essays in Anthropology, Psychiatry, Evolution, and Epistemology*. Chicago: Chicago University Press.
Bielo, James S. 2008. 'On the Failure of "Meaning": Bible Reading in the Anthropology of Christianity'. *Culture and Religion* 9 (1): 1–21.

Bielo, James S. 2009. *Words Upon the Word: An Ethnography of Evangelical Bible Study*. New York: SUNY Press.

Brown, Bernardo. 2017. 'In Search of the Solemn with Sri Lankan Migrant Priests'. *Australian Journal of Anthropology* 28 (2): 180–94.

Carapanzano, Vincent. 2000. *Serving the Word: Literalism in America from the Pulpit to the Bench*. New York: New Press.

Chua, Liana. 2012. 'Conversion, Continuity, and Moral Dilemmas among Christian Bidayuhs in Malaysian Borneo'. *American Ethnologist* 39 (3): 511–26.

Clarke, Peter B. 2000. *Japanese New Religions in Global Perspective*. Richmond: Curzon Press.

Daswani, Girish. 2011. '(In-)dividual Pentecostals in Ghana'. *Journal of Religion in Africa* 41 (3): 256–79.

Doak, Kevin. 2011. 'Introduction: Catholicism, Modernity, and Japanese Culture'. In *Xavier's Legacies: Catholicism in Modern Japanese Culture*, edited by Kevin Doak, 1–30. Vancouver: University of British Columbia Press.

Dumont, Louis. 1980. *Homo Hierarchicus: The Caste System and its Implications*. Chicago: Chicago University Press.

Engelke, Matthew. 2004. 'Discontinuity and the Discourse of Conversion'. *Journal of Religion in Africa* 34 (1–2): 82–109.

Fisch, Michael. 2001. 'The Rise of the Chapel Wedding in Japan: Simulation and Performance'. *Japanese Journal of Religious Studies* 28 (1–2): 57–76.

Ghanbarpour, Christina. 2015. 'Legacy of a Minority Religion: Christians and Christianity in Contemporary Japan'. In *The Changing World Religion Map: Sacred Places, Identities, Practices and Politics*, edited by Stanley Brunn, 2025–44. Dordrecht: Springer.

Goffman, Erving. 1974. *Frame Analysis: An Essay on the Organization of Experience*. Cambridge, MA: Harvard University Press.

Hannerz, Ulf. 1987. 'The World in Creolisation'. *Africa* 57: 546–59.

Hirsch, Eric. 2008. 'God or *Tidibe*? Melanesian Christianity and the Problem of Wholes'. *Ethnos* 73 (2): 141–62.

Kan, Sergei. 1991. 'Shamanism and Christianity: Modern-Day Tlingit Elders Look at the Past'. *Ethnohistory* 38 (4): 363–87.

Keane, Webb. 2007. *Christian Moderns: Freedom and Fetish in the Mission Encounter*. Berkeley: University of California Press.

Keene, Donald. 1955. *Anthology of Japanese Literature, from the Earliest Era to the Mid-Nineteenth Century*. New York: Grove Press.

Keller, Eva. 2005. *The Road to Clarity: Seventh-Day Adventism in Madagascar*. New York: Palgrave Macmillan.

Leach, Edmund. 1954. *Political Systems of Highland Burma: A Study of Kachin Social Structure*. Cambridge, MA: Harvard University Press.

Leach, Edmund. 1972. 'Melchisedech and the Emperor: Icons of Subversion and Orthodoxy'. *Proceedings of the Royal Anthropological Institute of Great Britain and Ireland for 1972*: 5–14.

LeFebvre, Jesse R. 2015. 'Christian Wedding Ceremonies: "Non-Religiousness" in Contemporary Japan'. *Japanese Journal of Religious Studies* 42 (2): 185–203.

Lienhardt, Godfrey. 1982. 'The Dinka and Catholicism'. In *Religious Organization and Religious Experience*, edited by John Davies, 81–95. London: Academic Press.

Malley, Brian. 2004. *How the Bible Works: An Anthropological Study of Evangelical Biblicism*. Walnut Creek, CA: Altamira Press.

Meyer, Brigit. 1999. *Translating the Devil: Religion and Modernity among the Ewe in Ghana*. Trenton, NJ: Africa WorldPress.

Moeran, Brian. 1986. 'One over the Seven: *Sake* Drinking in a Japanese Pottery Community'. In *Interpreting Japanese Society: Anthropological Approaches*, edited by Joy Hendry and Jonathan Webber, 226–42. Oxford: Journal of the Anthropological Society of Oxford.

Moeran, Brian. 1997. *Folk Art Potters in Japan: Beyond an Anthropology of Aesthetics*. London: Routledge.

Mullins, Mark. 1998. *Christianity Made in Japan: A Study of Indigenous Movements*. Honolulu: University of Hawai'i Press.

Mullins, Mark. 2011. 'Between Inculturation and Globalization: The Situation of Catholicism in Contemporary Japanese Society'. In *Xavier's Legacies: Catholicism in Modern Japanese Culture*, edited by Kevin Doak, 169–92. Vancouver: University of British Columbia Press.

Nakane, Chie. 1970. *Japanese Society*. Berkeley: University of California Press.

Ortiz, Fernando. 1995. *Cuban Counterpoint: Tobacco and Sugar*. Durham, NC: Duke University Press.

Paglia, Camille. 1990. *Sexual Personae: Art and Decadence from Nefertiti to Emily Dickinson*. London: Yale University Press.

Rambo, Lewis. 1993. *Understanding Religious Conversion*. New Haven, CT: Yale University Press.

Reid, David. 1981. 'Remembering the Dead: Change in Protestant Christian Tradition through Contact with Japanese Cultural Tradition'. *Japanese Journal of Religious Studies* 8 (1–2): 9–33.

Reid, David. 1989. 'Japanese Christians and the Ancestors'. *Japanese Journal of Religious Studies* 16 (4): 259–83.

Robbins, Joel. 2004. *Becoming Sinners: Christianity and Moral Torment in a Papua New Guinea Society*. Berkeley: University of California Press.

Robbins, Joel. 2007. 'Continuity Thinking and the Problem of Christian Culture'. *Current Anthropology* 48 (1): 5–38.

Robbins, Joel. 2010. 'Anthropology, Pentecostalism and the New Paul: Conversion, Event and Social Transformation'. *South Atlantic Quarterly* 109 (4): 633–52.

Robbins, Joel. 2012. 'Transcendence and the Anthropology of Christianity: Language, Change, and Individualism. Edward Westermack Memorial Lecture (October 2011)'. *Suomen Antropologi: Journal of the Finnish Anthropological Society* 37 (2): 5–23.

Rumsey, Alan. 2004. 'Book Review: Christianity, Culture Change, and the Anthropology of Ethics'. *Anthropological Quarterly* 77 (3): 581–93.

Sahlins, Marshall. 1985. *Islands of History*. Chicago: University of Chicago Press.

Sahlins, Marshall. 1992. 'The Economics of Develop-Man in the Pacific.' *Res: Anthropology and Aesthetics* 21 (1): 12–25.

Scott, Michael W. 2005. '"I Was Like Abraham": Notes on the Anthropology of Christianity from the Solomon Islands'. *Ethnos* 70 (1): 101–25.

Shaw, Rosalind, and Charles Stewart. 1994. 'Introduction: Problematizing Syncretism'. In *Syncretism/Anti-Syncretism: The Politics of Religious Synthesis*, edited by Charles Stewart and Rosalind Shaw, 1–16. London: Routledge.

Sosen to Shisha ni tsuite no Katorikku Shinja no Tebiki [Guidelines for Catholics with Regard to the Ancestors and the Dead]. 1985. Episcopal Commission for Non-Christian Religions. Tokyo: Catholic Bishops' Conference of Japan, 1–32.

Stewart, Charles. 2007. 'Creolization: History, Ethnography, Theory'. In *Creolization: History, Ethnography, Theory*, edited by Charles Stewart, 1–25. London: Routledge.

Suter, Rebecca. 2015. *Holy Ghosts: The Christian Century in Modern Japanese Fiction*. Honolulu: University of Hawai'i Press.

Swyngedouw, Jan. 1984. 'Japan's Roman Catholic Church and Ancestor Veneration: A Reappraisal'. *Japanese Religions* 13 (2): 11–18.

Swyngedouw, Jan. 1985. 'The Japanese Church and Ancestor Veneration Practices: The Mahayanization of Japanese Catholicism?'. *Japan Missionary Bulletin* 39 (2): 56–65.

Uchimura, Kanzō. 1985. *How I Became a Christian: Out of My Diary, by a 'Heathen Convert'*. Tokyo: Keiseisha.

Vaté, Virginie. 2009. 'Redefining Chukchi Practices in Contexts of Conversion to Pentecostalism'. In *Conversion after Socialism: Disruptions, Modernisms and Technologies of Faith in the Former Soviet Union*, edited by Mathijs Pelkmans, 39–59. New York: Berghahn.

Vilaça, Aparecida. 2014. 'Culture and Self: The Different "Gifts" Amerindians Receive from Catholics and Evangelicals'. *Current Anthropology* 55 (S10): 322–32.

Viveiros de Castro, Eduardo. 2011. *The Inconstancy of the Indian Soul: The Encounter of Catholics and Cannibals in Sixteenth-century Brazil*. Chicago: Prickly Paradigm Press.

Werbner, Richard. 2011. 'The Charismatic Dividual and the Sacred Self'. *Journal of Religion in Africa* 41 (2): 180–205.

Whitehouse, Harvey. 2000. *Arguments and Icons: Divergent Modes of Religiosity*. Oxford: Oxford University Press.

6

Writing as Rupture: On Prophetic Invention in Central Africa

Ramon Sarró

Introduction

In this chapter I would like to pay attention to dynamics of ruptures linked to prophetic imagination in Africa. Prophets bring new religious discourses and convince followers that they have to abandon old religious cultures and convert to these innovative ones. Tempting as it is to analyse the prophetic work as rupture, as an effort at redirecting people's imagination towards the 'new world' and towards the future, it would yield a very partial view on the work of prophetic imagination. In several prophetic movements I have been studying in West and Central Africa, the invitation of the prophets is not only to make a break with the past, but to critically reassess the past in order to understand the predicaments of the present too (Sarró 2018a). In other words, rupture and repair, to borrow the phrase from Rowlands, Feutchwang and Zhang's chapter, are more often than not the two sides of the same coin, especially in places where the past is remembered with a combination of pride and suffering, as is often the case in Africa.

The dyad of prophecy and invention is mediated by the unknown (Paine 1995). The ways prophets bring the unknown into the familiar could be analysed in many different social fields, but in this chapter I will focus on only one: writing systems. Writing has been seen by many scholars, certainly those endorsing Pan-Babylonists and other civilizational views of humanity, as the historical rupture par excellence. Indeed, a very popular book stated in its title that 'history begins at Sumer' (Kramer 1956), precisely because anything prior to the emergence of history was – and according to many authors today still is – considered as human 'pre' history. The emergence of writing works like a totemic operator that distinguishes a certain 'we' from a certain preliterate 'they' and that has been used to explain (or mystify?) the transition from mythical existence to logical thinking. Although as far as philosophy of history goes this is today an outmoded problematic epistemology, the fact remains that access to writing is regarded in many parts of the world as one of the most important achievements that individuals and societies may boast, their true coming of age.

But how do you access the alphabet? There are two ways: either you learn to use an existing alphabet or you invent your own from scratch. The invention of the alphabet has been a topic of research of both historians and anthropologists. Ethnographic evidence shows that in many places creative individuals, very often considered as prophets by their publics, have invented their own way to transcribe sounds into graphic symbols. The most famous individuals studied by anthropologists would include Sequoyah, a Seneca Indian who, despite being illiterate, was able to invent a syllabary (Foreman 1938), that of the Hmong prophet Shong Lue, who invented an alphabet in Vietnam (Smalley et al. 1990) and that of Souleymane Kante, whose visions gave birth to the N'ko alphabet in Mande West Africa (Vydrine 2001). Building on those cases, over the last decade, I have been investigating the emergence of an alphabet in Congo and the biography of the man who invented it through divine revelation.

Like many other alphabets, this one is closely connected to a prophetic movement, in this case to the Church of Simon Kimbangu, an institution based on the message of the prophet Simon Kimbangu (1887–1951). Since 1921 this Church has been making great efforts at bringing something 'new' to the Bakongo people of central Africa, while at the same time making them proudly aware of their cultural roots. The writing system, Mandombe (an expression that can be glossed as meaning 'the writing system of the Africans'), was invented by a man called Wabeladio Payi (1958–2013). In 1978, after having some dreams in which Simon Kimbangu promised to send a mission for him, young Wabeladio spent nine months praying in a room, and in 1979 finally received a revelation. He realized that the lines separating the bricks on the wall against which he was praying could be interpreted in such a way as to give rise to graphic symbols, 'graphemes' to use his word.[1] In a subsequent dream, God told him that his mission was to investigate the graphic symbols of the wall.

Wabeladio then started to investigate the mathematical and geometrical properties of the different figures he could draw with the lines of the wall. In 1985, six years after his initial revelation, he wrote an insightful unpublished report on the relationship between creativity (in art and technology) and geometry (Wabeladio Payi 1985). By 1994 he started to ascribe phonographic qualities to the symbols he was creating, and a proper alphabet (a syllabary at first) was born. It was, therefore, a very long process, which lasted many years, although in the popular imagination of his followers his invention is telescoped to the 1978 dream and presented as an invention of a 'sudden genius' instead of a long process of investigation, incubation and experimentation.[2] In his inventive process, Wabeladio started by analysing the mathematical and geometrical aspects of the lines and of the figures, making an intellectual regression to what I would call 'the elementary forms of rupturing life'. Like the pre-Socratic philosophers, like Ramon Llull, like Descartes, like the Cubists, Wabeladio realized that if you really want to start anew, you must start from geometry. And, indeed, he became a sophisticated geometer, offering something that was so absolutely new that people could not relate to it at all, and only a few understood what he was doing. The names of the graphemes he was inventing were, at first, *sui generis* concepts, bearing total independence from any other graphic system, and with no cultural connotations at all for any possible public. The very concept of *mandombe*, a Kikongo word, was not invented until 1994. Between 1978 and 1994, Wabeladio was referring to its invention as *écriture imbriquée*, a clever pun as the French *imbriquée* means both 'overlapping' and 'made out of bricks'. In the 1990s, he started to rename all the elements of the writing system, including the name of the system itself. Thus, the names of the two basic elements upon which the entire alphabet rests, which resemble 5 and 2, were changed from *solita* and *aldo* (two entirely invented concepts) to *pakundungu* and *pelekete*, two onomatopoeic nouns of great connotation in the 'affliction cult'-oriented culture of the Bakongo. *Pakundungu* represents the grave sound and *pelekete* the acute sound of the two *ngoma* (drums) that must be present in all Kongo ritual. The names of the more complex graphemes he developed, upon which syllables are constructed, were renamed from *canne* ('walking cane', in French) to *mwuala* ('royal sceptre', in Kikongo). This renaming and cultural rerooting on his invention in the Kongo imagery was a rather late development. At the beginning, and for a long time, no matter how impressed people were with the young man's drawings and three-dimensional geometries, they could not *relate* to the invention, and Wabeladio was a rather solitary thinker with little impact. He even had to make a break with his matrilineal family, who were convinced the young man was wasting his time with the invention and suspected he was either bewitched or mad. He only started to gain public acceptance when he managed to rephrase his quasi-surreal language and imagery in a way that resonated with people's histories and experiences, and particularly with the messianic matrix inherent in Kongo cultural roots.

Kimbanguism and the spread of Mandombe

Since its beginning in 1978, the Mandombe alphabet and art have been strongly associated with the Kimbanguist Church, and they are taught in Kimbanguist centres in the Democratic Republic of Congo, in its neighbouring Republic of Congo (Brazzaville), in Angola and in the diaspora. A succinct description of this Church is therefore in order.

Kimbanguism was born among the Bakongo people in 1921, when Simon Kimbangu, a young man educated at the Baptist mission of Wathen (Ngombe-Lutete) and often described in colonial sources as a 'prophet', started to heal, make prophecies and even, oral history claims, make miracles in Lower Congo, then part of Belgian Congo. He became especially famous after allegedly having brought one dead woman to life on 6 April 1921. This is considered by members of the Church today as the official date of the start of his miraculous activities. Why Kimbangu was considered a prophet and whether he can be, sociologically or theologically, considered a prophet is a debate within the Kimbanguist Church itself. The official line within the Church today is that Simon Kimbangu was the incarnation of the Holy Ghost (Kayongo 2005); whether he can or cannot be considered a prophet is becoming less and less relevant.

The fame of Kimbangu, healing and making miracles on top of the hill of N'kamba, spread like bushfire throughout the Lower Congo regions. According to some accounts, thousands of people from the entire region and also from the French colony of Congo and the Portuguese colony of Angola came every day to be healed by him.[3] People made long pilgrimages in order to deliver or destroy ritual objects linked to traditional cosmology, in a clear effort to abandon practices and start a new society afresh. As soon as the movement began on 6 April, the Belgian government decided to ban it, under pressure not only from local authorities but also from Catholic and Protestant missionaries, as well as from merchants who feared the movement might have a negative effect on their activities. Kimbangu was taken and imprisoned in September 1921, following two months of fierce persecution in the hills and forests around N'kamba. The Kimbanguist movement, however, continued clandestinely and despite persecution by the Belgian authorities (MacGaffey 1983; Diangienda Kuntima 1984; Mélice 2009, 2010).

The Kimbanguist Church was finally recognized by the Belgian state in 1959, just one year before Independence, and it became one of the two major religious institutions in independent Congo (or, as it would later be known, Zaire, and today the Democratic Republic of Congo) under Mobutu's rule in the 1960s. Today, it is still one of the major Churches in the Democratic Republic of Congo, as well as being a huge international institution. Its members often assert that the total number of Kimbanguists worldwide is around 17 million, but a complete census has not yet been undertaken. Moreover, at the moment, an internal schism is making it difficult to establish precise numbers and memberships (for the schism, see Sarró et al. 2008; Mélice 2011; Apo Salimba 2013).

The Church's slogan is 'Kimbanguism: Hope of the World', and its theology is indeed very much based on messianic hope (Sarró and Mélice 2010; Sarró and Santos 2011; Sarró 2015), with a political theology centred on the restoration of the Kingdom – identified both with the Kingdom of God and the Kingdom of Kongo – around the holy city of N'kamba (also known as N'kamba-New Jerusalem). N'kamba was Simon Kimbangu's birthplace and is today the spiritual and administrative centre, as well as the most important pilgrimage site, of the Church. It offers a paradigmatic case for the study of political theology and for theoretical comparisons with other messianic-oriented religious communities based on notions of suffering and on the restoration of a divine-political kingdom.

In 1960 Kimbangu's coffin was transferred from Lubumbashi, where he had died nine years earlier, to a mausoleum built in his natal village of N'kamba. In the late 1960s the Kimbanguist Church was inducted into the Ecumenical Council of Christian Churches, and N'kamba was officially declared the Church's central headquarters. It would be impossible to summarize the current configuration and theology of the Church in the space of this chapter, but it is important to emphasize that the suffering of past Kimbanguists is very present in the Church's liturgy and symbolism. Thus, for example, there are said to be 37,000 seats in the main temple in N'kamba, which equals the number of Congolese families who were forcibly displaced and taken away from their homes by the colonial authorities in a futile effort to put an end to the movement.

Today, Kimbanguists form one of the biggest religious communities in the Democratic Republic of Congo, and also in the Republic of Congo and Angola. This fact cannot be stressed enough in understanding Mandombe's widespread acceptance in the public sphere. Over the last twenty years Mandombe has been used within the Church to transcribe Biblical and other texts. And, by the time Wabeladio passed away, there was a fierce debate, especially in the Democratic Republic of Congo, about whether Mandombe should be 'secularized' and taught outside Kimbanguist circles too. Wabeladio created CENA (the Center for the Study of Mandombe) in 1995. Between 1996 and 2012 CENA created teaching centres (called *nsanda*) across the national territory, covering the entire Lower Congo, but also parts of Bandundu, Province Oriental, the two Kivus, Equator, Kasai and many countries outside the Democratic Republic of Congo. In Kinshasa, each of the 22 local municipalities (or 'communes' as they are called) had one teaching centre by the time Wabeladio died. It is probably fair to say that some 10,000 certificates were granted by the different teaching centres over that period. This means that 10,000 people had learned the rudiments of Mandombe by 2012. These rudiments could be acquired in three months by literate people, but could take up to six months if the students did not know how to read and write. Mandombe teachers were always connected to professional pedagogues so as to improve their teaching techniques. 'For those who are literate, we explain the principles of Mandombe, but for those who are illiterate, we teach them to draw without any theory whatsoever', one of the teachers explained in an interview in 2012. There was never a shortage of teachers, for one thing learning Mandombe did was to encourage people to become teachers of the alphabet.

In a tour I did with Wabeladio across the Lower Congo in summer 2012, I noticed the enthusiasm of some elderly people in truly remote places in the forests of Mayombe who, while being illiterate in the Roman alphabet, could nevertheless write and read in Mandombe (although I did not find anybody who could read with fluency). I was equally, if not more, impressed by the enthusiasm of young people who worked in the *nsanda* on a cooperative basis, having their own cassava field and orchards. The different *nsanda* I visited in the urban and rural areas that year in Lower Congo – including Mbanza Ngungu, Kinsantu, Matadi, Boma, Muanda, and several small forest villages between Boma and Tchela – were all quite big, and in some of them I was received by thirty or forty people. The word I heard most often when asking why they were learning Mandombe was 'identity'. Mandombe was an alphabet sent by God to a Mukongo man, and it was their duty and pride, as Bakongo, to learn how to read it and write it.

Such huge numbers of enthusiastic people do not mean, however, that all of them used Mandombe. As Wabeladio explained to me, a lot of people learned it but they very rarely used it and ended up forgetting how to.[4] In order to encourage people to keep using it, the Mandombe

League was created in the late 1990s. This encouraged Mandombe users to write to each other. Because, obviously, postmen were not expected to be able to read an address written in Mandombe, these letters were sent through CENA itself. They were taken from the *nsanda* in the sender's village to Kinshasa; from Kinshasa they went to the *nsanda* in the recipient's village. This allowed the people at the headquarters of Mandombe in Kinshasa to keep tight control of the League's progress. Up to 2012 they were very happy with the huge number of letters that were circulating among the different centres every year. The League also organized social visits to help people to get to know each other. In 2011, for instance, Wabeladio hired a van in Kinshasa and took many Mandombe students to pay a friendly visit to some *nsanda* in the southern province of Bandundu.

Mandombe: the world on the wall

In 1978, when he was 21 years old and a Catholic, Wabeladio had a series of disturbing dreams in which he saw the late prophet Simon Kimbangu calling him. Against the will of his Catholic family, he decided to go to N'kamba-New Jerusalem, the Holy City of Kimbanguism (in Lower Congo), to find out why he was having the dreams. The journey to N'kamba was full of mysteries, especially when Wabeladio got stuck to the ground for several hours in the middle of the path, unable to move; a 'miracle' (his own words) still today haunting him. Yet it was also fruitless. On his way back from the Holy City, he decided to report the mysterious trip to the leader of the Church, Joseph Diangienda Kuntima (Kimbangu's son), who lived in Kinshasa. The latter told Wabeladio: 'My father [Simon Kimbangu] is preparing you for a mission; you have to pray and pray and the mission will be revealed to you.'

Wabeladio then went to the town of Mbanza Ngungu, where part of his family was based, and prayed for nine months in a small room, until one day he noticed that the lines between the bricks on the wall were drawing the two figures 5 and 2, as bricks do. He sensed that the message was hidden in these two figures. That night, he dreamt that an insect was drawing with its saliva the figures 5 and 2 repeatedly on his skin, until his entire body looked like a wall.

That was the confirmation, and from then on he started to 'study the symbols' as he says, a process that would take him 'from the simple to the complex' (i.e. from the two elementary symbols 5 and 2 to a complex and mysteriously symmetrical script and numerological system).

I have no room to describe all the implications of Wabeladio's invention of Mandombe, which became a very popular alphabet to transcribe Kikongo and Lingala, as well as a very ingenious form through which to create art by following the geometrical principles underneath Mandombe. Some artists in Kinshasa have specialized in Mandombe art, also called Kimbangula. By 2009, when I met Wabeladio Payi, the alphabet was being taught in hundreds of specialized centres all across the Democratic Republic of Congo, as well as in Congolese diasporas in Africa and Europe.

The fact that Wabeladio's invention was grounded on a brick wall is in itself a good place to start drawing some implications from his work. It is of course a coincidence that he saw the writing on a wall in 1979, the same year that Pink Floyd were producing their album *The Wall*, but it is a thought-provoking coincidence. Take archaic walls such as those of Jericho's falling apart, or that in the cavern described by Plato, which deludes us into believing in shadows, or take modern ones such as the vile one separating Thisbe from her lover Pyramus, the ambivalent one in the 1909 poem by Robert Frost 'Mending Walls' (Frost 1914), the exasperatingly never-ending one in Kafka's novella *The Great Wall of China*, written in German in 1917 (Kafka 2007); take the walls that gave power to imagination by becoming canvases for so much rebellious graffiti in Paris 1968 (Besançon 1968). Whenever and wherever they appear, walls and bricks have been used as metaphors for several aspects of human existence. There has also been a close connection between spirituality and walls. Thus, in the Old Testament's Book of Daniel we learn about King Belshazzar, who sees a mysteriously disembodied hand write on his wall the Hebrew words *mene mene teke uparshim*, an apocalyptic message that only the prophet Daniel could decipher (Daniel 5: 13–24).

The connection between seeing forms on walls and getting inspiration – divine or artistic – is very old. Leonardo da Vinci made a method out of it, instructing young artists to look for accidental stains on walls in their search for art forms (Turner 2011). Walls have also been very important for the development of new forms of art in the twentieth century. In a letter to A. Pieyre de Mandiargues in 1957, Jean Dubuffet, an artist to whom I will return, wrote that he got inspiration just by looking at walls, and that all his art was linked in one way or another to walls (Webel 2008). But probably the most astonishing connection between walls and artistic creativity is the work of Fernando Oreste Nanetti (1927–94), an Italian artist who spent much of his life in a mental hospital in Tuscany on whose walls he inscribed more than 70 metres of drawings and texts (Peiry 2016).

Bricks and walls are indeed good to think about and to imagine. British psychologist Liam Hudson proposed a brick test to assess individual creativity. It consisted in asking subjects what things could be made out of bricks (Hudson 1966). Some people could give more than 15 different answers to the question. I doubt, however, that anyone ever answered: 'an alphabet'. In their recent book on creativity, John Kounios and Mark Beeman write: 'If you look at a brick, you'll probably think of it as a part of a building or a wall. But you could also think of it in other ways: as a paving stone, a doorstep, a paperweight, or a walnut cracker' (Kounios and Beeman 2015, 8). Other ways there are indeed, but surely it is still Stone Age compared with Wabeladio's usage of bricks as the bases for an alphabet!

In truth, Wabeladio did not invent the alphabet with the bricks, but rather with the mathematical relations in the lines between bricks. As in some spiritual ladders imagined by medieval thinkers such as Ramon Llull's (which consisted of seven steps, and then God as the eighth, final one), the materiality of the brick (or of the stone in Llull's case) was the first step towards the most immaterial principles and ultimately towards knowledge of God. In his writings, of which sadly only very few remain, he argued that for 'creative imagination' (his words) to construct beauty it must abide by arithmetical principles. Here he would have been a good interlocutor of Paul Valéry. In an article on aesthetic invention in which he wrote against romantic views that glorify pure, boundless imagination, the French poet and thinker argues that not even the imagination of the poet is entirely free of constraints, as he or she too has to comply with strict rules of composition (Valéry 1957).

Theoreticians of creativity seem to agree that invention does not work out of the blue. It works by invoking and playing with knowledge and images stored in our mind and in a dialectical relationship with the surrounding human and physical environment. Some authors have argued that madness is an exception, and that 'outsider artists' can create truly innovative art because they are free from any connection with other people and free from the 'asphyxiating culture', ready to deliver themselves to the invigorating faculty of forgetfulness, as Dubuffet, the founder of the *art brut* movement, put it (1968). A lot of writing on delusion and on the so-called *art brut* follows this problematic assumption and portrays outsider artists as the maximum exponents of genius, free from the subjugation of received aesthetics and from other structures of domination and subordination. Dubuffet's idea that artists must develop their 'faculty of forgetting' to get away from the tyranny of culture and develop genius is suggestive. Unfortunately, he never told *how* one develops such a faculty.

The view that connects true artists with mad people, so dear to Dubuffet, needs to be qualified in two ways. First, very often what we find in outsider art is not a free association of disconnected elements, but on the contrary an obsession with detail, repetition, geometry and symmetry. This was characterized in 1922 as the 'decorative urge' (*Smucktrieb*) by Heidelberg psychiatrist Hans Prinzhorn, one of the founders of the study of what was later to be known as outsider art (quoted in Cardinal 1972, 18). Secondly, we should remember that, as Lévi-Strauss put it in *Tristes Tropiques*, 'human societies, like individual human beings (at play, in their dreams, or in moments of delirium), *never create absolutely:* all they can do is to choose certain combinations from a repertory of ideas which it should be possible to reconstitute' (Lévi-Strauss 1955, 160; my emphasis). Notice that Lévi-Strauss, who was surely aware of the usages that surrealism and other rebellious art schools were making of delusion, notes that his denial of absolute creation includes delirium. Clearly inspired by Lévi-Strauss, French physician and philosopher Henri Laborit wrote in an essay on discoverers: 'Most likely, creative imagination does not create anything; it discovers relations of which one was still not aware' (Laborit 1970, 38; my translation). This capacity to combine, to find new relations, has ever since Lévi-Strauss and Laborit been explored more systematically by creativity scholars. Kounios and Beeman write: 'We define creativity as the ability to reinterpret something by breaking it down into its elements and recombining these elements in a surprising way to achieve some goal' (2015, 9), a definition that not only accords very well with the notions expressed by Lévi-Strauss and Laborit, but one that is also very appropriate when thinking about the invention of Wabeladio, based as it was on breaking down the perceived wall into its composite elements and then reconstructing something different out of the elements. In a study on technology and invention, Brian Arthur (2009) stresses the cumulative effect of these combinations and reinterpretations: the more we innovate through combination, he argues, the more elements we create for future combinations to emerge. It may therefore be problematic to thwart incipient innovations such as Mandombe, since nobody really knows what further combinations they will give rise to in the future, and therefore what greater inventions we may be averting with our early judgement. Wabeladio once told me that should he have the conditions to develop his invention, it would be very useful in the future to develop architecture and even the construction of spaceships. Sadly, he died at the moment when the University of Kinshasa was finally showing some real interest in his creativity and scientific promise, and had hired him despite his lack of any formal university degree.

Connection and combination seem to be at the heart of most theories of creativity. I would like to propose a more balanced view in which *disconnection* is at least as important as connection. I believe that invention consists in a double act of separation, a double rupture. Firstly, the inventor must disconnect elements from their context of origin (as Wabeladio separated lines from the bricks) so that they can be 'originally' recombined; secondly, they must disconnect the final product from specific influences (in the case of Wabeladio, he received a lot of technical feedback from Kinshasa artists, mathematicians, linguists and theologians). Only an artful disconnection between the process of creation and the final product will yield a product that will appear to the public as having been created by an individual genius (with the help, in this case, of God). One could put this idea in dialogue with Gell's notions of technology/enchantment (Gell 1994) or Graeber's works on fetishes and creativity (Graber 2005), but also with theories of influence and artistic creativity. In two different but related studies on those topics, literary critic Harold Bloom (1973; 2011) has argued that influences are accompanied by anxiety; authors must present themselves as original, even knowing they are building on models and ideas created by someone else. What he called 'anxiety of influences' he could as well have called 'anxiety of inventors'. Inventors have to make sure that *their* invention will not be attributed to anybody else. They also have to make sure that the influences are duly acknowledged, but in such a way that the resulting work is perceived, first and foremost, as *their* creation, not as a sum of different parts. Furthermore, for their invention to be a contribution to humanity, they have to disconnect the result from their own personal or parochial concerns and link it instead to universal concerns. Wabeladio offers a paradigmatic example. He learned from God, he learned from the landscape and from the built environment, and he learned from his peers and from scholars. He took very good notice of the comments and feedback he received and made every single effort to meet university professors in Kinshasa and elsewhere to discuss with them, and he deeply impressed some of them. His life was one of learning, but nobody doubts, not even those who helped him with the most technical aspects, that Mandombe is Wabeladio's invention.

Absolute beginners

Rupture was a fundamental aspect of Wabeladio's life and work, and the burgeoning literature on rupture in anthropology has indeed helped me understand his relationship with his background and ambitions. This literature has been refreshing as it has allowed us to understand why and how so many thousands of young people today want to lose their roots and live as 'absolute beginners' (to borrow the title of a famous novel on London youth in the 1950s; MacInnes 1959), usually in urban areas far away from their rural traditionalist elders. That said, an exaggerated stress on rupture may have two limitations. One is that we risk portraying rupture as being irreversible or definitive in cases where it is not. Very often a *longue durée* approach shows that rupture is dialectical. One breaks up now to make up later, as Wabeladio did with his tradition and even with his maternal family, with whom he split when he was in his mid-twenties but reconnected two decades later. The other pitfall is that by insisting on the importance of rupture today we may lose sight of its relevance to understand the past and its role in the making of history in general. Humans have always been rupturists. Socrates, the founder of Western philosophy, was condemned to death for persuading youths in Athens to follow their ethical principles and make a clean break with their elders' instructions. The Old Testament (let alone the New Testament, where rupture with kin ties and obligations is explicit in many of Jesus' teachings) is full of young people rebelling against their elders. More recently, one of the interpreters of the birth of modern history, Alexis de Tocqueville, highlighted, in his *The Old Regime and the Revolution* (Tocqueville 1856), on the force of breaking with the past for the birth of modern France (although his main point was, precisely, that even the revolutionaries ended up creating a continuity with the past rather than a rupture with it).[5] Robespierre was reported to have said 'in order to achieve our mission, we need precisely the opposite of which existed before' (Guigon 2007). Not to mention the glorification of the *écart absolu* by Fourier and other utopian and revolutionary thinkers, later inherited by Dadaists, surrealists (Guigon 2007) and, especially, proponents of *art brut* such as Dubuffet and his follower Michel Thévoz, author of an insightful essay on the connection between *art brut* and the invention of alphabets aptly entitled *Le language de la rupture*, the language of rupture (Thévoz 1978). Let me finish this digression on rupture with an apocryphal phrase attributed by Dadaists to Descartes in 1918 (on the cover of the third issue of their journal *Dada*): 'I do not want to know if there have been men before me.' Although scholars have proved that the founder of modern philosophy never wrote this thought, at least not in these exact words (Behar and Carassou 1990, 91), the idea is certainly in the spirit of his philosophy, especially of his 1641 *Metaphysical Meditations*. He needed to ground his certainty on himself, not on the authority of tradition. Now, the paradox is: why did Dadaists, who were also trying to make a break with the past, need the *authority* of Descartes? Even when breaking with tradition, people need a tradition from which to unpick stitches. We are inescapably historical animals.[6]

Like Descartes' case, Wabeladio's is particularly good in showing that for ruptures to be effective, they need to be solidly grounded. His efforts to root his new certainty in geometry were an avatar of many prior historical ruptures, also grounded on mathematics or geometry. Think about the importance of geometry for the birth of Western philosophy in pre-Socratic thinkers such as Pythagoras, breaking up with prior mythical models. Consider Renaissance thinkers such as Leonardo da Vinci breaking away from medieval cosmology by grounding human beings on the certainty of numbers. Think about the (religious) importance of geometry in the fathers of modern philosophy such as the above-mentioned Descartes, or Pascal, or Spinoza, for whom geometry was a secure way to ground the human in a supra-individual order of reality in the new post-medieval world, in which humans were detached from the great chain of beings and in which they had to look for certainties within themselves, not in the expanding infinite universe.

Wabeladio's life tells us that he was advancing solidly in the path of creativity by making more and more complex associations. The death of the creator froze the elaboration of a writing system that was in constant transformation. Its evolution might be usefully compared with that of the Vietnamese writing system invented by the prophet Shong Lue (Smalley et al. 1990). Despite being a revelation, Shong Lue kept transforming it, and different versions of it existed at different times, the last one being the easiest and most effective. Surely Mandombe would have continued to be transformed too, and I suspect that it would have evolved towards simplification. As I witnessed in a presentation in Kinshasa in 2011, Wabeladio was often accused by his detractors of having created a too cumbersome writing system. He agreed that the writing was a bit too difficult, and he was in fact working towards a way to make the syllables less complex. He told me that God had sent him some ideas in a dream as to how to simplify the writing, and he was putting them to work. This was the reason why he did not want Mandombe to be computerized. Whoever invented a software for Mandombe would stop the flow of creativity and deter Wabeladio from improving the invention. He would only accept the introduction of software if this was done by someone working very close to him, so that he could keep on introducing the necessary modifications, many of which came directly from God. This had not happened by the time of his death. However, some people have invented different software possibilities (at least one in France and one in Canada) and I am sure that, if Mandombe is to persist, one form or another of computerization will become standard in the future.

The presence of the persona of Wabeladio in his invention can be understood in two opposite ways: secular and spiritual. One could argue that Wabeladio wanted people to know that he and nobody else had invented Mandombe. Like Ulysses shouting his name to Polyphemus after having blinded him (a moment that, according to Horkheimer and Adorno [2002], was like the birth certificate of the Western self), Wabeladio wanted Mandombe to be shouting his name to us: 'Remember, Wabeladio was the name of he who created me!' That would be one plausible interpretation. But having known the man, I would insist on the other interpretation. Wabeladio wanted his biography to be known because it was the only way in which to erase himself from his invention. By making sure everybody knew the extraordinary revelation he received in 1979, he was making sure we understood that his invention was rooted in a transcendent domain. In his public presentations (or 'demonstrations', as he called them), Wabeladio used the concept of 'we' quite often. Thus, he would not say '*I* thought that by rotating the false element I could generate new keys' but rather '*we* thought that by rotating … '. In a lecture he gave in Matadi in 2011, someone in the audience asked him why he was using the first person plural. Wabeladio answered that it was because he was not doing this by himself, but with the spirit of God working through him. One could argue that for him, as for Spinoza, mathematics was a supra-individual structure, a matrix weaving the entire world, an infinite geometrical grid providing individuals with a sense of dependence on a transcendent order.[7]

Conclusion

Wabeladio was indeed an 'absolute beginner'. He made himself from scratch the day he observed two symbols on a wall of bricks, and he offered 'the new', in the form of an alphabet and of an artistic system, to his Bakongo publics. At first, the concepts he invented to refer to his invention were totally out of the blue, and the materiality on which the invention was based (the brick) was, as far as Kongo traditions of making go, rather unusual. His life was accompanied by conversion from Catholicism to Kimbanguism and by painful rupture with his family, especially his mother's brother, the authority in the family. His invention, Mandombe, is a paradigmatic locus where the need for inventors to be clever at making their invention is realized, but they have to be even more clever at presenting the final product to the public. They have to present it in a way that the influences, the roots of the invention, are concealed, perhaps forgotten, lest they are accused of copying, not creating from scratch. I could say with Deleuze that they have to inscribe *difference* upon *repetition*, but I will rather say with Harold Bloom that they have to inscribe *genius* upon *influence*.

Wabeladio noticed that he had to keep on experimenting with connections and disconnections if he wanted people to follow him. If he continued with his incomprehensible language and imagery, he would be taken as mad (as indeed he was for a long time). He rescued himself out of madness by reconnecting his original invention with something even more original, like the sounds of the healing drums of the Bakongo. But it was a very clever move, for it gave legitimacy for his publics to accept Mandombe and to see him as its 'inspired inventor' (a category used by Simon Kimbangu Kiangani, the head of the Kimbanguist Church, to refer to Wabeladio in 2005), bringing together his prophetic dimension with his creative one. As Robert Paine argued (Paine 1995), the voice of prophecy (Ardener 1987) and the logics of scientific discovery are different but complementary dimensions of our relationship with the unknown. Wabeladio brought together the two. Like a prophet, he received from God and revitalized culture. But he also explored three-dimensional, descriptive geometry with true scientific spirit and methods. Elsewhere I have described prophets as 'masters of connection' (Sarró 2018a) and, following Dozon (1995), I have characterized their imagination as a work of synthesis. With his unique capacity to synthesize and to connect the seemingly unconnectable, Wabeladio simultaneously introduced the new and revalued the old.

Notes

1. In this chapter I offer some theoretical reflexions on prophetic invention, without entering into the very complex descriptive geometry of Mandombe as a graphic system that gives rise to both art and writing. The inner geometrical workings and the aesthetics of Mandombe have been dealt with in another place (Sarró 2018b).
2. For a genealogy of the Western notion of 'genius' and a criticism of the suddenness of inventions attributed to a genius, see Robinson (2010; 2011).
3. A good collection of early sources on Kimbanguism is currently being most carefully edited by Jean-Luc Vellut (2005; 2010). A very detailed account of the early days of Kimbanguism, based on Baptist sources, is the unpublished doctoral thesis by Mackay (1985).
4. Such being 'hard to learn, easy to forget' must of course be a common feature of scripts in general, and not only of Mandombe.
5. Caroline Humphreys offers, in her chapter, a thoughtful view of French Revolution as rupture. This works as a good companion to the 1962 historical novel *El Siglo de las Luces* by Cuban writer Alejo Carpentier, which offers not only a powerful reflection on the making of modern Europe,

but also on the role of rupture, and of the symbolism of the guillotine in particular, in the making of the Atlantic world.

6. At least 'we' are the relatively healthy people, psychiatrically speaking. Some psychiatrists, such as Eugene Minkowski (1927), argued that in schizophrenic delusion historical consciousness disappears, and the temporal atrophy is compensated for by a spatial hypertrophy. For the schizophrenic patient, according to Minkowski, everything is here, now, and 'here' becomes a hyperconnected space where *everything* can be contemplated, like seeing 'the world in a grain of sand', as the famous poem by William Blake goes.

7. I am grateful to some comments in this Durkheimian direction that both Maurice Bloch and Bruce Kapferer made in different presentations they heard about the mathematical aspects of Mandombe.

References

Apo Salimba, M.L. Armand. 2013. *Histoire de la dissidence au sein de l'Eglise Kimbanguiste à la lumière de '26=1'*. Kinshasa: Éditions culturelles africaines.

Ardener, Edwin. 1987. 'The Voice of Prophecy'. In *The Voice of Prophecy, and Other Essays*, 134–54. Oxford: Berghahn.

Arthur, W. Brian. 2009. *The Nature of Technology: What It Is and How It Evolves*. London: Allen Lane.

Behar, Henri, and Michel Carassou. 1990. *Dada: Histoire d'une subversion*. Paris: Fayard.

Besançon, Julien. 1968. *Les Murs ont la Parole: Mai 1968*. Paris: Tchou.

Bloom, Harold. 1973. *The Anxiety of Influence: A Theory of Poetry*. Oxford: Oxford University Press.

Bloom, Harold. 2011. *The Anatomy of Influence: Literature as a Way of Life*. New Haven, CT: Yale University Press.

Cardinal, Roger. 1972. *Outsider Art*. New York: Praeger.

Diangienda Kuntima, Joseph. 1984. *L'Histoire du Kimbanguisme*. Paris: Editions Entraide Kimbanguiste.

Dozon, Jean-Pierre. 1995. *La Cause des Prophètes: Religion et Modernité en Afrique Contemporaine*. Paris: Seuil.

Dubuffet, Jean. 1968. *Asphyxiante Culture*. Paris: J.J. Pauvert.

Foreman, Grant. 1938. *Sequoyah*. Norman: University of Oklahoma Press.

Frost, Robert. 1914. *North of Boston*. London: David Nutt.

Gell, Alfred. 1994. 'The Technology of Enchantment and the Enchantment of Technology'. In *Anthropology, Art, and Aesthetics*, edited by Jeremy Coote, 40–63. Oxford: Clarendon Press.

Graeber, David. 2005. 'Fetishism as Social Creativity: or, Fetishes are Gods in the Process of Construction'. *Anthropological Theory* 5: 407–38.

Guigon, Emmanuel. 2007. 'L´écart absolu'. Accessed 1 April. http://www.charlesfourier.fr/spip. php?article384.

Horkheimer, Max, and Theodor Adorno. 2002. *Dialectic of Enlightenment*. Translated by Edmund Jephcott. Stanford, CA: Stanford University Press.

Hudson, Liam. 1966. *Contrary Imaginations: A Psychological Study of the English Schoolboy*. London: Methuen.

Kafka, Franz. 2007. *The Great Wall of China and other Short Stories*. London: Penguin. Translated from the German by Malcolm Pasley.

Kayongo, Léon N. 2005. 'Kimbanguism: Its Present Christian Doctrine and the Problems Raised by It'. *Exchange* 34 (3): 135–55.

Kounios, John, and Mark Beeman. 2015. *The Eureka Factor: Creative Insights and the Brain*. London: Penguin.

Kramer, Samuel N. 1956. *From the Tablets of Sumer*. Indian Hill, CO: The Falcon Wing's Press.

Laborit, Henri. 1970. *L'Homme Imaginant: essai de biologie politique*. Paris: Union Générale d'Éditions.

Lévi-Strauss, Claude. 1955. *Tristes Tropiques*. Paris: Plon.

MacGaffey, Wyatt. 1983. *Modern Kongo Prophets: Religion in a Plural Society*. Bloomington: Indiana University Press.

MacInnes, Colin. 1959. *Absolute Beginners*. London: McGibbon and Kee.

Mackay, D. J. 1985. 'The Once and Future Kingdom: Kongo Models of Renewal in the Church at Ngombe Lutete and in the Kimbanguist Movement'. PhD thesis. Aberdeen: University of Aberdeen.

Mélice, Anne. 2009. 'Le kimbanguisme et le pouvoir en RDC: Entre apolitisme et conception théologico-politique'. *Civilisations* 58 (2): 59–79.

Mélice, Anne. 2010. 'La désobéissance civile des kimbanguistes et la violence coloniale au Congo belge'. *Les temps modernes* 65 (658–9): 218–50.

Mélice, Anne. 2011. 'Prophétisme, hétérodoxie et dissidence: l'imaginaire kimbanguiste en mouvement'. PhD thesis. Liège: University of Liège.

Minkowski, Eugene. 1927. *La schizophrénie: Psychopathologie des schizoïdes et des schizophrènes.* Paris: Payot.

Paine, Robert. 1995. 'Columbus and Anthropology and the Unknown'. *Journal of the Royal Anthropological Institute* 1 (1): 47–65.

Peiry, Lucienne. 2016. 'Il soliloquio lapidario di Nannetti'. *Quaderni d'altri tempi* 64. Accessed 30 January. http://www.quadernidaltritempi.eu/rivista/numero64/mappe/q64_m04.html.

Robinson, Andrew. 2010. *Sudden Genius? The Gradual Path to Creative Breakthroughs.* Oxford: Oxford University Press.

Robinson, Andrew. 2011. *Genius: A Very Short Introduction.* Oxford: Oxford University Press.

Sarró, Ramon. 2015. 'Hope, Margin, Example: The Kimbanguist Diaspora in Lisbon'. In *Religion and Diaspora,* edited by Jane Garnett and Sondra Housner, 226–44. London: Macmillan.

Sarró, Ramon. 2018a. 'Prophecy'. In *The International Encyclopedia of Anthropology,* edited by Hilary Callan. Hoboken, NJ: Wiley. https://doi.org/10.1002/9781118924396.wbiea2318.

Sarró, Ramon. 2018b. 'Entre Art et Écriture: l'Invention du Mandombe en Pays Kongo'. *Terrain: Anthropologie et Sciences Humaines* 70: 104–25.

Sarró, Ramon, Ruy Blanes and Fátima Viegas. 2008. 'La guerre dans la paix: ethnicité et angolanité dans l'Eglise kimbanguiste de Luanda'. *Politique Africaine* 110: 84–101.

Sarró, Ramon, and Anne Mélice. 2010. 'Kongo-Lisbon: Dialectics of Centre and Periphery in the Kimbanguist Church'. In *Chrétiens Africains en Europe,* edited by Sandra Fancello and André Mary, 43–67. Paris: Khartala.

Sarró, Ramon, and Joana Santos. 2011. 'Gender and Return in the Kimbanguist Church of Portugal'. *Journal of Religion in Europe* 4: 369–87.

Smalley, William A., Chia Koua Vang and Gnia Yee Yang. 1990. *Mother of Writing: The Origin and Development of a Hmong Messianic Script.* Chicago and London: University of Chicago Press.

Thevoz, Michel. 1978. *Le Langage de la Rupture.* Paris: PUF.

Tocqueville, Alexis de. 1856. *The Old Regime and the Revolution.* Translated by John Bonner. New York: Harper and Brothers.

Turner, Christopher. 2011. 'The Deliberate Accident in Art: Blots'. *Tate Etc.* 21: 1–7.

Valéry, Paul. 1957. 'L'Invention Esthétique'. In *Oeuvres I, Variété, Théorie poétique et esthétique,* 1412–15. Paris: Éditions Gallimard.

Vellut, Jean-Luc, ed. 2005. *Simon Kimbangu 1921: de la prédication à la déportation. Les Sources. Vol 1. Fonds missionnaires protestants (1): Alliance missionnaire suédoise.* Brussels: Académie Royale des Sciences d'Outre-Mer.

Vellut, Jean-Luc, ed. 2010. *Simon Kimbangu 1921: de la prédication à la déportation. Les Sources. Vol 1. Fonds missionnaires protestants (2): Missions baptistes et autres traditions évangéliques.* Brussels: Académie Royale des Sciences d'Outre-Mer.

Vydrine, Valentin F. 2001. 'Souleymane Kanté, un philosophe-innovateur traditionnaliste maninka vu à travers ses écrits en n'ko'. *Mande Studies* 3: 99–131.

Wabeladio Payi, David. 1985. 'Méthode de découverte du style imbrique de construction par composition'. Unpublished report. Kinshasa: Association nationale des inventeurs du Zaire.

Webel, Sophie. 2008. *Jean Dubbufet o el Idioma de los Muros.* Madrid: Círculo de Bellas Artes.

7

Slow Rupture: The Art of Sneaking in an Occupied Forest

Stine Krøijer

Introduction

In 2012, a group of radical environmental activists took up residence in a little forest in the Ruhr district in Germany to counter the expansion of lignite mining in the area. Like many other environmental activists across Europe, the group had lost confidence in the ability and willingness of politicians to come up with solutions to catastrophic climate change and environmental destruction. After a decade of spectacular summit protesting from 1999 to 2009, during which the extra-parliamentarian left mainly directed their protests at meetings of heads of state, the global financial institutions and later the United Nations (UN) climate negotiations (Graeber 2002, 2009; Juris 2008; Krøijer 2013, 2015; Maeckelbergh 2009), radical environmental activists in Europe turned their anger directly towards the largest carbon emitters. Among these so-called 'carbon bombs' is the German electricity utility company RWE (Rheinisch-Westfälisches Elektrizitätswerk AG), which, according to the company itself, is one of Europe's largest emitters of carbon dioxide and is responsible for running an 85 square kilometre lignite mine adjacent to the old growth forest occupied by activists. In order to prevent the continuous expansion of the mine, activists have established a number of tree-sits in the forests, and engage in a mix of ecotage (sabotage on behalf of the environment) and civil disobedience directed at mining installations.[1] In the forest occupation where I did fieldwork, tree-sitting and other direct actions went hand in hand with experiments in alternative, sustainable livelihoods based on the conviction that people must rewild and harmonize their life with nature.

This chapter takes its point of departure from this change of focus in environmental activism, which today exceeds the approaches historically favoured by radical left or anarchist circles. Already in 2001, after the summit protests in Genoa where an activist was shot and killed at close range by the Italian police, the Italian *Disobedienti* called for the abandonment of summit protesting, a rethinking of tactics and a return to the building of local alternatives and autonomies in villages, neighbourhoods and social centres (Krøijer 2015, 140). After failed attempts at influencing the austerity measures of the European Union in the context of the financial crisis that swept the continent after 2007, and a few years of UN climate 'summit hopping', activists such as those in the small forest in Germany have increasingly redirected their time and attention to local environmental struggles. Based on my on and off fieldwork since 2014 in the German anti-coal movement and in the forest occupation, this chapter analyses the implications of taking the climate struggle to the mines and power plants, as well as to daily life in such contexts, and describes the forms of activism that have flourished after 'the anarchist travelling circus' (Goaman 2013) abandoned the scene of the heads of state. I describe how 'slowing down' – instead of relying on spectacular confrontations and clashes with the police and the heroic narratives about it (cf. Krøijer 2015) – has become a strategy for producing and staging a rupture with the structures of domination inherent to capitalism that are perceived also to impede, in various ways, actions that address the climate crisis. This change in the temporality of rupture and the slowness with which it is performed is, I argue, intimately tied to efforts aimed at developing a different, closer relationship to nature, to rewild or even become nature oneself. In this line, dwelling in trees, mimicking animals and learning so-called 'primitive' living skills are ways of living and acting that aim to create a radical break *within* capitalism. By cultivating their connections to non-human beings, such as trees and wild boars, the activists enact what I call a 'slow rupture'. The performance of slow ruptures both challenges ideas of rupture and revolution found on the radical left as well as standard anthropological thinking about rupture. In this sense, the new forms of action produce a form of rupture with rupture.

The introduction to this volume argues that the Modern World began with a rupture. This modern form of rupture is epitomized by the French and Russian Revolutions, tied as they were to the epochal idea of the 'progress of man' (*sic*) through the sudden, radical and complete change afforded by the revolutionary moment. These historic events have made a strong imprint on political thinking about radical change and anthropological ideas about what rupture is and could be, which have lingered in anthropological writing on the subject. This is particularly clear in the work of the Manchester School where Max Gluckman's distinction between revolutions and rebellions has haunted anthropology, in the sense that it demands from researchers the passing of judgement on the extent to which social uprisings, protests, upheavals, crises and proclaimed revolutions are producing enduring and fundamental social change (Gluckman 1963, 8; Turner 1969, 125–32).

One way in which to challenge the association between rupture and revolution is pursued by Humphrey (this volume). She provides a view of the cuts, contradictions and ruptures within the French Revolution, which impeded the construction of a collective revolutionary subject and narrative. Inspired here by Isabelle Stengers's 'cosmopolitical proposal', I intend to go another way by arguing that it is possible to influence the fundamental nature of something without this change being either sudden or complete. In addressing the philosophy of history, Stengers argues for the slowing down of reasoning 'to arouse a slightly different awareness of the problems and situations mobilizing us' (Stengers 2005, 994). Following this, slowing down might in itself be a move that challenges conventional ways of thinking, enacting and scaling rupture. The radical environmental activists described here are involved in an operation analogous to that of Stengers by producing a pause or moment of hesitation in their own 'politics as usual' (cf. Ranciére 2010). This political moment neither produces a total replacement of one system with another – nor is it simply a 'carnival of desire' (see introduction to this volume) – but is a new form of politics-with-nature that breaks altogether with the progressive ambition inherent in modern ideas of rupture.

In the following, I shall briefly provide a bit more background about the forest occupation before turning to two ethnographic scenes: a sneaking workshop convened during a 'skill-sharing camp' held in the forest occupation to reach out to broader activist circles; and a conversation with two tree-sitting activists about how to do politics with trees. My aim in engaging with these two scenes is to consider the scale that we use to measure rupture and explore how the slowness involved in constructing new more-than-human political subjectivities in the forest occupation also awakens the brutal realization that something must change.

A forest occupation

Germany's Ruhr district, with its enormous deposits of coal and lignite, became the powerhouse of early northern European industrialization. Located near the border with France, Belgium and the Netherlands, this resource-rich area is a site of recurrent acts of conflict, but after the Second World War a shared concern with the smooth distribution of the area's raw materials also came to play an important role in the establishment of the European Coal and Steel Community, the precursor of the European Union. In the post-war period, urban areas in the Ruhr district underwent rapid economic development based on mining. Even today, the wider Metropol Rhine-Ruhr is home to some of Germany's largest open-cast lignite mines, mainly owned and operated by the electric utility company RWE.

In 2012, a group of radical environmental activists occupied the remainder of what was originally a 5,500-hectare old-growth forest adjacent to a large mine in the area, with the hope of slowing down or even stopping its continuous expansion. In 1978 RWE bought the forest, which had been managed as *bürgerwald* (a forest common) for the previous 500 years; after the change in ownership, clear-cutting of the land and forced relocation of several villages commenced. The expansion of the mining operation is projected to continue until 2040, which, together with the company's enormous carbon emissions, has created a strong sense of disillusionment among environmental groups and organizations. The lack of political willingness to address the root causes of climate change, place a carbon tax on emissions and invest in green energy transition has contributed to the emergence of a strong German anti-coal movement since 2014. It was after one of the first annual summer camps of the movement that activists established a more permanent occupation and built a number of tree-sits in the forest's slow-growing oak and beech trees to curb the advancing cutting line on what was left of the highly rich and biodiverse forest.

The forest occupation is made up of various tree-sits and a base camp, which is today located on a little piece of land at the edge of the woods lent to the activists by a local farmer, who is also a strong opponent of the mine as he is about to lose his land to the diggers. At the outset the main purpose of the camp was to support the tree-sitters by providing food and water supplies, to coordinate internal communication and security, serve as a space to store utensils, building and climbing equipment, and coordinate and maintain relations with local villagers and the broader, by now international, anti-coal movement. Activists in the forest occupation have also participated in ongoing lawsuits concerning the future of the forest, political advocacy and information campaigns both in the Rheine-Ruhr region and internationally, and in the coordination of several large direct actions in the area under the slogan *Ende Gelände*.[2] These mass direct actions have drawn a large international attendance of people willing to break the law by trespassing on private property in order to call attention to the demand for Germany to leave its fossil fuels in the ground, and particularly to the highly problematic effects of lignite or brown coal mining.[3] In the week prior to the COP23 (the name for the 23rd Conference of the Parties to the United Nations Framework Convention on Climate Change) in Bonn in 2017, 4,000–5,000 activists refrained from protesting outside the climate summit venue in order to join a mass action on mining, which stopped all work at the Hambach mine for three days.

Activists living in the forest occupation share this commitment to take action on major carbon emitters, but over the years have come to do so through different means. Already in 2015, few activists in the forest occupation found it worth even considering joining the protests connected to the COP21 in Paris or argued actively against prioritizing these one-off spectacular protests. Instead, they passionately advocated the view that it is more important 'to build alternatives', for example by spending time building mud houses for people to keep warm in the base camp during the cold winter months. There, the 'System Change, Not Climate Change' slogan of the broader climate justice movement is increasingly enacted through the sharing of more mundane living skills that should enable and make feasible a life 'in the wild', and preparing for if or when dramatic climate change alters the fundamental conditions of life even in such places as Germany (Krøijer 2019).

Each year prior to the cutting season – which in Germany runs from 1 October to 28 February and is the time when a landowner is allowed to clear the land – activists of the forest occupation organize a skill-sharing camp where visiting activists can share their skills and activist tactics by signing on to a daily schedule of workshops. Some of these activities are 'action skills', such as tree climbing and climbing rescuing techniques, building of platforms in trees and tripods for blockading roads, as well as 'sneaking'. Others are concerned with 'living skills' such as the collection of mushrooms and wild herbs, scavenging and dumpster diving, house-building with clay, fire starting, and so on. The celebration of skill-share gatherings is not limited to Germany, but can be found in most Earth First! circles and rendezvous, and among anarcho-primitivists in the USA (Austdal 2016). The aim of all this, I have been told, is to liberate human and non-human beings who have been 'civilized' and 'domesticated' by agricultural progress and industrial capitalism. As I highlight further later, this process also includes the construction of a new and 'wilder' political subjectivity. One way to accomplish human liberation of this kind is by burning identity papers, taking on aliases and cover names from their life in the forest.[4] Another parallel way to strive towards this goal, which is the subject of the present chapter, is to become enmeshed in nature by intensifying experiences of interconnected political being. In what follows, I expose two scenes from activist life in the forest to explore this point.

The art of sneaking

Owen is leading the sneaking class on a late October evening. He is an experienced activist, who has been living in the forest on and off for four years, interrupted only by occasional jobs as a doorman at punk-rock venues in a large German city. Participants in the class are mainly newcomers from Spain, Britain and Sweden, most of whom are planning to stay on in the camp for the winter and cutting season. They have been instructed to show up in either camouflage or black clothes, preferably also bringing a torch, which should not be used unless 'something unexpected' occurs. Owen is also taking a mobile phone, making it possible to connect with the camp group 'in case for some reason we are not back before midnight', he states. Owen tells the group that the sneaking skill-share class will probably be completely uneventful, but that RWE's security personnel sometimes patrol the forest. 'They will almost always beat you severely if they catch you', a Spanish girl adds.

Owen tells the participants that the art of sneaking rests on the ability to move slowly sideways, rolling on one's feet at every step in order to avoid the sound of snapping brushwood. To acquire night vision it is important to focus on the darkness and use one's arms to slowly slide low-hanging branches to the side without making unnecessary noise. The destination of the sneaking expedition is an old road separating the activist-controlled part of the forest from the cutting area near the rim of the mine. First the group moves along a relatively illuminated path to train their skills, then they turn north through a darker section of the forest. After the first half hour of sneaking the group makes a stop. 'Now we will move along a meadow', Owen says. 'We will squat down once in a while to listen for sounds and noises.' Participants are also instructed to look out for flashing lights, the sign of approaching security guards. 'They usually wave their torches at chest height, which also means that you can avoid them by keeping an eye out for animal tracks', Owen explains, pointing towards an almost invisible track below the ferns on the side of the footpath. 'Get down on your knees and creep along. This forest is full of wild boars. If you are attacked you can hide below the scrubs like a piglet and get up on the other side and just run off. The guards will not usually follow you because they are scared of being lured into an ambush', he says.

After an hour and a half, the group reaches the side of the road. Some hundred metres away, mine security has a checkpoint from where they can overlook the road. 'You need to get to the other side of this abandoned road if you want to reach the mine', a young Swedish woman who calls herself Lynx explains to me. Many people in the camp take on an animal or plant name which, on an instrumental level, serves to conceal individual identity, but in which there also seems to be an effort to come closer to or become animal or plant-like. We are asked to squat down and wait behind the tree line. From the bushes ahead of us we hear some strange sounds and grunting noises. Lynx grabs my arm, 'What is it?' she asks. 'What do we do if a wild boar charges out at us?' Actual boar attacks on humans are rare, but they can occur during the rutting season and may result in multiple penetrating injuries to the lower part of the body. Lynx is ready to flee, but after a few moments Owen appears from the bushes, waving everybody forward. If it were not for the tension of the situation, the mistake would probably have produced laughter. The group makes a few crossings of the road, training to cross simultaneously and run in a straight line in order to appear as one, or at least make the exact number of activists indiscernible from the security check point. After the exercise at the roadside, the group makes a disorderly retreat, moving quickly along the forest trails towards the camp. Owen's mobile phone rings and he flashes his torch. The forest turns pitch black and we continue blindly, while Lynx complains: 'If he wants us to develop animal senses, why does he turn on the bloody torch? It will take us at least 45 minutes to recover.'

Sneaking skills are useful if one wants to avoid arrest prior to an ecotage action or plans to build a new tree-sit near the cutting line. Sneaking is a tactic of avoidance, and when practised in a forest it gives a sense of both escaping and blending in with the surroundings. Scrubs, bushes, grasses and trees offer shelter, but if we are thinking like an impetuous wild boar, the vegetation can also be taken as the point of departure for a fast and relentless attack. Sneaking, in other words, opens up the question whether it is possible to think of a slow or even sneaking rupture. Rupture and revolutions are moments usually associated with speed, with rapid, fundamental social and structural change as against slow reform processes (Dunkerley 2007, 23–6). The speed of revolutionary moments has been re-enacted numerous times through the protests of the radical left and the alter-globalization movement over the past century, but the sneaking workshop exemplifies how a reinvention of forms of politics is under way in which slowness entails a rupture with radical left politics as usual, and with its tradition of vanguardism. The Occupy Movement already played on slowness – stressing encampment and permanence in public space rather than rapid and spectacular appearance – thereby turning existing forms of protest inside-out (Krøijer 2015, 215). In the forest occupation slowness is linked to nature, blending in with the forest and engaging in sympathetic magic (Taussig 1993) with wild boars and their piglets to draw from their power and bodily capabilities. Indeed, the most 'untamable' rupture of our time has to do with coming closer to nature and seems to involve more than human agency or human-animal assemblages. This changing temporality of rupture is tied to this 'becoming-animal', to paraphrase Deleuze and Guattari (1987, 242), and in the following scene I explore how activists develop a sense of interconnectedness with the trees through tree-sitting. Cultivation of nature sensibilities and becoming-animal requires time, but also lead to a break with socio-centric ideas of radical change.

Adding arms to trees

After the skill-share camp in October, I do not return to the forest occupation again until early January, at the height of the cutting season. Soon after my arrival I run into Lynx, who has stayed on in the forest occupation and proves to have had ample chance to train her sneaking skills. When we first met in October, she was eager to learn to climb and to experience 'how little she could live on', preferably in a tree-sit, but now she explains that the situation in the forest has developed into a rather 'brutal version of hide-and-seek' between activists, police and the mining company's private security forces. The security personnel of the mine sometimes patrol the forest in groups, hunting people to and from the tree-sits, cutting down climbing ropes, or hanging 'lynched' dolls from branches, supposedly to generate fear and awe. More than once these encounters have led to physical confrontations, and recently an activist known as Fledermaus was badly hurt. 'Things have escalated quite a bit since then', Lynx explains: 'we did not have a lot of discussion about it; it just seemed necessary'. As a result, some people have increasingly engaged in small sabotage actions, such as damaging the pumping stations that are used for lowering the groundwater level in the entire area, short-circuiting cables on the coal railway line transporting lignite from the mine to one of several power plants, and arson of mobile and radio antennas in the area (Krøijer, in preparation). Lynx has spent most of her time occupying different tree-sits, which in her view is a political act in and of itself, but she has also occasionally 'been out on nightly walks to avoid falling into winter torpor', as she phrases it.

Lynx is sleeping in a tree in Beech Town, a group of 30 metre copper beeches some 15 minutes' walk from the base camp. Her tree-sit is called Aquarium due to the many windows in the 6 square metre treehouse and the transparent plastic roof over the bed, which provides ample view of the sky through the naked top branches. The little treehouse, which is tied with ropes onto strong branches, is located some 25 metres above the forest floor. During the night, the distant noise from the mine gets mixed with the rustling sound of the branches and the wind, which today makes the entire tree sway lightly. Lynx enjoys being in the tree, she explains in the course of the evening, but, in contrast to some of the other tree-sitters, she finds it difficult to just be in the tree slumbering for several consecutive days.

During a long morning stretching into the early afternoon, we rest, talk and make coffee in the Aquarium, while observing the forest from above. 'Can you see those little beeches and shoots down below?' she asks me, and continues: 'in a sense trees are like people, they help each other out, they create community.' I ask her if she considers the trees to be living beings, which she confirms and then adds: 'We talk about the trees as living beings when we are building the tree-sits: whether the tree looks healthy, if it is dead or has dead branches. What we see now is that big healthy trees fall over because their roots do not get sufficient water.' The marvel of how the forest grows, and of the interdependence between trees, is in other words soon superseded by more sombre predictions: 'The trees in this forest are in a sense already dead', she exclaims, thereby repeating a phrase I have heard many times in the camp. 'They are suffering from water shortage due to the low groundwater level around the mine. It is visible from their shorter leafing period', she explains, admitting that, in this light, their attempt to save the forest does not make much sense, as the trees will die anyway. Nonetheless, she argues, by being in the tree-sits, occupying the trees, she and other activists are 'adding arms to trees', thereby 'improving the part of their defence system that they have not naturally developed'. In making this argument she implicitly draws on recent popular and scientific studies of trees (see for example Simard et al. 1997, 2012; Wohlleben 2016), but also points to how a new political assemblage of people and trees might increase the chance of curbing the advancing logging machines.

After some hours of doing nothing in particular, we visit another activist named Acorn, who lives in a large oak tree and who has been part of the forest occupation since its beginning in 2012. Acorn sticks her head out of a window far above ground as we approach and invites us up for a cup of tea, even though she warns us of the cold she has developed over the past few days. The treehouse, which she built with the help of a friend, is constructed on three platforms: a middle landing platform to unhook one's climbing gear from the rope reaching the ground 25 metres below, a top platform with a roof constructed over a dome of hazelnut branches coated with old blankets, hay and a tarp, and a lower platform with a 500 kg cement block with a lock-on inside to slow down the police's attempt to arrest and remove her from the tree in case of eviction. She has been working on her nest over the autumn, to keep warm during winter and to have 'a quiet place to withdraw to', she explains.

Acorn shows us around and comments that a great titmouse jumps in from the little east-facing window almost every morning to look for breadcrumbs. 'The Nest' has a large mattress and a little kitchen corner with a gas cooker and a few utensils, but apart from this there is only a shelf with books and some papers. 'It is so quiet in the forest', she comments. 'Soon you can observe the leaves sprout, first hand, see the trees seed and later observe when their leaves turn purple. Being in the tree is just the most peaceful place to be', a statement that at first surprises me due to the noise from the mine and the threat of eviction. She describes the tree as her 'safe-space', a term drawn from queer-feminist theory that defines such spaces as sites to avoid, rework or challenge mainstream stereotypes (Roestone Collective 2014). I realize that the tree-home offers her the tangible safety that avoiding encounters with the private security forces entails, and peace from the sometimes heated debates and radical activities in the base camp, but that it also allows for an exploration of a different kind of 'intersectional' relation to trees.[5] 'It is very different from sleeping in the camp', she says, and offers me this place to stay for a couple of days, to try it for myself, while she travels to visit her mother in a large German city.

Her comment points to a salient difference in the forest occupation between those activists that see the occupation of the trees as the most important form of action to stop the expansion of lignite mining, and activists in the camp who either favour direct actions or spend most of their time experimenting with alternative, sustainable livelihoods (Krøijer, in preparation). Acorn is in her late twenties, has long blond hair collected in plaits below a green hunter's cap, and when she is on the ground she is black clad, wearing a harness or belt with climbing gear and a knife. She is also usually smiling, outgoing, and does most of the public relations work, but over the years she has grown increasingly concerned with what she calls 'sustainable activism'. This, she explains, does not primarily concern environmental sustainability, but how to endure in activism over time: 'Many of the people that started the forest occupation, back when Monkey Town existed, are gone now.[6] They simply burned out, got too sad when the trees were felled, or the repression just got to them. I know my tree ... not that I own it ... but I intend to be here when Day X comes.' Acorn explains that during the cutting season a number of interim tree-sits are put up, and will be shortly, but that they have agreed it can only be done if people are committed to occupying them until Day X; that is, when they are evicted by force. She tells the story of how two winters ago she occupied such an interim tree-sit that was constructed on an open iron fence, while writing a diary on a toilet roll, which she still saves. After two exhausting weeks she was arrested by climbing police.

The most important point Acorn wants to convey by introducing the issue of 'sustainable activism' is how the tree holds a promise of emotional and physical renewal. This was not her motivation for occupying the old oak tree years back, but a feeling of responsibility and interdependence that has emerged from years of co-living. The cultivation of these human–tree relations is so far only to a limited extent mediated by language: the hesitation I often experienced in conversations with activists included a careful avoidance of religious and spiritual vocabulary to describe their experiences and political project as well as a deliberate attention on steering clear of the tree symbolism and romanticism of the Third Reich (cf. Crapanzano 2004, 234). Instead the alliance with trees is discreetly cast as a relation of solidarity between the dying and oppressed, joining together in the renewal of radical politics. Before heading down, Acorn points to the cement block below us and explains the 'emergency procedures' if the police arrive with their 'cherry pickers', lifts used to evict the tree-sits.

Scales of rupture

Over the years, fieldwork among anarchist groups and radical environmentalists in Europe has led me to ponder about the scale on which rupture should be measured. In the literature on revolutionary change, adjectives such as 'sudden', 'radical', 'complete' and 'fundamental' are used to describe the nature of rupture and the transformation it entails of society and its political institutions (Dunkerley 2007). Are tree-sitting, sneaking and building eco-friendly mud-houses in a forest occupation, instead of going to protest at the climate summit in Paris, radical practices that enable fundamental transformations, and if so in what way? Akin to the Danish jihadist described by Kublitz (this volume), the role of rupture in the renewal of political practice does not follow a linear perception of time. But to scrutinize the performance of slow rupture, it is first necessary to identify how the systemic structures of capitalism are envisioned among activists and activist writers.

As I have described in more detail elsewhere (Krøijer 2015), anarchist groups and radical environmental activists describe capitalism as having systemic qualities; it is a coherent, pervasive and dynamic system, but unlike Marx's prediction, it is not seen as likely that it is going to break owing to its own inherent contradictions (cf. Marx 1974). Several writers close to the movement have developed these thoughts most consistently: in *Empire* (2000), Michael Hardt and Antonio Negri describe the imperial and systemic qualities of capitalism, and how it comes to permeate all aspects of life; in *The Shock Doctrine* (2008) and *No Is Not Enough* (2017), Naomi Klein outlines how the capitalist system in fact grows stronger and even expands from its recurrent crises. In agreement with this, radical environmental activists see political processes, such as the UN climate talks for example, as machines for 'greenwashing' the status quo. In the German anti-coal movement, activists describe the fossil fuel industry and the political elite, but also normal people's passivity as coinciding in upholding a carbon-fuelled economy. As an example of this system-preserving alliance, the way in which RWE and other private energy companies in 2015 managed to reverse a government proposal aimed at placing a carbon tax on coal-fired power plants is frequently mentioned. Even so-called Green Capitalism, which still relies on a logic of growth and progress, is described as just another version of the same, almost all-encompassing system that essentially seems to exist at 'the end of history' (cf. Fukuyama 1992). Increasingly, the view of capitalism as historic endpoint has nonetheless over the last years come to rest uneasily with more apocalyptic outlooks on the future, including the expectation of a total system collapse owing to capitalism's own systemic death drive (Austdal 2016; Krøijer 2019).

In the light of this totalizing view of capitalism, any rupture has to be internal to the system. There is, in other words, no outside vantage point from where the system can be attacked in its totality (Krøijer 2015). The forest occupation in the heart of Germany's industrial centre can, like many other anarchist and left radical projects and protest events, be conceptualized as an attempt to establish an alternative space in the centre of capitalism. The anarchist writer Hakim Bey used the concept 'the temporary autonomous zone' to characterize an already existing anarchist practice, namely the liberation of a place in space, time and imagination (Bey 1991, 99). These alternative spaces or occupied zones are interstitial, and are hence opened up 'at an internal distance' to the system they seek to transform (Krøijer 2015, 10; see also Critchley 2007; Gibson-Graham 2006). By being internal, the activist theory of change displays similarities to Edward N. Lorenz's theory of the butterfly effect (1963, 1972; Prigogine 1997), which refers to the idea that a butterfly's wings create tiny perpetuations that may ultimately create, alter or accelerate large-scale weather effects, such as a tornado, in another location within a dynamic system. In Lynx's account of a confrontation at a bridge described above, she talks of escalation in quantitative terms as the growth and escalation of conflict with mining security personnel, but these momentary escalations are also accompanied with doubt as to the effectiveness of confrontations. Apparently insignificant or mundane acts might potentially create large-scale or delayed systemic effects, but the lack of predictability produces not only hope among activists that their actions might matter, but also concerns about how to endure and sustain activism over time, as illustrated by Acorn's comments on the matter. This strategy of destabilization relies, as Greenhouse phrases it, on the 'heat of the moment' (this volume), which unsettles time and social relations without a clear view of its consequences.

Independent of the processes that might be judged as escalating (capitalist collapse, climate change or just change), environmental activism seems to be slowing down without becoming less radical. Here I have focused on 'the art of sneaking' to illustrate this point. Compared with walking, sneaking involves a different temporal rhythm, and whereas walking and wandering is a particular form of onward movement described extensively by generations of phenomenologists and practice theorists (De Certeau 1984; Mauss 1992 [1934]; Pink 2008; Ingold and Vergunst 2016), sneaking is a tactic of avoidance, which on a very tangible level constantly establishes lines of flight. Crucially, sneaking does not rest on the expectation that something better lies ahead (cf. Tsing 2015, 23–4); in the forest occupation it is a necessary skill for operating within enemy territory, and it implies a bodily defiance of the idea of progress.

The question then is if sneaking is less radical than 'storming the Winter Palace' in both practical political and analytical terms. Protest events of the radical left have historically been modelled on the revolutionary moment of the armed assault during the October Revolution in Russia in 1917, by orchestrating spectacular moments of bodily confrontations with the police in the streets of Europe. These moments were often saturated with aggressive macho aesthetics and display of militancy on both sides of the confrontation. On a different plane, this to a large extent also holds for anthropological 'turns', the celebration of paradigmatic ruptures and rowdy attitudes in theoretical debates.

In thinking differently about the pace of rupture, Isabelle Stengers's call for the need for a slowing down of reasoning can be helpful, insofar as it advocates a form of analytical abstention and hesitation with political ramifications. Similarly, Marilyn Strathern has argued that the idea of incompleteness is one of the most important things to draw from feminist theory (Strathern, cited in Holbraad and Pedersen 2017, 143). The forms of activism described here involve an abandonment of both male and human vanguardism and a deliberate cultivation of slower, less complete and even sneaking radical transformations. Slowing down is accomplished by immersing oneself in the forest, and developing and assembling these more-than-human subjectivities that are following a different temporal rhythm. It is likely that some of Stengers's thoughts are already entangled with activist practices, as she has been visiting anarchist projects in France in the company of an American neopagan and alter-globalization activist known as Starhawk.[7] Cultivating incompleteness, recognizing interdependence, and creating much-needed spaces of hesitation are necessary in both theory and practice to break with totalitarianism, ingrained ideas of progress predicated on exploitation of nature and non-human beings, but also with the kind of progressiveness that in spite of the supposed radicalism tends to reproduce existing power relations. In this light, I find that the challenge still remains to pluralize and develop a more incomplete anthropological take on rupture that avoids taking the break inherent to violent overthrowing of power as its model.

This new hesitation in activist practice becomes further visible by considering how they are not only changing in pace, but also in their objective. If the ultimate rupture of past revolutionary movements consisted in overthrowing governments, installing a different societal order and creating 'a New Man', then the fundamental object of rupture is still political subjectivity (Buck-Morss 2002; Fernandes 2010; Holbraad 2014), but with the important addition that in projects such as the forest occupation this new political subject is more-than-human. Acquiring animal senses and learning to think like a wild boar, temporarily reassembling human and tree forms of agency to procure new defence mechanisms, or mimicking rather naïve versions of indigenous people's life skills (see also Austdal 2016; Krøijer in preparation) to enable a life in the wild all suggest a break with anthropocentric, heroic tales of rupture. Re-wilding as practised in the forest occupation is not only directed at the environment or nature, but at making more feral human beings and thereby remaking their relationship to other beings. It challenges the domestication of people – through citizenship, expensive lifestyles, and conventional thinking – but also the perception of nature as an object for exploitation.

As Cronon has suggested, wilderness is here seen as a refuge that should be recovered (Cronon 1995, 69), a space for other life-making projects, but also a space where humans are able to regain their physical and mental strength and become other. In the forest occupation the wild is not the last bastion of rugged (male) individualism, as in the classical American visions of the frontier (ibid., 75), but the land for forming new communities of humans and trees based on mutual help and inter-species solidarity. In this logic, fundamental change is not only experienced to be in the hands of human beings, but emerges through human and non-human ways of being in the world that entails new assemblages of species and gendered beings. The attempts at 'becoming-animal' is full of hesitation and cautious *rapprochement* and failure; a new radical subjectivity that relies on both self-imposed and unstable shape-shifting and attempts at redefinitions of the sensible world as instrument of struggle.

Acknowledgements

This chapter was first presented at the Rupture Conference, University College London in February, 2017. I thank Bjørn Enge Berthelsen, Helene Risør, and colleagues at the Pontifica Universidad Católica de Chile (conicyt/fondap/15110006) for comments on previous versions of the chapter. The research has been made possible thanks to the Danish Council for Independent Research, grant no. 1321-00025B and grant no. 4001–00223. I am most indebted to friends and activists who have shared their experiences with me.

Notes

1. Tree-sitting is a direct action tactic first developed by Earth First! in the USA. Activists live on platforms in tall trees to prevent them from being cut down by loggers (Hill 2000; Jordan 1998; Taylor 1995; Wall 1999).
2. The slogan *Ende Gelände* is an imperative that loosely translates 'here and no further!', playing on the double meaning of 'an area coming to an end' and a practice in an area that needs to end or be terminated.
3. Brown coal or lignite is a soft, low-grade coal with a wood-like texture. It has a lower carbon content and lower calorific value than conventional 'black' coal (Kopp 2016).

4. In this chapter, I have used different aliases to secure the anonymity of people, but have tried to stay with the general ethos of the names already used in the forest occupation. I have also slightly altered some events and places to avoid the association of certain actions with individual persons.
5. Intersectionality is the concept used in feminist theory to describe the intersection of different forms of oppression (such as class, race, ethnicity and gender). Here I use the term slightly differently, namely to highlight the intersection between humans and nature, and how this relation is experimented with to lessen human dominance.
6. Monkey Town is the name of the first forest occupation and base camp established in a forest meadow. The base camp and the first tree-sits were evicted and cleared in 2014, and the trees that had been occupied were felled.
7. Starhawk is mentioned in Stengers's writings on cosmopolitics (2005), and has engaged in discussions with Stenger during her visits to anarchist collectives (Zad Collective 2017).

References

Austdal, Tord. 2016. 'World Making in the Mountains: Post-Apocalyptic Utopianism in Southern Appalachia'. PhD dissertation. Bergen: University of Bergen.

Bey, Hakim. 1991. *TAZ: The Temporary Autonomous Zone, Ontological Anarchy, Poetic Terrorism*. Brooklyn, NY: Automedia.

Buck-Morss, Susan. 2002. *Dreamworld and Catastrophe: The Passing of Mass Utopia in East and West*. Cambridge, MA: MIT Press.

Crapanzano, Vincent. 2004. *Imaginative Horizons: An Essay in Literary-Philosophical Anthropology*. Chicago: University of Chicago Press.

Critchley, Simon. 2007. *Infinitely Demanding: Ethics of Commitment, Politics of Resistance*. London: Verso.

Cronon, William. 1995. 'The Trouble with Wilderness, or Getting Back to the Wrong Nature'. In *Uncommon Ground: Rethinking the Human Place in Nature*, edited by William Cronon, 69–90. New York: W. W. Norton.

De Certeau, Michel. 1984. *The Practice of Everyday Life*. Berkeley: University of California Press.

Deleuze, Gilles, and Félix Guattari. 1987. *A Thousand Plateaus: Capitalism and Schizophrenia*. Minnesota: University of Minnesota Press.

Dunkerley, James. 2007. *Revolution and the Power of History in the Present*. London: Institute of Latin American Studies.

Fernandes, Sujartha. 2010. 'Revolutionary Praxis in a Post-Neoliberal Era'. *Interventions* 12 (1): 88–99.

Fukuyama, Francis. 1992. *The End of History and the Last Man*. New York: New Press.

Gibson-Graham, J. K. 2006. *The End of Capitalism (As We Knew It): A Feminist Critique of Political Economy*. Minneapolis: University of Minnesota Press.

Gluckman, Max. 1963. *Order and Rebellion in Tribal Africa*. New York: The Free Press.

Goaman, Karen. 2013. 'The Anarchist Travelling Circus: Reflections on Contemporary Anarchism, Anti-Capitalism and the International Scene'. In *Changing Anarchism: Anarchist Theory and Practice in a Global Age*, edited by Jonathan Purkis and James Bowen, 163–80. Manchester: Manchester University Press.

Graeber, David. 2002. 'The New Anarchists'. *New Left Review* 13: 61–73.

Graeber, David. 2009. *Direct Action: An Ethnography*. Edinburgh: AK Press.

Hardt, Michael, and Antonio Negri. 2000. *Empire*. Cambridge, MA: Harvard University Press.

Hill, Julia Butterfly. 2000. *The Legacy of Luna: The Story of a Tree, a Woman and the Struggle to Save the Redwoods*. San Francisco, CA: Harper.

Holbraad, Martin. 2014 'Revolución o muerte: Self-Sacrifice and the Ontology of the Cuban Revolution'. *Ethnos* 79 (3): 365–87.

Holbraad, Martin, and Morten Axel Pedersen. 2017. *The Ontological Turn: An Anthropological Exposition*. Cambridge: Cambridge University Press.

Ingold, Tim, and Jo Lee Vergunst. 2016. 'Introduction'. In *Ways of Walking: Ethnography and Practice on Foot*, edited by Tim Ingold and Jo Lee Vergunst, 1–20. London: Routledge.

Jordan, John. 1998. 'The Art of Necessity: The Subversive Imagination of Anti-Road Protest and Reclaim the Streets'. In *DiY Culture: Party and Protest in Nineties Britain*, edited by G. McKay, 129–51. London: Verso.

Juris, Jeffrey. 2008. *Networking Futures: The Movements against Corporate Globalization*. Durham, NC, and London: Duke University Press.

Klein, Naomi. 2008. *The Shock Doctrine*. London: Penguin Books.

Klein, Naomi. 2017. *No Is Not Enough: Resisting Trump's Shock Politics and Winning the World We Need*. New York: Penguin.

Kopp, Otto C. 2016. 'Lignite'. *Encyclopedia Britannica*. Accessed 5 December. https://www.britannica.com/science/lignite.

Krøijer, Stine. 2013. 'Security Is a Collective Body: Intersecting Temporalities of Security around the Climate Summit in Copenhagen'. In *Times of Security: Ethnographies of Fear, Protest and the Future*, edited by Martin Holbraad and Morten Axel Pedersen, 33–56. New York: Routledge.

Krøijer, Stine. 2015. *Figurations of the Future: Forms and Temporalities of Left Radical Politics in Northern Europe*. Oxford: Berghahn Books.

Krøijer, Stine. 2019. 'Miner la vie: Une région allemande d'extraction du charbon'. *Terrain* 70.

Krøijer, Stine. In preparation. 'Civilization as the Undesired World: Anarchists, Primitivists and Indigenous Peoples in Times of Climate Crisis'.

Lorenz, Edward N. 1963. 'Deterministic Nonperiodic Flow'. *Journal of the Atmospheric Sciences* 20: 130–41.

Lorenz, Edward N. 1972. 'Predictability: Does the Flap of a Butterfly's Wings in Brazil Set Off a Tornado in Texas?' Paper delivered at the AAA Section on Environmental Sciences, MIT, MA. Accessed 3 February 2011. http://eaps4.mit.edu/research/Lorenz/Butterfly_1972.pdf.

Maeckelbergh, Marianne. 2009. *The Will of the Many: How the Alterglobalization Movement is Changing the Face of Democracy*. New York: Pluto Press.

Marx, Karl. 1974. 'Forord'. In *Skrifter i udvalg. Bidrag til kritik af den politiske økonomi*. Copenhagen: Rhodos.

Mauss, Marcel. 1992 [1934]. 'Techniques of the Body'. In *Incorporations*, edited by J. Crary and S. Kwinter, 455–77. New York: Zone Books.

Pink, Sarah. 2008. 'Walking with Video'. *Visual Studies* 22 (3): 240–52.

Prigogine, Ilya. 1997. *The End of Certainty: Time, Chaos and the New Laws of Nature*. New York and London: The Free Press.

Rancière, Jacques. 2010. *Dissensus: On Politics and Aesthetics*. London: Bloomsbury.

Roestone Collective. 2014. 'Safe Spaces: Towards a Reconceptualization'. *Antipode* 46 (5): 1346–65.

Simard, Suzanne W. et al. 1997. 'Net Transfer of Carbon between Ectomycorrhizal Tree Species in the Field'. *Nature* 388: 579–82.

Simard, Suzanne W. et al. 2012. 'Mycorrhizal Networks: Mechanisms, Ecology and Modelling'. *Fungal Biology Reviews* 26 (1): 39–60.

Stengers, Isabelle. 2005. 'The Cosmopolitical Proposal'. In *Making Things Public: Atmospheres of Democracy*, edited by Bruno Latour and Peter Weibel, 994–1003. Cambridge, MA: MIT Press.

Taussig, Michael. 1993. *Mimesis and Alterity: A Particular History of the Senses*. Oxford: Routledge.

Taylor, Bron. 1995. 'Introduction'. In *Ecological Resistance Movements: The Global Emergence of Radical and Popular Environmentalism*, edited by Bron Raymond Taylor, 11–34. New York: SUNY Press.

Tsing, Anna. 2015. *Mushroom at the End of the World: On the Possibility of Life in Capitalist Ruins*. Princeton: Princeton University Press.

Turner, Victor. 1969. *The Ritual Structure: Structure and Anti-Structure*. Piscataway, NJ: Transaction Publishers.

Wall, Derek. 1999. *Earth First! and the Anti-Roads Movement: Radical Environmentalism and Comparative Social Movements*. London and New York: Routledge.

Wohlleben, Peter. 2016. *The Hidden Life of Trees: What They Feel, How They Communicate Discoveries from a Secret World*. Vancouver: Greystone Books.

Zad Collective. 2017. 'Starhawk and Isabelle Stengers on the Zad'. Accessed 7 August. https://zad-forever.blog/2017/08/07/starhawk-and-isabelle-stengers-on-the-zad/.

8

The Rhythm of Rupture: Attunement among Danish Jihadists

Anja Kublitz

Introduction

We have spent the afternoon in the basement of a housing project in a Danish town watching YouTube videos of jihadi anasheed (militant Islamist hymns), a sub-genre of Islamic a cappella songs accompanied by pictures that call upon Muslims to take up arms and defend their sisters and brothers. We started out in Palestine before jumping to Afghanistan, Chechnya and Syria. The videos – which were neither chronologically nor causally arranged – echoed each other with pictures upon pictures of Muslim suffering and revolt. After three intense hours, Khaled and I decided to take a break and stepped up into the courtyard.[1] We are smoking cigarettes while we watch the sun set behind the wide green lawn at the end of the grey blocks.

Then Khaled says, 'You know, this is where we expect the buses to arrive.'

'Which buses?' I ask.

'The buses that will take us to the borders when they deport us', he responds.

'Is this what happened in the Middle East?' I ask, sidestepping what I know.

'No', Khaled explains. 'This is what happened to the Jews in Europe. They were picked up in buses and taken to the concentration camps. In the Middle East you are shot next to your house.' The sky has turned red and we are silent again.

Then I say, 'You know, they are also waiting for the buses in Copenhagen.'

'Really?' Khaled exclaims. 'I thought it was just here.'

'No', I reply. 'Behind most of the ghettos there are lawns just like this one, and that is where people expect the buses to arrive.' Then I add, 'You know, in *Mjølnerparken*, the buses actually did arrive.'

Khaled looks at me.

'Yeah', I continue, 'one month after Omar.' ['Omar' refers to a young Danish Palestinian from the housing project Mjølnerparken who, in 2015, shot two people in the centre of Copenhagen in what was deemed a terrorist attack, before he himself was shot dead by the Danish police.] 'One month after Omar, the anti-terror police turned up in large numbers with machine guns and face shields and several big buses. The police formed lines so nobody could escape and chased people out of their homes and into the buses. Then the police searched the apartments. Everybody thought that this was it, that they were being deported.'

'But they weren't?' Khaled asks.

'No', I respond. 'They were allowed back in their apartments, except for two who were arrested.'

We finish our cigarettes and return to the basement and the moving images of different formations of colonial powers – Israel, Russia, France, the United States – and the interwoven oppression of Muslims around the globe and across time. All accompanied by beautiful a cappella songs that cut through the existing political order and, in the words of God, call upon Muslims wherever they are to join the jihad and alter the course of the world.[2]

In this chapter I want to address the abundance of the past in the present that leaves my interlocutors gasping for air but also ripe for radical change. I will try to show the recursive ruptures, which are always new again, and the broken continuities that do not allow the past to remain past but instead make it reappear, reflecting and intensifying the present. Based on 13 years of on-and-off fieldwork among immigrant families in Danish housing projects and two years of fieldwork among Danish jihadists, I want to explore why Khaled and other Danish youngsters have joined Islamic militant organizations in the Middle East.

The jihadi anasheed YouTube videos, I suggest, offer an emic scale of rupture that can be used to understand why young Danish Muslims feel called upon to radically change their lives and set off to war. The videos are characterized by the contrapuntal rhythms of a cramped colonial present (the images) and the voice of God (the soundtrack).[3] The divine words (Hirschkind 2006, 39) emerge as if from nowhere. They are not related to the grim imagery of war and killings; instead the a cappella voices reveal a whole other dimension, where the world is not chaotic, brutal and unjust but beautiful, coherent and self-evident. Unlike the images of violent colonial and post-colonial encounters situated in specific times and places,[4] God is out of time and place and simultaneously omnipresent.[5] The wider implication of this is that my interlocutors do not refer to the event of the Arab Spring as the Arab Spring but as a miracle.[6] For them, the event was defined neither as being Arab (indicating a place) nor spring (indicating a time) but as being godly. According to them, it was this miracle that made them wake up and radically change their lives. As such, the Arab Spring was able to cut through the existing spatio-temporal colonial order exactly because it was not delimited by space and time but offered a glimpse of a harmony that was there already, perfectly made, and which my interlocutors could choose to join.

Analytically, this chapter thus contributes to the body of literature that is concerned with ruptures as radical transformative events. Inspired by St Paul's miraculous conversion to Christianity and especially the interpretations of this event by the philosophers Alain Badiou (2003; 2007) and Giorgio Agamben (2005), anthropologists have studied Christian conversions as singular disruptive events that through the grace of God 'make the continuum of history explode' (Robbins 2011, 185; see also, among others, Meyer 1998; Harding 2000; Robbins 2004, 2007, 2010; Engelke 2004, 2010; Marshall 2009, 2010; and Bialecki 2009, 2017). Within this literature – and most explicit in the work by Joel Robbins – rupture is opposed to and theorized against continuous, causal, linear time (Robbins 2007, 12). In this chapter I have taken the liberty of using this notion of rupture as but *one* – although widely adopted – example of how change might come about; namely, as the tipping point between continuity as linear and change as singular. Within my ethnography, I argue that rupture takes a different form; that of intersecting rhythms. The difference between Robbins's and my own conceptualization do not, I believe, pertain to different religious cultural forms. Instead, I suggest they reflect our different ethnography, the different questions we pursue and that Robbins – and many of the anthropologists who study Christian conversions – has studied ruptures within singular lifespans, whereas I have studied them across generations (Kublitz 2011; 2016).[7]

That the young jihadists watch jihadi anasheed videos not only of the present uprising in Syria but also of past revolts in Palestine and Afghanistan reflects the fact that although they are born in Denmark, the majority of Danish jihadists are children of refugees and immigrants from the Middle East and North Africa, and have grown up in the shadow of the failed uprisings and revolutions of their parents' generations. In other words, if we study my interlocutors' families across generations or my young interlocutors' sampling of jihadi anasheed videos, it turns out that ruptures are not singular events but recurrent.

Contributing to the present discussion of rupture as an analytical prism through which to study radical transformations (Holbraad, Kapferer and Sauma, this volume), this chapter therefore introduces a different conception of change and continuity than that described in the literature on Christian religious ruptures (Robbins 2007; 2011). In the lives of my Danish jihadists and their families, continuity cannot be described as progressive and linear, nor can change be described as a singular disruptive event. Instead I argue – inspired by the jihadi anasheed videos and my long-term fieldwork – that rupture can be conceptualized as the intersection between two contrapuntal rhythms. I have borrowed the term 'contrapuntal' from the field of music, where it is used to describe music consisting of multiple, sometimes opposing, melodies that can interrupt each other. Edward Said used the term to describe hegemonic colonial culture in juxtaposition with its counter-hegemonic counterpart (Said 1993). Here I use it to describe how ruptures unfold in my interlocutors' lives as the rhythm of a mundane colonial history on repeat that is interrupted by the rhythm of recurrent extraordinary counter-hegemonic events. The enduring colonial history (Stoler 2016) is experienced by my interlocutors as a repetition of the same (which is why they await the buses), whereas the repetitive ruptures across generations – such as revolutions and miracles – are experienced by the respective generations as introducing difference.[8]

I argue that the lives of my interlocutors and their families offer a different notion of change and continuity from the widely adopted dichotomist conceptualization. My ethnography attests that people's everyday lives can be so marked by changes (in this case, forced migration and continuous violations) that any continuity understood as a chronological progressive sequence of past, present and future has collapsed, and that radical ruptures can come in series as a continuous repetition of extraordinary transformative events (see also Kublitz 2013; 2016).

Ethnographically, this chapter explores how the Arab Spring and the ensuing uprisings in Syria paved the way for the becoming of European jihadists. The Danish jihadists are part of a larger population of European citizens who since 2011 have set off to the Middle East to take up arms, with the clear aim of overturning oppressive secular regimes and substituting them with righteous Islamic ones. Since 2012 approximately 150 so-called foreign fighters have left Denmark (Center for Terroranalyse 2018, 5) out of a total of approximately 4,000 foreign fighters from the European Union (van Ginkel and Entenmann 2016, 3). Despite the fact that European jihadists are extremely exposed politically, almost no empirical studies have been conducted among them. Whereas a growing body of policy papers has been released (see among others Bakker and de Leede 2015; Hoyle et al. 2015), scholarly publications are primarily limited to political and historical studies (see for instance Kepel 2015; Roy 2017) and analysis of jihadists' cultural artefacts, such as their clothing, poetry, and YouTube videos (see among others Hegghammer 2017).[9] Taking as my point of departure the cases of two young Danish men who have fought in the Middle East, this chapter thus offers unique insight into the motivations and practices of European jihadists.

Denmark affords an especially fertile vantage point for such a study because, relative to the size of its population, it produces the second largest number of jihadists in Europe (Neumann 2015) and the highest percentage (approximately 50 per cent) of returned foreign fighters (van Ginkel and Entenmann 2016, 29). Furthermore, Denmark has only recently begun to prosecute jihadists, and it has therefore been possible to conduct fieldwork among those who have returned. I present here the cases of Khaled and Amr who, respectively, joined the Free Syrian Army (FSA) and Islamic State (IS). I have chosen these specific cases to highlight the similarities of ideas and practices across the spectrum of different political organizations. Although the ideologies of FSA and IS are very different and even antagonistic, my ethnography shows that the choice of which political and military groups my interlocutors joined was more dependent on chance and social network than ideology (see also Sageman 2004). In these specific cases Khaled, who joined FSA, an organization that from its outset was defined by its goal of bringing down the government of Bashar al-Assad, was more engaged in Islamic religious and political ideas than Amr, who joined IS.

Mimicking the composition of the jihadi anasheed videos, the rest of this chapter is structured as a cross-cutting between events that my interlocutors consider to be divine and an enduring colonial present (Stoler 2016). In what follows I will therefore introduce the miracle of the Arab Spring that made my interlocutors radically change their lives before offering insight into my interlocutors' everyday lives, in which there seems to be no change in sight. I will then return to the many changes that the miracle introduced, before discussing how the recurring ruptures are always new again by comparing the current miracle with the revolutions of my interlocutors' parents' youth. I argue that the miracle of the Arab Spring introduced a change of change that not only paved the way for a different experience of time (cf. Robbins 2007; 2011) but also offered an attunement to a divine present beyond the mundane progression of history.

The miracle of the Arab Spring

The day after Hosni Mubarak was removed from power, Khaled decided to quit his criminal activities in Denmark and move to Egypt. Back then, in 2011, he declared himself a socialist. Since then, Khaled has not only stopped his criminal activities, changed his political convictions, lived in Egypt for half a year and been part of the revolution; he has also travelled to Syria twice in order to fight against Bashar al-Assad and has, in his own words, become an Islamist. Like my other jihadist interlocutors, Khaled was neither politically active nor religiously observant before the Arab Spring. Rather he was an established criminal with a good head and a gift for numbers, who at an early age got a central position as an accountant for the local gang and the drug market in his city. Although Khaled was not politically active back in 2011, he became so when the Arab Spring took off. According to him, he simply stopped his criminal activities. 'So you just stopped from one day to the next?' I asked him. 'Yes', Khaled responded, and continued:

> I did. When I was a criminal, you had this idea that people in the Middle East are idiots, and that you have these corrupt regimes and nobody does anything about them. And you had no hope of return, because who had imagined that Mubarak would be overthrown in 14 days or that Gaddafi would be killed like that, and that the people would wake up? Nobody had expected that. Nobody had imagined that. It wasn't realistic. I found out that you should not necessarily think about what is realistic. You should not be limited by what is realistic.

When I conducted this interview in 2015, I thought of the Arab Spring as a political event. Only later did I realize that my young interlocutors do not differentiate between worldly events and God. Two years later, therefore, I asked Khaled, 'Do you remember that you said that the Arab Spring was beyond imagination?' 'Yes', Khaled replied, 'It was a miracle. A miracle.'

In a similar way, Amr explained why he decided to join IS in 2014. Like Khaled, Amr grew up in a housing project. According to him, he had been a troublemaker all his life and was engaged in a number of criminal activities before he decided to turn his life around in 2011. Like Khaled, he describes the fall of Mubarak as a miracle. When I ask him what he means by this, he responds, 'A miracle is something that happens without the human capacity to organize or plan it. It wasn't us. It wasn't the Muslims who planned the Arab Spring. The Egyptians only had to take one step, then God opened the possibilities ... It was obvious.'[10] Amr started to visit the local mosque and explained, 'As a Palestinian, when I started practising Islam, I also brought that, you know, *hamas* along – you know, enthusiasm, the idea that we want to make a difference. Not just talk, but do something.' The continuous onslaught of violence against Syrian civilians by Assad made Amr decide to join IS.

What is striking in the narratives of Khaled and Amr, as well as those of my other interlocutors, is that setting off to Syria is not so much about heading for 'an elsewhere' as it is about reaching for 'an otherwise' (Povinelli 2011a; 2016).[11] The rupture initiated by the Arab Spring is not considered or spoken of as a rupture of reverse migration or of going to war but rather as a rupture of religious awakening (see also Roy 2017, 30). Although all of my interlocutors have grown up in Muslim households and have some knowledge of and experience with Islamic traditions, they were not practising an Islamic way of life before 2011. According to them, the miracle of the Arab Spring took them by surprise and made them 'wake up', a phrase that is not accidental, since Islamic revival is also referred to as Islamic awakening. In many ways my interlocutors' narratives of the miracle as 'beyond imagination' are exemplary of how the event has been theorized – using St Paul's conversion as a model – as instigating an unexpected, fundamental break with what has come before and as paving the way for new modes of being and acting in the world (Badiou 2007; Robbins 2004; Bialecki 2009). Since God by definition is beyond mundane imagination, unexpectedness or shock is evidence in itself of a divine event (Bialecki 2009, 116, 121). As Bialecki writes: 'God is about surprise' (2017, 96; see also Jules-Rosette in Harding 2000, 38; Robbins 2010, 643).

Before I elaborate on how the Arab Spring and God introduced a new world order, I want to show why my interlocutors so happily embraced an event that was beyond imagination. The housing projects where my interlocutors grew up are not places for miracles; rather they are places where even modest changes seem out of reach. Before I return to God, I will therefore introduce the colonial history on repeat.

The block – camp – ghetto

A joint is being passed around. Adham turns to me with bloodshot eyes and says, 'We are non-humans; we are hyenas.' Mohammed continues, 'We always stand here. Every day. If you are first "under the block", you do not get out of "the block".' 'But you got out', says Adham, lighting up and looking at Khaled. 'You got away.' 'Well … I'm still here', Khaled replies, and looks down. 'That's true', Adham says, 'You are still here.'

'The block' to which the youngsters refer has a double meaning. It refers both to the housing project as such and the concrete balcony of staircase 145, which offers shelter from the rain and a place to hang out. 'The block', somehow, also refers to the end of the world. It is not a place to start; rather it is where you end, where today resembles tomorrow, and where socio-economic mobility seems out of reach (Kublitz 2015). The block is also home, and that explains why Khaled has returned.

The majority of Danish jihadists' parents arrived in Denmark in the wake of failed revolutions and uprisings. Khaled's father was a prominent figure in the Muslim Brotherhood in Syria, which fought against Syrian president Bashar al-Assad's father. Amr's family has fled twice: first in 1948 when they were expelled by the newly declared Jewish state, and then again in the 1980s after the Palestinian revolution in Lebanon.[12] In Denmark the refugees were settled in housing projects where they still live today, 30 years on – sometimes together with their grown children who cannot afford their own apartments.

Among my interlocutors, there is a profound, shared experience of – despite their families escaping their homelands – never managing to escape the past. This is not only because the majority of their neighbours in the housing projects come from the Middle East and North Africa. More importantly, the relationship between the projects and the Danish state, to my interlocutors, echoes the past and present relations between Europe and the Middle East and Africa, and the past relation between Europe and its minorities. In her book *Duress: Imperial Durabilities in Our Times* (2016), Ann Stoler writes about the trouble with temporalities. She argues that conventions of past, present and future occlude how imperial regimes endure and reappear in the present (Stoler 2016, 35). She encourages us to study the multiple temporalities in which people live (Stoler 2016, 25). In a similar vein, Rebecca Bryant describes how the present becomes uncanny, strangely familiar, when it relapses into the repetition of a traumatic past that does not allow for anticipation of the future (Bryant 2016, 21). The abundance of the past in the present is quite tactile for my interlocutors. Based on my ethnography, however, I have come to believe that the uncanniness of my interlocutors' present reflects not only that the past keeps returning in the present but also that the future is anticipated in the present – just as more of the same. As the prelude to this chapter showed, my interlocutors expect the buses to arrive any day. To them, the past and the future are embedded in the blocks themselves and in their relation to the Danish state.

The housing projects are not only referred to as blocks but also as refugee camps (in Arabic, *mukhayyam*) and ghettos. The many labels do not simply evoke past or distant sites of containment and confinement but are also ways of highlighting the multiple temporalities that are contracted in the concrete blocks and green lawns. It is only because the refugee camps are present in the ghettoes that the Palestinians use the same terms for 'inside' and 'outside' as they did for the camps in Lebanon, and that 'going outside' does not mean leaving your apartment but venturing outside of the project. It is only because the Jewish ghettos are present in the blocks that the green lawns are not only sites for recreational activities but also pickup spots for extermination camps. The ghetto-cum-camp-cum-block, of course, also points toward another present constellation, namely the empire-cum-colonial state-cum-welfare state. During a conversation when Amr expanded on the merits of IS, where the citizens pay taxes and the poor are taken care of, I couldn't help commenting that it very much sounded like the welfare state. Amr simply replied, 'The problem is that when you say "democracy", all I hear is imperialism, imperialism, imperialism.' Amr, of course, refers to the United States' and Europe's – including Denmark's – past and present 'democratic interventions' in the Middle East, most recently in Afghanistan, Iraq and Syria. But he also refers to the Danish state's interventions in the housing projects, which are equally characterized by policies of abandonment (Povinelli 2011b; Kublitz 2015), such as cuts in social benefits and welfare services, and increasing control and surveillance (Kublitz 2013), sometimes in the form of a kind of colonial care, as when immigrant children are removed from their parents (cf. the French empire's children's colonies in Stoler 2016, 86).

The first time I visited Khaled in the housing project where he grew up, he singled out the 'institution-children'. 'There', he pointed, 'there's another one.' The 'institution-children' refers to the immigrant children who were forcibly removed from their families by the welfare state. Khaled explained, 'You can recognize them because they are a head taller and broader than the rest of us. They grew up with three meals a day: oatmeal and potatoes. We often only got one meal a day.' I asked, 'Was it better to grow up in an institution?' 'No', Khaled replied. 'Those who were put in institutions never got out again. They grew up without their parents, among young criminals. My brother, for instance, he never got out; he is still in and out of prisons, even though my mother brought him Arabic food several times a week.'

Stoler suggests that we think of 'the colony' not as a specific geographical site but as a principle of managed mobilities (Stoler 2016, 117), where being at risk and being a risk is a fuzzy political line (2016, 121). The block-cum-camp-cum-ghetto is exactly such a formation, where it is unclear and changeable who is the hunter and who is being hunted (ibid., 121). Today in the housing projects, people who belong to rival gangs or refuse to cooperate are not only threatened or beaten but also kidnapped, systematically tortured and, increasingly, killed.[13] The youngsters do not experience that they can get any help from the police, that is, the Danish state, who on the contrary label the youngsters as gang members. Therefore they find themselves caught between the gangs and the police, which my interlocutors also refer to as a gang, owing to their form of organization and violent practices. The youths' practices of guarding the neighbourhood, their experiences with confinement and their parents' experience of being unable to protect their children all echo and replicate the families' previous experiences with wars (Kublitz 2013).

It is against this backdrop of a claustrophobic present – where previous and current constellations of force and fear have turned the present and the anticipated future into bare repetitions of the past (Bryant 2016; Deleuze 2009, 24) – that my young interlocutors received the uprisings in the Middle East as a miracle that radically changed the world and introduced new avenues for action.[14]

Striving in the way of Allah

According to my jihadist interlocutors, the fall of Mubarak and the subsequent uprisings in the Middle East made them radically change their lives or, as some of them phrase it, made them 'wake up'. Today they explain their previous criminal activities as the result of growing up in a capitalist society that primarily values the pursuit of money, a kind of false consciousness. My interlocutors, though, did not turn toward Marx but toward God (cf. Kublitz 2016). Whereas the European states tend to focus on the young people's movement to the Middle East, the individuals themselves consider their journey as just one way of striving in the way of Allah (jihad). The Arab Spring did not just set my interlocutors on the move to the Middle East but made them start praying, join humanitarian organizations and engage in community work. When they did join various political and militant organizations in the Middle East, their primary goal was not to take up arms but to alleviate the suffering of their Muslim brothers and sisters, and to join the struggle for a new Islamic order. And they were not disappointed. Khaled joined a faction under the Free Syrian Army and, although food was scarce, he was elevated by his many conversations with brothers from all over the world. They spent most of their time smoking cigarettes and discussing how they would liberate Muslims and create a future Islamic order. Amr, who joined IS, was impressed by how he and other foreign jihadists were welcomed by the local citizens, by how organized IS was, the low crime rate, and the firm but just law enforcement. Khaled returned to Denmark because he realized that the revolution would take years and because he wanted to take a course in journalism that would equip him with qualifications that are in demand by the militant organization in Syria. Amr returned because he missed his fiancée.

Today Amr has given up his criminal activities. He is now married, attends a mosque, works for a cleaning company, and is striving daily to improve his *iman* (faith). As he explains, 'You know, sometimes it goes up, sometimes it goes down, sometimes it is stronger, sometimes it is weaker. Right now it is OK, but it could be better. It has to go a little bit more up before it … you know.' Khaled is back at the block, although not as a drug dealer. Instead, he runs free workshops on art and photography for other young people. Like Amr, he is striving to improve his faith and make up for his past misdeeds.

To my interlocutors, the Arab Spring introduced a rupture, a break in the current contraction of past, present and future that allowed for both personal redemption and a radically different experience of time (cf. Marshall 2009). As such, my interlocutors' transformations resemble other conversion stories that highlight the intervention of God and the event, especially Joel Robbins's description of Pentecostal conversions (Robbins 2011; 2010; 2007). Robbins, however, describes conversion among the Upramin as a rupture that renders the present disjointed from the past (Robbins 2010, 637). The miracle of the Arab Spring was that it rendered the future disjointed from the present. To my interlocutors, the events of the Arab Spring introduced a cut in the existing social relations that made my interlocutors see God's actions and plans and allowed them to imagine a new political order. Not unlike the a cappella songs in the jihadi anasheed videos, the miracle of the Arab Spring created a caesura in the stalemate of the present and introduced a different future that did not replicate the past. As Khaled states, 'I believe that the whole world is in the midst of a spiritual evolution. What happens in the Middle East is because of this. *Yani* [you know], I dare, I do not fear anymore, I can. I believe in justice. It's an avalanche and it's not gonna stop. Most Muslims are convinced that we will rule the new world order.' Or in Amr's words, 'From an Islamic point of view, it is perfect that all the refugees arrive now. In 20 years from now, somebody else will rule Denmark …

Venligboerne [meaning 'the friendly people', a civil movement welcoming refugees in Denmark] are sweet, but what are they going to offer? Nude bathing? Soon the refugees will understand the system here and they will turn toward Islam.'

The miracle and the revolution

What surprised me the most when I started out my current fieldwork in 2015 was my interlocutors' optimism. I had expected to meet disenchanted returned jihadists who, confronted with the brutality and opportunism of war, had decided to return home. But this is not what I found. And although time has left a ruined Syria, a severely diminished IS, and a Gaza that is deemed 'unlivable' by the UN, the spirit of my interlocutors has not declined. The reason for this, I believe, is the rupture that the miracle of the Arab Spring sparked. On an individual level, my interlocutors underwent a change when they stopped pursuing profit through selling drugs and other criminal activities and instead started pursuing *iman* (faith) through helping their sisters and brothers, attending mosque, and building an Islamic state. Although both profit and faith can be quantified and are somewhat precarious in that you can gain or lose them (Mittermaier 2013), they nevertheless involve radically different practices and world views.

I do not believe, however, that this turn toward faith in itself explains why my interlocutors are happy with the current state of the world. Rather, I have come to believe that their optimistic stance reflects the miracle as a specific change of change in itself (Højer et al. 2018). Whereas the interlocutors and I can easily agree that the revolutions of their parents failed, they look totally baffled when I refer to the current developments as failures. If revolution is history's locomotive – following Martin Malia (2006) and Reinhardt Kosseleck (2004) – the revolutions of their parents failed because history ended up repeating itself. In the specific cases of Khaled and Amr, the generation of Khaled's parents did not succeed in overthrowing Syrian president Hafez al-Assad. On the contrary his son, Bashar al-Assad, has committed even worse crimes against the Syrian population than his father did during his lifetime. Similarly, the Palestinian revolution led by the generation of Amr's parents did not succeed in challenging the occupation by Israel, whose stranglehold on the occupied Palestinian territories has only increased as the Palestinian political leadership has collapsed. If the uprisings and revolutions of my interlocutors' parents were supposed to move history forward, the Arab

Spring, on the other hand, was received by my interlocutors as a miracle, a messianic event, because it pulled the brake on the locomotive of history and made history on repeat explode – to paraphrase Robbins's reading of Walter Benjamin (Robbins 2011, 185). To my interlocutors, the miracle of the Arab Spring was not that it moved history ahead but that it offered a glimpse of a divine world that was there already, perfectly made, and which my interlocutors could choose to join. Unlike the revolution, the miracle offered attunement to a divine present beyond the mundane progression of history. Having lost faith in the world, my interlocutors started believing in God.

Today my interlocutors' practices are characterized by both an urgent need to act and a more laid-back attitude, reflecting temporalities that we might call *immediacy* and *telos*. On the one hand, these youngsters are immediately affected by violent events, which they think of as urgent potentialities to restore justice and worship God. Simultaneously, many understand their current actions through the future Islamic governance that inevitably will come. These two perspectives are not exclusive. When I asked Khaled why one should bother to fight in Syria, or do other good deeds, if an Islamic order was going to arrive anyway, he explained, 'If you want to fly, you can stand like this [both legs solidly planted on the ground], but you can also lift one of your legs, like this. Then you are already halfway there.'[15] Standing on one leg with his arms reaching for the skies, Khaled is ready for take off. The recent political developments, with Brexit and Trump, have convinced my interlocutors that the End of Time (*Akhir al-zaman*) is near (see Greenhouse, this volume). And who knows? Maybe this miracle that comes as a whole new configuration of God and brutal practices of justice will topple the world and once and for all abolish the current political order. Or maybe Khaled has gone nowhere, but is just the son of an immigrant, trying to keep his balance in the basement of a ghetto while he repeats the tragedy of his parents. What I do know is that, to my interlocutors, the revolutions might have come to an end (Haugbølle and Bandak 2017), but the miracle has just begun.

The rhythm of rupture

In the basement of a Danish housing project, Khaled and I are watching another jihadi anasheed video, this time of a gloomy, endless desert with no trees or buildings in sight. In the midst of the sand dunes, a young man in his twenties is sitting dressed in a traditional white Afghan outfit of loose linen trousers, a tunic and a folded turban, a Kalashnikov lying casually in his lap. The chorus fades out as the camera zooms in on the young man, who is quietly crying. In eloquent Arabic he bemoans that he had to leave his mother. Khaled turns towards me and says, 'Most people cry when they watch this video. It is very hard to leave your mother.'

In an article on the genealogy of jihadi anasheed, Behnam Said traces the poetry of the contemporary militant hymns. According to him, the jihadist poetry brought forth in the Islamist hymns can be seen as an extension of a nineteenth-century anti-colonial poetry style. Furthermore, the many anasheed used today in videos by militant Islamic organizations can be traced back to the late 1970s and early 1980s, the decades that are known as the era of Islamic resurrection (Said 2012, 865; see also Hirschkind 2006). Mirroring Said's historical analysis of jihadi anasheed, my ethnography on Danish jihadists questions whether one can understand the latest rupture of the Arab Spring as a clear-cut break with the past (Robbins 2011; Engelke 2004; Meyer 1998).

Although my young interlocutors distance themselves from their parents and do their best to get rid of 'the muck of the past' (Shah 2014; see also Kublitz 2011) by refusing to recognize any resemblance whatsoever between their parents' failed revolutions and the current miracle, I do not believe that this should lead us to conceptualize this latest rupture as a singular event. The jihadi anasheed videos give them away. Not only does the composition of the videos that display the present uprisings and military battles in Syria mimic the composition of the many other jihadi anasheed videos from past battlefields in Palestine, Chechnya and Afghanistan (Said 2012), but my interlocutors also view them as one batch, in a non-chronological order, and do not distinguish them according to where or when they took place but according to the intensity of affect they cause, such as whether they make you cry (see also Hirschkind 2012). If we zoom out from the singular radical rupture within a specific life span and observe ruptures across generations – or through the practice of watching jihad anasheed videos – the multiple ruptures come across as a repetitive rhythm. My ethnography, therefore, questions not only the young interlocutors' emic understanding that they are embarking on a fundamentally different journey from that of their parents, but also current theories that celebrate ruptures as *singular* moments of radical discontinuity (Badiou 2007; Robbins 2004). Although each rupture does introduce a radical change to the history on repeat, the ethnography indicates that they are also recurrent. The question then becomes, how can each rupture be at once new, as my interlocutors insist, and recurrent?

The answer, I believe, is that the singular ruptures are related exactly by way of the affect they cause – the difference they enforce in the world. In this way, my ethnography is more aligned with a Deleuzian reading of change than that of a Badiouan. Whereas Alain Badiou argues that change emerges through events that give birth to the new (Badiou 2007), Gilles Deleuze argues that change comes about through repetitions that introduce a difference in kind (Deleuze 2009). In the lives of my interlocutors the singular rupture is defined as such because it introduces a change that attempts to overthrow the history on repeat. Whereas this change has to be a change of change in order to come across as new in relation to previous ruptures – like the difference between a miracle and a revolution – the singular rupture is nevertheless related by exploding the history on repeat. Secondly, the multiple ruptures are related and recognizable by way of their form: through the events of violent uprisings. If one removed the soundtrack and texts from the jihadi anasheed videos, the pictures themselves would come across as interchangeable. The single rupture, in other words, does not only come as a surprise, in the sense that it is unexpected, but also has to be recognizable. When my interlocutors so radically and happily turned their lives upside down in the wake of the Arab Spring, it was not only because the miracle offered them a way out of their current predicament, but also because they recognized it as an event that could potentially change the world as they knew it – just as the jihadi anasheed songs are each distinct but nevertheless adhere to the same rhythm and pitch (Said 2012; Pieslak 2017), or as the rhythm of rupture is repeated with a difference across generations.

Inspired by the miraculous event of St Paul, Christian religious ruptures have been conceptualized as singular and in opposition to history as continuous and linear (Robbins 2007; 2011). My ethnography offers a quite different conceptualization of rupture. In the lives of my Danish jihadists' families, continuity cannot be described as progressive and linear, nor can change be described as a singular disruptive event. Instead I suggest that rupture can be conceptualized as the recurring intersections between two contrapuntal rhythms: the rhythm of a colonial history on repeat and the rhythm of anti-colonial struggles. It is important for me to underline that the notion of history on repeat does not refer to an exotic mythical time (Lévi-Strauss 1966), but is the tragic outcome of the broken continuities of my interlocutors' lives, where past, present and future violations echo each other (Bryant 2016). Likewise, the recurrent ruptures cannot be understood only as a repetitive joyous celebration of the new (see Holbraad, Kapferer and Sauma, this volume), but are first and foremost the dire consequence of the fact that although my interlocutors and their parents did manage to introduce radical changes to the enduring colonial history, they have not managed to circumvent it – yet.

By way of conclusion, I suggest that if we want to understand the current turn of the world with its populist and religious movements (see also Greenhouse and Pedersen, this volume), it might be helpful not to think of rupture as singular but rather as the outcome of contrapuntal rhythms. Not only because we might learn from the past, but first and foremost because it might help us to recognize what indeed is new.

Acknowledgements

This chapter is based on research carried out with the generous support of Aalborg University's talent programme and the Danish Research Council for Independent Research (DFF–4001–00223). The chapter has benefited from the comments of John Dulin, Andreas Bandak, Mark Sedgwick, Charles Hirschkind, Michael Ulfstjerne, Marlene Spanger and Steffen Jensen. I also want to thank the editors for their useful suggestions.

Notes

1. All names used in this article are aliases to secure the anonymity of the participants.
2. *Jihad* means 'to struggle in the way of Allah'.
3. In this chapter I treat God as an object equivalent to other objects, such as the welfare state. I do so because it reflects how my interlocutors experience the world. As Jon Bialecki writes in relation to Christian charismatic evangelism, God is an object by way of how people refer to him and rely on him (2017, 77), and, I would add, by way of the effects and affects that my interlocutors believe he causes. See also Amira Mittermaier (2011, 28; 2012, 256) for a similar approach and Bialecki (2014) for a critique of 'methodological atheism'. Furthermore, my interlocutors believe that the anasheed, like the Quran, reveal the word of God.
4. My interlocutors are very much in line with Stoler's (2016) understanding of recurring colonial durabilities. For instance, the Syrian secular regime's dictatorship and suppression of its citizens and Islamist opposition has led my interlocutors to consider it on a par with previous secular colonial rule and aligned with contemporary imperialist regimes (see also Gartenstein-Ross and Vassefi 2012, 835).
5. As creator, Allah necessarily stands outside creation. But Allah is also present in creation, acting in it and directing it, as the Quran explains at length (personal communication with Professor Mark Sedgwick and the interlocutor Khaled).
6. My interlocutors use the Danish term *mirakel* (miracle). However, if requested they would translate it into the Arabic *muajiza*.
7. When I have chosen this Christian-inspired theoretical framework anyway, it is first and foremost because the jihadist interlocutors to a certain extent conceive of the Arab Spring as a disruptive event along the lines of Badiou's understanding; and because the ethnography in noticeable ways resonates with descriptions of Christian conversions (especially within Pentecostalism), reflecting how my interlocutors are not only influenced by Islam but equally by Christianity and popular culture (cf. Larkin 2008). See also Saba Mahmood, who writes that despite the fact that the Islamic piety movement is antagonistic toward secularism, it presupposes many secular concepts and is far more hybrid than its participants will acknowledge (Mahmood 2012, xv).
8. In *Difference and Repetition* (2009) Gilles Deleuze distinguishes between two kinds of repetitions: repetitions of the same, which he refers to as 'material repetitions' (2009, 24), and repetitions that involve a difference and thereby pave way for the new.

9. Several online studies have been carried out, though (see for instance Navest et al. 2016), as well as ethnographic studies among jihadist families (see for instance van San 2018).
10. Mittermaier describes how her Egyptian Sufi interlocutors believe that the uprising was driven by a divine force; that it was God who moved the people to dispose of Hosni Mubarak (2017; see also Gartenstein-Ross and Vassefi 2012, 835).
11. Elizabeth Povinelli's work is dedicated to an anthropology of the otherwise, to describing 'forms of life that are at odds with dominant, and dominating, modes of being' (Povinelli 2011a, 1). Based on fieldwork among aboriginals in Australia, she analyses alternative potentialities of social existence to the current 'settler late liberalism' (Povinelli 2016, 18). In a similar way, the jihadist interlocutors are experimenting with forms of life that are otherwise to (and transcend) what they perceive as the dominant imperialist and capitalist mode of governance.
12. The Palestinian revolution (*al-thawra*) lasted from 1969 to 1982. It consisted of a number of Palestinian popular uprisings that succeeded in liberating the refugee camps in Lebanon and paved the way for the Cairo Agreement, which handed over control of the camps from the Lebanese government to the Palestine Liberation Organization.
13. In 2016, ten people with gang connections were killed. In 2017, 25 people were wounded and three killed in the so-called gang war. In comparison, ten people with gang connections were killed between 2008 and 2013 (Lauritzen and Dreyer 2016).
14. Mahmood also partly describes the Islamic revival of the 1970s as a response to the failure of postcolonial Arab regimes (2012, xi). In a very different context, that of the Pentecostal movement in Nigeria, Ruth Marshall describes the Pentecostal revival as a response to postcolonial radical insecurity and the related unreliability of human relations (2010, 216; 2009, 3).
15. Along similar lines, Marshall writes that Christian conversions are seen as a way of hastening the fulfilment of God's plan (2009, 66).

References

Agamben, Giorgio. 2005. *The Time that Remains: A Commentary on the Letter to the Romans*. Stanford, CA: Stanford University Press.
Badiou, Alain. 2003. *Saint Paul: The Foundation of Universalism*. Stanford, CA: Stanford University Press.
Badiou, Alain. 2007. *Being and Event*. London and New York: Continuum.
Bakker, Edwin, and Seran de Leede. 2015. *European Female Jihadists in Syria: Exploring an Under-Researched Topic*. The Hague: International Centre for Counter-Terrorism.
Bialecki, Jon. 2009. 'Disjuncture, Continental Philosophy's New "Political Paul" and the Question of Progressive Christianity in a Southern California Third Wave Church'. *American Ethnologist* 36 (1): 110–23.
Bialecki, Jon. 2014. 'Does God Exist in Methodological Atheism? On Tanya Lurhmann's *When God Talks Back* and Bruno Latour'. *Anthropology of Consciousness* 25 (1): 32–52.
Bialecki, Jon. 2017. *A Diagram for Fire: Miracles and Variation in an American Charismatic Movement*. Berkeley: University of California Press.
Bryant, Rebecca. 2016. 'On Critical Times: Return, Repetition, and the Uncanny Present'. *History and Anthropology* 27 (1): 19–31.
CTA (Center for Terroranalyse). 2018. *Vurdering af terrortruslen mod Danmark*. Copenhagen: Politiets Efterretningstjeneste.
Deleuze, Gilles. 2009. *Difference and Repetition*. London: Continuum.
Engelke, Matthew. 2004. 'Discontinuity and the Discourse of Conversion'. *Religion in Africa* 34 (1): 82–109.
Engelke, Matthew. 2010. 'Past Pentecostalism: Notes on Rupture, Realignment, and Everyday Life in Pentecostal and African Independent Churches'. *Africa: Journal of the International African Institute* 80 (2): 177–99.
Gartenstein-Ross, Daveed, and Tara Vassefi. 2012. 'Perceptions of the "Arab Spring" within the Salafi-Jihadi Movement'. *Studies in Conflict & Terrorism* 35 (12): 831–48.
Harding, Susan Friend. 2000. *The Book of Jerry Falwell: Fundamentalist Language and Politics*. Princeton: Princeton University Press.
Haugbølle, Sune, and Andreas Bandak. 2017. 'The Ends of Revolution: Rethinking Ideology and Time in the Arab Uprisings'. *Middle East Critique* 26 (3): 191–204.

Hegghammer, Thomas. 2017. *Jihadi Culture: The Art and Social Practices of Militant Islamists*. Cambridge: Cambridge University Press.

Hirschkind, Charles. 2006. *The Ethical Soundscape: Cassette Sermons and Islamic Counterpublics*. New York: Columbia University Press.

Hirschkind, Charles. 2012. 'Experiments in Devotion Online: The YouTube Khutba'. *International Journal of Middle East Studies* 44 (1): 5–21.

Hoyle, Carolyn, Alexandra Bradford and Ross Frenett. 2015. *Becoming Mulan? Female Western Migrants to ISIS*. London: Institute for Strategic Dialogue.

Højer, Lars, Anja Kublitz, Stine Puri Simonsen and Andreas Bandak. 2018. 'Escalations: Theorizing Sudden Accelerating Change'. *Anthropological Theory* 18 (1): 36–58.

Kepel, Gilles. 2015. *Terror in France: The Rise of Jihad in the West*. Princeton: Princeton University Press.

Kosseleck, Reinhart. 2004. *Futures Past: On the Semantics of Historical Time*. New York: Columbia University Press.

Kublitz, Anja. 2011. 'The Sound of Silence: The Reproduction and Transformation of Global Conflicts within Palestinian Families in Denmark'. In *Mobile Bodies, Mobile Souls: Family, Religion, Migration in a Global World*, edited by M. Rytter and K.F. Olwig, 161–80. Aarhus: Aarhus University Press.

Kublitz, Anja. 2013. 'Seizing Catastrophes: The Temporality of Nakba among Palestinians in Denmark'. In *Times of Security: Ethnographies of Fear, Protest and the Future*, edited by Martin Holbraad and Morten Axel Pedersen 103–21. London and New York: Routledge.

Kublitz, Anja. 2015. 'The Ongoing Catastrophe: Erosion of Life in the Danish Camps'. *Journal of Refugee Studies* 29 (2): 229–49.

Kublitz, Anja. 2016. 'From Revolutionaries to Muslims: Liminal Becomings across Palestinian Generations in Denmark'. *International Journal of Middle East Studies* 48: 67–86.

Larkin, Brian. 2008. 'Ahmed Deedat and the Form of Islamic Evangelism'. *Social Text* 26 (3): 101–21.

Lauritzen, Kirstine B., and Pernille Dreyer. 2016. 'Banderneer blevet mere brutale'. *BT*. Accessed 2 December. https://www.bt.dk/danmark/koldblodige-og-brutale-bandemedlemmer-i-danmark-de-er-den-vaerste-gruppe-vi-overho.

Lévi-Strauss, Claude. 1966. *The Savage Mind*. Chicago: University of Chicago Press.

Mahmood, Saba. 2012. *Politics of Piety: The Islamic Revival and the Feminist Subject*. Princeton: Princeton University Press.

Malia, Martin. 2006. *History's Locomotives: Revolutions and the Making of the Modern World*. New Haven, CT: Yale University Press.

Marshall, Ruth. 2009. *Political Spiritualities: The Pentecostal Revolution in Nigeria*. Chicago: University of Chicago Press.

Marshall, Ruth. 2010. 'The Sovereignty of Miracles: Pentecostal Political Theology in Nigeria'. *Constellations* 17 (2): 197–223.

Meyer, Birgit. 1998. 'Make a Complete Break with the Past'. *Historische Anthropologie* 6 (2): 257–83.

Mittermaier, Amira. 2011. *Dreams That Matter: Egyptian Landscapes of the Imagination*. Berkeley: University of California Press.

Mittermaier, Amira. 2012. 'Dreams from Elsewhere: Muslim Subjectivities beyond the Trope of Self-Cultivation'. *Journal of the Royal Anthropological Institute* 18: 247–65.

Mittermaier, Amira. 2013. 'Trading with God: Islam, Calculation, Excess'. In *A Companion to the Anthropology of Religion*, edited by J. Boddy and M. Lambek, 274–93. Oxford: Wiley.

Mittermaier, Amira. 2017. 'The Unknown in the Egyptian Uprising: Towards an Anthropology of al-Ghayb'. *Contemporary Islam*. Accessed 25 August. https://link.springer.com/article/10.1007/s11562-017-0399-1.

Navest, Aysha, Martijn de Koning and Annelies Moors. 2016. 'Chatting about Marriage with Female Migrants to Syria: Agency beyond the Victim versus Activist Paradigm'. *Anthropology Today* 32 (2): 22–5.

Neumann, Peter. 2015. 'Foreign Fighter Total in Syria/Iraq Now Exceeds 20,000; Surpasses Afghanistan Conflict in the 1980s'. *International Centre for the Study of Radicalisation and Political Violence (ICSR)*. Accessed 26 January. http://icsr.info/2015/01/foreign-fighter-total-syriairaq-now-exceeds-20000-surpasses-afghanistan-conflict-1980s/

Pieslak, Jonathan. 2017. 'A Musicological Perspective on Jihadi Anashid'. In *Jihadi Culture: The Art and Social Practices of Militant Islamists*, edited by T. Hegghammer, 63–81. Cambridge: Cambridge University Press.

Povinelli, Elizabeth. A. 2011a. 'Routes/Worlds'. *e-flux* 27: 1–12.

Povinelli, Elizabeth. A. 2011b. *Economies of Abandonment: Social Belonging and Endurance in Late Liberalism*. Durham, NC: Duke University Press.

Povinelli, Elizabeth. A. 2016. *Geontologies: A Requiem to Late Liberalism*. Durham, NC: Duke University Press.

Robbins, Joel. 2004. *Becoming Sinners: Christianity and Moral Torment in a Papua New Guinea Society*. Berkeley: University of California Press.

Robbins, Joel. 2007. 'Continuity Thinking and the Problem of Christian Culture: Belief, Time and the Anthropology of Christianity'. *Current Anthropology* 48 (1): 5–38.

Robbins, Joel. 2010. 'Anthropology, Pentecostalism, and the New Paul: Conversion, Event, and Social Transformation'. *South Atlantic Quarterly* 109 (4): 633–52.

Robbins, Joel. 2011. 'On Messianic Promise'. In *Echoes of the Tambaran: Masculinity, History and the Subject in the Work of Donald F. Tuzin*, edited by D. Lipset and P. Roscoe, 183–96. Canberra: ANU E Press.

Roy, Olivier. 2017. *Jihad and Death. The Global Appeal of Islamic State*. London: Hurst.

Sageman, Marc. 2004. *Understanding Terror Networks*. Philadelphia: University of Pennsylvania Press.

Said, Behnam. 2012. 'Hymns (Nasheeds): A Contribution to the Study of the Jihadist Culture'. *Studies in Conflict & Terrorism* 35 (12): 863–79.

Said, Edward W. 1993. *Culture and Imperialism*. London: Vintage.

Shah, Alpa. 2014. '"The Muck of the Past": Revolution, Social Transformation and the Maoist in India'. *Journal of the Royal Anthropological Institute* 20: 337–56.

Stoler, Ann Laura. 2016. *Duress: Imperial Durabilities in Our Times*. Durham, NC, and London: Duke University Press.

Van Ginkel, Bibi, and Eva Entenmann, eds. 2016. *The Foreign Fighters Phenomenon in the European Union: Profiles, Threats & Policies*. Hague: International Centre for Counter-Terrorism.

Van San, Marion. 2018. 'Belgian and Dutch Young Men and Women who Joined ISIS: Ethnographic Research among the Families They Left Behind'. *Studies in Conflict and Terrorism* 41 (1): 39–58.

9

Earthquake Citizens: Disaster and Aftermath Politics in India and Nepal

Edward Simpson and Michele Serafini

While some earthquakes pass almost unnoticed, others become dramatic markers of history and time, signalling the rise or fall of civilizations. Part of this power lies in the violent ability of earthquakes to shake individual and collective certainties – and for someone or something to capitalize or prosper on that uncertainty. The Lisbon earthquake of 1755 caused Voltaire, Rousseau and others to herald the death of God (Voltaire 1988, 2005; Kendrick 1956). The same events directed Kant's (1764) then revolutionary thought on the nature of rationality and the sublime. Mill (1848) provocatively saw earthquakes as periods of 'accelerated consumption', a form of 'quantitative easing' – to use a contemporary term – given by nineteenth-century nature. Lenin (1970) saw parallels between the political potential of disaster and revolutionary crisis.

Recent literature turns back to the eventful nature of earthquakes (and disasters more generally). Naomi Klein (2007), for example, describes 'the shock doctrine' of opportunistic capital at work; Solnit (2010) sees the positive revolutionary potential of disasters as people are brought together in common humanity. In these formulations, the earthquake is always a moment of total rupture into which history and politics collapse as something new – good or bad – is produced in the aftermath.

In this chapter, we use contemporary earthquake ethnography and accounts of other disasters from the secondary literature to look at the kinds of actions that accompany earthquakes. In particular, we look at the changing relations between citizens and their states in the wake of tectonic shifts. One of these earthquakes took place in Gujarat, western India, in 2001; the other in Nepal in 2015. We look for patterns in action and commonality at macro-, intermediate and individual levels.

The material presented is based on ethnographic research conducted over a decade in Gujarat by Simpson and between 2015 and 2017 in Nepal by Serafini. We write in the first person when referring to research undertaken on specific earthquakes and together in the rest of the chapter. Along the way, we pause to examine the rupturing of other catastrophic events such as the philosophical aftermath of the earthquake in Lisbon and falling bombs and rocks. In all cases, we describe how initial moments of cooperation gave way, in the longer term, to conflict, contested identity politics and radical conservatism, and to a general sea change in the big politics of our regions. We do this with the aim of tracing some of the mechanics of rupture in the wake of an earthquake to observe the intimate as well as the political bearings of the philosophers' moral disquisitions. Rupture is here taken as a sudden and widespread crisis of judgement (Roitman 2013). Akin to the situation described by Greenhouse (this volume), we see how different scales of doubt and relativity are brought together in friction by the little events that permeate the lives of those who survive. If an earthquake becomes a moment of total change, that happens because the same words, funds and policies are given to the puzzled eyes of those who have just endured loss and suffering.

There is a large literature on disasters and survival that we will not pretend to review here.[1] Two studies stand out to us from the rest as seminal and eloquent: Robert Jay Lifton's (1967) account of surviving the Hiroshima bomb and Barbara Bode's (1989) descriptions of living through an earthquake in Highland Peru in 1970. Both writers (psychologist and anthropologist respectively) attempted to place the intimate and personal aspects of survival within a broad landscape of policy and social change. They had a deep understanding of the worlds they were writing about and could consequently see the multiple connections between things and meaning that were confused by disaster. They describe situations where categories and boundaries are blurred, where rival ideas and persons interact and produce unintended outcomes. Themes common to survivor literature such as anger, rehabilitation policy, budgets and shame all live together, sometimes in the same breath.

Bode recounts changes in individual mentality and structure. The disaster occurred two years after a coup in which General Velasco Alvarado took over the revolutionary leadership of the country. His 'Inca socialism' or 'Peruanismo' strove for freedom from the shackles of America and the doctrines of socialism and capitalism. Alvarado saw it possible to make a new human morality, resurrecting the Indian past and elevating suitable national heroes. Part of his vision was to integrate the marginal sierra culture of Indian peasants (of which the earthquake-affected region was part) into the coast-dominated national sphere. Bode suggests the General seized upon the disaster as a springboard to implement his imagined future. The Catholic Church too had expanded its presence in the valley in the years before the earthquake. Marxist inspired, the political hermeneutics of the gospel also came down squarely on improving the lot of the oppressed. Revolutionary and religious forces interpenetrated and stood united in an attempt to overturn the old hierarchical structures and to build a new egalitarian state.

Bode sees deliberate political will and the spread of neoliberal bureaucracy as keys to the transformation of the valley. The disaster became a providential mandate for redesigning all that had been. The state formed new branches to oversee reconstruction and the formation of a new social order. At the same time, changes were afoot at a more intimate level. The Catholic Church took 'progress' to mean that false and sinful religious practices, such as the worship of local deities, were to be extinguished. In response, the survivors repeatedly protested, fearing the foreign aesthetic and design being given to their town.

Lifton's post-bomb psychology suggests that links between survivors and those who spectate is not metaphorical; rather, we are linked by psychological components in which the growing spectacle of holocausts of the twentieth century has imposed on us all a series of immersions in death which mark our existence. Lifton's 'death imprint' or 'death spell' relates to imagery and the conditions of death: the jarring awareness of the fact of death, in his case the grotesque and sudden burning and then slow disintegration of A-bomb bodies.

Similarly, the televised tsunami of 2004 encouraged us to imagine what it is to drown, with waves bubbling and chattering into concrete hotels, but then continuing to rise and swell and rise; laughter and surprised cries eventually cease, the brown wave swelling into Bandar Aceh carrying away the town. In our minds alone we could never quite reach the end of the fantasy. Unlike waves, the death imprint of those in earthquakes, as we shall see, is characterized by crushing, falling, the fear of falling again and the kind of gasping anxiety produced as certainties move under our feet: madness, submission and images of collapsed things that should be standing (Simpson 2013).

Lifton describes the impossibility for the survivor of catastrophe to complete what Freud (1917) called the 'work of mourning' because there is no time to prepare for the theft of life. Survivors of Hiroshima mourn for their dead as well as the dead of others, objects and lost symbols, but also for beliefs that have been shattered, for a way of life that has vanished. Yet they mourn in vain; the survivor mourns for his former self, for what he was before the intrusion of death and the emergence of a life impaired by mourning and the guilt of survival. The consequence of the survivor's defence against death anxiety and the guilt of survival is the cessation of feeling. We may characterize this lack of feeling as an affective anaesthesia and as a key element in a broader disaster syndrome.[2]

Lifton describes the toxic combination of neediness and mistrust among bomb survivors: those surrounding them appear as disingenuous (what he calls 'counterfeit nurturance'). In addition, they suffered 'contagion anxiety': if I come too close to you, I will experience your experience of annihilation and later your death, and I do not want that. I do not want to suffer more. We take from Lifton the idea that individual survival carries with it the structural conditions that lead to a more general social fragmentation.

If we marry the ideas of Bode and Lifton, we can see three distinct but related forms of post-disaster dynamic. There is opportunity in the rupture for the structural reform of countries and regions: the reconstruction loan with certain conditions attached from an international bank, but also the expansion of state bureaucracy. On the same scale, there is chance for nation-building and large-scale ethnic politics, the march of the generals or the reform of the religious. Secondly, on the ground, there is the interface between local institutions, whether public or private, and those affected by the disaster. Here, there might be a tug of ideas, a competition of rival agendas or an impulse to reform and development (however understood); or there might be resistance to change via the solace of identity politics, whether in the form of nostalgia for a golden age or in the invigoration of ethnic, religious or linguistic boundaries. The means and methods are manifold. Finally, there is the individual struggle for survival. Nuclear bombs might carry with them their own particular psychology; nevertheless, as we shall see, other disastrous situations bring guilt and energy to those who survive. There are many other levels between the three, but in a broad sense they give some indication of the varying harmonies of violence that a disastrous moment of rupture can produce.

In our material, earthquakes emerge as peculiar moments in which these different levels come to reverberate, thus producing the possibility for change or for a renewed attention towards past things. The loose discourses of power of the everyday come to have a tighter grip on the intimate life of a survivor. Habitual behaviours may also be forgotten in the name of reconstruction. Latent conflicts may find the symbolic resources for building new and radicalized forms of ideology. Crisis, in the way Roitman (2013) has conceptualized it, may justify policies that would not be allowed to fly in normal times. In this sense, the tectonic rupture of an earthquake leaves space for the production and reproduction of rupturing narratives of human manufacture.

Gujarat

The earthquake in Gujarat took place in January 2001, a time when many things in India were changing fast. I (Simpson) had conducted research in Gujarat before the disaster. Partially because of this, my attention was drawn to my friends who had survived. When I first visited after the earthquake in the second half of 2001, it was obvious that the overwhelming concern of those I knew was the endemic sense of uncertainty about the future. They were also struggling to interact with the many who had come from elsewhere to use the moment of shock to profit and to change the order of things.

Looking back, many people I know well had their lives fundamentally changed by the earthquake; or at least the earthquake now plays a prominent role in the way people make sense of their lives. Friends or family died, they consequently grieved and remembered. There are plentiful rags to riches stories and conspicuously fewer tales of those being deprived of their riches for lives of impoverishment. Over the years, the earthquake gradually became a marker of time: a point at which things changed direction, not radically and without reference to the past but rather as a form of filter through which some things did not pass while others grew in amplified form. The earthquake has become an origin myth, albeit told with knowledge of the previous state of things.

At a broad level, and deeply significantly, the earthquake in Gujarat brought a new chief minister to power. Narendra Modi, who is now the Prime Minister of India, was able to dislodge his predecessor in 2001 in the name of the earthquake. Keshubhai Patel, Modi claimed, was unable to manage post-earthquake reconstruction in the region. Modi took charge of Gujarat – never having faced an election – on 7 October 2001, some nine months after the disaster. As reconstruction got under way, he took a keen interest, visited many times, and gave some of his most well-known speeches at inauguration and anniversary ceremonies. Through reconstruction, his administration worked hard, as we will see, to build support for their Hindu nationalist project, developing particular partnerships, holding strategic renaming ceremonies, and promoting new heroes and history for the region.

In the intervening 17 years, change has been profound. The different scales and types of policies co-opted to restructure the region have allowed for the formation of new kinds of citizens and consumers as well as religious and cultural subjects. Post-earthquake reconstruction permitted the ideas and values of Hindu nationalism to be built prominently into the landscape. Public–private partnerships were introduced for village reconstruction as a condition of loans from development banks. Hundreds of partnerships across the region provided opportunity for cultural and religious organizations to build villages as they saw fit. New temples and forms of organized religion were thus presented to the villagers, often appearing to have state sanction because the responsibility for clearing up after the calamity was generally regarded to be the responsibility of government. The combination of loss and trauma caused by the earthquake, the promise of wealth and abundance brought by the 'sponsoring' organization and the general uncertainties of the times meant that new ideas found a welcome home in some villages. Generally speaking, organizations with an elective affinity with the nationalist interests of the ruling government received contracts for the most prestigious and influential reconstruction projects. The earthquake thus became a mechanism for entrenching religious and political values into the fabric of provincial society through reconstruction.

Elsewhere, land and water were made readily available for the new industries that targeted the affected area to avail of tax concessions. Against this backdrop, the transformation of the once commonplace, the mundane and everyday, in the aftermath was, in many ways, as dramatic as the rapid loss of the conspicuous and noteworthy in the moment of ruin brought about by the earthquake. The shock of the disaster established the condition for the creation of new possibilities, namely an industrial society underpinned by the cultural politics of Hindu nationalism.

The longer I watched and listened, the more it was obvious that it was not the disaster itself but the doctrines of the interveners that were truly shocking: shock-doctrine-SHOCK. I say this because in urgent and confused circumstances, the gaze of those on the ground is distracted from normal things by spectacle. Rules may be suspended (caste, religious distinction), and new ones (building, planning and tax) introduced. In Gujarat, 'aftermath time' was marked most strongly by the struggle of the affected with those who intervened, the doctrine-SHOCK era. In this sense, aftermath time had both psychological and moral connotations, as new arrangements and ideas were battling to find a new peace with pre-existing ones. Those bewildered by the earthquake often called the aftermath 'the second earthquake', suggesting it too was terrible.[3]

At the institutional level, as I have already mentioned, the conditions placed on loans by the development banks (Asian and World) created the most generalized framework for reconstruction. These conditions demanded the reorganization of local government and the privatization or semi-privatization of many local services, including planning. Reconstruction also necessitated private insurance and bank accounts for the beneficiaries of housing assistance. At other times, such radical measures would have been debated and contested; however, in the heat and confusion of the moment these measures came into force almost unnoticed.

The industrialization of the region is the most visible consequence of the state's home-grown reconstruction policies (tax breaks and permitted land grabs). In the shadows of these interventions there were other technocratic, linguistic and bureaucratic aspects to the post-earthquake interventions. The awe of technology contributed to the pacification of the affected, as the new district hospital was mounted on springs. The swift instrument of town planning cut through old societies, encouraged people to learn how to read maps, and to adopt nationalist and suburban mentalities. Signs of reconstruction appeared in Hindi, the national but previously invisible language in the region. Others brought religious and cultural ideas in their relief trucks.

When viewed as a whole, there were a number of serious contradictory pulls in the competing policy frameworks. For example, professionals in post-disaster reconstruction are often frustrated by the inability of their industry to learn from past calamities. As we will see in the Nepal material, such amnesia has been routinized by the 'disaster paradigm', or, the set of pre-existing knowledge and expectation that disasters engage. Emphasis is placed on the uniqueness of the circumstances of each disaster. Concern lies with the cultural conditions of the affected region or, similarly, the specificity of patterns of risk or vulnerability. In essence, risk/vulnerability is 'memory bumped forward' (Jasanoff 2010) or 'the taming of chance' (Hacking 1990), which, given that local conditions are always unique, necessarily means each disaster must be different. Therefore, we might reason, all societies are affected by disaster, but this or that society has not been affected by this or that disaster before. The disaster industry thus operates under the tense conditions of its own making: on one hand all disasters are unique, while on the other the standard codes and forms have been produced in an attempt to give those working in the industry a memory and a frame in which to work.

In short, the bewildered lived among varying superimposed spheres, as different ideological forms were traced one over the other. Some new formulations of meaning took root and displaced others; some failed (but not many). And so, in the aftermath, those who intervened with new ideas and technologies created deep anxiety, or perhaps ambivalence, among the local population over whether change and modernization had been a cause of the disaster or were in fact predestined to be the primary consequences of reconstruction.

Until recently, the decayed frames of colonial famine and flood relief measures influenced contemporary post-disaster interventions in India.[4] Private trusts and charities had also developed parallel structures to channel compassion and cash to the affected. From a laissez-faire approach to disaster relief in the late nineteenth century, the twentieth century has seen the emergence of increasing state intervention and control in the aftermath of natural disaster.[5] The earthquake in Gujarat was but one of the shocks that found the existing state of affairs wanting, and prompted the state to reform the old policies and design national codes for future bad happenings.[6] Consequently, doctrine came in many layers, from diverse sources and often with contradictory aims and tensions. Banks, national and state governments, local administrative units, private sector and humanitarian organizations all contributed their own favourite ingredients to the mix.

At the third or most intimate level there were other dynamics at play. For some, there was grief and mourning for people with names and personalities. For others, the moment of the earthquake left scars of incomprehension, which later became madness or recurrent foreboding. But the most general sense was that history had imploded into a rumbling moment and meaning had collapsed. At first, a sense of intensified community or humanity seemed to be blooming, as people helped and talked to those they usually ignored. This sensation was on the whole short-lived, and in the months and years to come other dynamics took hold. Following the aforementioned earthquake in Peru, the spirit of 'brotherhood' lasted two or three days.[7] Similar reports were provided by those we met in Gujarat and Nepal. At first, people helped one another. After a few days, some said as many as 15, older patterns were restored. Secrecy ran through the town as compensation schemes and rumours of new property made people greedy and jealous. After a few years, a smug euphoria emerged as people were wealthy and had goods and cash aplenty. There was a short phase in which regional identity was promoted as a way to counter those who had come from the outside with foreign ideas. On the whole, however, survival tended to push people apart rather than bringing them together, a trend that was mirrored in the concrete plans to reduce the population density of the town through mass-suburbanization.

As months passed and new loyalties and configurations appeared, initial moments of cooperation gave way to other kinds of rupture running through the aftermath. The population of Gujarat is far from homogeneous, and the different cultures of eastern and western parts of the state came firmly into contact through reconstruction. Most doctrine was brought from the east, where the big cities and centres of government are to be found. The 'truths' and 'realities' with which doctrines and policies were supposed to engage were generally not the 'truths' or 'realities' of local people themselves. At various times, the state and other doctrinaires began to see the people as ungrateful when they protested about what they were being offered. Often it was said that the people of Kutch in the west, where the earthquake had had most effect, did not have enough culture or education to see the benefits in the new reconstructed scheme of things. Those who came from the east to reconstruct the west brought with them the authority of state power and a greater sense of a 'Gujarati culture'. They also came with the knowledge that those in the west were victims, and this contributed to their sense of self-confidence.

Over those years of research, it was possible to see how those who intervened in the aftermath brought with them various understandings of tragedy and right and wrong, in addition to some well-formed ideas (however misplaced) about the kind of people they had come to help. Conversely, those affected by the disaster struggled to differentiate between those who had come to intervene. Were all interventionists the same? Were there good and best organizations? It took a long time for the contours of that particular landscape to become visible.

In Gujarat, we see policy and organizations that understood the importance of rupture and unsettlement for making things anew. Many of the interventions saw the earthquake as an opportunity for putting forward new ideas and ways of doing things. Some of these interventions were calculated and experienced, perhaps based on a knowledge of previous disasters; other interventions were tentative and formed more by the conditions of the moment than by a long-term plan. The earthquake shook things up, rendered visible the commonplace of what had been there. In the confusion, fear and avarice on the ground combined with state uncertainty and ready-made plans of development banks to distil the values of political nationalism through reconstruction.

Nepal earthquake: the grammar of bureaucracy

Between April and May 2015, two devastating earthquakes struck Nepal, causing almost 9,000 deaths and leaving a path of destruction. What followed was a period of significant change. For those who survived, there was pain in mourning, anger for delays and inequalities, and hope for better times to come. With time, the sorrow for what had been lost turned into new forms of expectation. Indeed, similarly to what happened in Gujarat, the earthquake proved functional in problematizing relations between citizens and the state, already fractious in normal times. As I (Serafini) happened to be in the country shortly after the earthquake, I observed these events at first hand and in raw form. Cognizant of what had happened in Gujarat some years earlier, I could focus on the everyday ruptures of life to see if the same history was going to be made again. In this section, I will not speak with the certainty that comes when the dust is settled and new scaffoldings are unveiled. Rather, I will look ethno-graphically at the points of juncture between the aforementioned scales of uncertainty and intervention to see how different ruptures were produced and tentatively bridged in the early aftermath of a tectonic shift.

As we have seen in the Gujarat case, an earthquake does not happen in a vacuum. Although devastation and death may suspend the normal rhythm of life, history does not collapse like a poorly built column in a low-rise housing block. Soon after the disaster, many villagers started reassembling things with the means they had at their disposal. There were those who rebuilt houses themselves and without fuss; those who found temporary refuge with relatives; and those who capitalized on private connections to reboot life without waiting for the government to act. In the decade prior to the earthquake, a growing and largely unregulated remittance economy had allowed households throughout the country to accumulate relative wealth under the puzzled eyes of a powerless state. Where neither investment in land, urban houses and commodities nor the repayment of loans had sucked dry the migratory economy, people often did not wait for either state or private aid to start rebuilding things. Bricks and corrugated tin sheets, after all, could just be retrieved from rubble. Where not available, they could be purchased. A World Bank report (Ratha et al. 2016, 16–17) clearly showed how remittances (and only those sent through formal channels) surged 20.9 per cent to $6.6 billion in 2015, and particularly so in the months following the earthquake in April – a steady growth from the 3.2 per cent rate of the previous year and way more than the $4 billion pledged by international donors for the reconstruction. For many of those who had relatives abroad at the time of tremors, remittances constituted a better short-term recovery scheme than any superimposed rehabilitation policy.

In the aftermath of the earthquake, the state entered into a crisis. It was not only that governmental buildings and the personnel of public offices had not been spared by tremors from ruination, but also that the quake revealed the fragility of governance in the country. In the wake of the disaster, in fact, foreign governments, volunteers and non-governmental organizations (NGOs) had sprung into action with an alacrity that could not be matched by the government. In less than two days, professional aid groups had come from everywhere, their uniforms and logos constituting a new landscape to be learned. Quickly and with minimal governmental intercession, emergency camps had been set up in playgrounds and open fields. Two weeks after the first tremors, Nepal seemed like a land of conquest. Chinese flags could be seen waving amidst the rubble of famous heritage sites; foreign armies and international NGOs (INGOs) were distributing tents, blankets and food under the uncertain guidance of improvised translators; Japanese teams of engineers were giving instructions on how to assess damage; and helicopters painted with the colours of the Indian flag were delivering aid from the sky, producing a mixture of awe and resentment amidst people on the ground.

Resentment took the form of what Bin Xu (2014), in relation to the Sichuan earthquake, has termed a 'consensus crisis'. The earthquake acted as an event that erased and restarted long processes of negotiation, interrupting silences and pushing people to speak out loudly about what had previously remained in the realm of unspoken dissatisfaction. Citizens everywhere could be heard asking 'hāmro sarkār kahā chha?' – 'where is our government?' In fact, discontent towards the government was not particularly novel. Twenty years of political instability, ongoing constitutional uncertainty and civil war had already made people wary of the state and its representatives. In some locations, the complete absence of elected administrative bodies for over two decades had exacerbated a feeling of distance and reciprocal unreliability. The earthquake, with its attendant delays and malpractices, further contributed to a general sense of inefficiency, unveiling a naked king. As one seasoned commentator of Nepali politics put it bluntly, the government was 'caught with its pants down' (D. Thapa 2015).

The perception of loyalties being stressed and torn apart was further strengthened by the sudden rupture of traditional tools of governance. At the time of damage assessment, what could have been potentially precious information templates – from cadastral maps of properties and registered households to disaggregated data concerning land ownership (*lalpurja*) and population – were largely ignored in favour of newer, internationally defined formats. As Yogesh Raj and Bhaskar Gautam have rightly noticed: 'just when ... state agencies needed to recover ... details and act swiftly to relieve people of their misery, they were struck by a severe bout of amnesia' (2015, 27). Instead of giving continuity to previous data, the machinery of assessment thus relied on standard formats developed within common international frameworks for disaster management. Pre-compiled documents written in English were used to ascertain the identities of victims; 'rapid visual assessment' practices were established with no cognition of the extreme variety of architectural styles and masonry in the country; clustering of life and people was done in a whimsical manner. What followed was confusion, drama and calculation; but also renewal in the form of an increasingly bureaucratized everyday life.

The menace to sovereignty produced by an impressive post-earthquake mobilization of people, foreign institutions and private charities was not unnoticed by the state. With the aim to regain control of the situation, a number of actions were taken by the government. Already during the emergency phase, the government attempted to centralize relief through the creation of a Prime Minister Relief Fund (a tradition across South Asia), through which all donations were to be channelled. At the same time, special provisions were issued to limit earthquake-related interventions only to NGOs and INGOs that had been present in the country prior to the disaster. In some instances, the state's suspicious attempts to control processes of aid distribution caused indignation and further troubles. A diplomatic crisis almost burst out upon accusations that the government was blocking vital supplies owing to peacetime customs rules. For some, the state's reactions to a crisis of legitimacy had the contrary effect of intensifying discontent amongst citizens and media alike. In such a situation of emergency, many people complained, the brokerage of relief by the state was taken as a harmful caprice. As the editor-in-chief of a popular English-language daily put it in a challenging tone, 'and now, eat nationalism!'

Yet, while an elite section of Kathmandu's civil society and almost the whole of the international press endlessly reproduced standard narratives of government failing and corruption, affected people began turning to the state for long-term compensation, rehabilitation and succour. For most, complaining about the state was just part of the story, good for gossip with friends at a tea stall or for searching a common ground of understanding with hungry journalists, but not the central component of what was going on.

As weeks passed by, a vast array of policies was formulated with the aim of bridging ruptures that had turned political. In the process, new ideas and frameworks came to parse everyday life and mould novel citizens and political subjects. Through these frameworks, the state was given the chance to re-enter into people's lives in a new attire and, for many, in an unprecedented way. Citizens were steadily transformed into earthquake victims (*bhukampa pidhit*). A resurgent culture of expectation was rearticulated in a new grammar, made of victims' identity documents, compensation schemes and expanding bureaucracy. While public outbursts of anger towards the government kept spilling out of the well-remunerated pens of both national and international journalists, many people on the ground began learning the new dialect of post-disaster recovery. A dialect, not a language, because it still seemed to draw on a well-rooted rhetoric of development (*bikas*) in the country:[8] *bhukampa pidhit* became the new *garib* (poor), while new terms such as 'resilience', 'transparency' and 'accountability' made their way into the mouths of many.

Despite being applied to a completely different setting, the same vocabulary of vulnerability, risk reduction and resilience that we had heard in Gujarat came to parse and intersect the myriad ways in which people talked about the seismic event. The institutional setting within which this new language had been first created and from which it was now being shouted out, indeed, conferred to certain words the power to stand for the overarching discourse on the earthquake.

The management of rupture has a comparative history of its own. Discussions abounded on how things could be 'built back better' (echoing the slogan first heard in the region after the 2004 tsunami). Specific issues that had been singled out as problems within a logic of vulnerability were given a general bearing, thus moving from being peculiar only to earthquake-affected regions to being applicable to the country as a whole. If recovery had to be followed by prosperity, and if short-cycled practices of resilience were to be strengthened by longer-term politics of security and risk reduction, new measures, plans and technologies had to be implemented nationwide. Envisioned changes had to encompass a multiplicity of scales, from more circumscribed fields such as those of house engineering or private banking to the broader ones of energy production and infrastructural expansion.

'Resilience' became an essential concept in the language of the aftermath, one that well signalled the complex tension between the state and its citizens in the wake of the disaster. Soon after the earthquake, both national and international media praised Nepalis for their 'resilience'. Like many other technical terms, it mainly appeared in English-language newspapers that winked to those who could use the word in their daily relations with donors and INGOs. Unsurprisingly, the term was also meant to praise those civil associations and common folk who had shown courage despite a weak and corrupt state.

The word comes from Latin *resilire*, which means 'to bounce back', 'to return to an original shape after a trauma'. Although historically used to designate elastic materials, it has recently been applied to human beings, signifying their capacity to return after depression, physical and moral traumas. Without the innate resilience of its citizens, it was said, Nepal would have had a much worst aftermath. Nepalese were resilient because they knew how to handle difficulties at a time of crisis, they were elastic enough to endure often blurry processes of distribution, they were liveable enough to face depression and face an absent government. It comes as no surprise that resilience soon became the adjectival hub of a nationalistic pride, especially for those who understood the meaning of the English term.

Yet, in order to justify intervention, the resilience concept was slowly reformulated in a twist which is shared with other post-disaster contexts (Benadusi 2013). Resilience became the conceptual aim of post-earthquake reconstruction, in line with an international rhetoric that had already been circulated for some years by institutions such as the United Nations, the World Bank, the United States Agency for International Aid (USAID) and the UK Department for International Development. 'Transparency' and 'accountability' (*pādarshitā* and *javaphdehitā* in Nepali-language newspapers) were included as essential tools for achieving the grand vision and pointed to what both the government and citizens alike had to develop. In the translation, some meanings were lost and others emerged. *Javaphdehitā* thus became the quality connoting the responsible person, in quite a practical sense of the one who responds to questions of any sort, or with a negative inflection of someone who has to take responsibility for a misdeed. In a context where the contact list on one's mobile phone is revealing of a person's social connectivity, *javaphdehitā* left the world of bureaucratic accountability and entered the pragmatic one of personal relations. Likewise, resilience became *suraksha* (security) as the ideal allowing the proliferation of different policies of control.

In order to have a strong and secure national recovery, the government attached side measures to rehabilitation policies. In the name of transparency and economic integration, remittances had to be controlled and regulated. At the presentation of the budget for Fiscal Year 2017/2018, Minister for Finance Krishna Bahadur Mahara clearly stated: 'Arrangements will be made toward making it mandatory for aspiring migrant workers to open a bank account before going for foreign employment' (Ghimire 2017). Following the earthquake, the state sought to regain legitimacy by creating conditions for domestic employment and by regulating that remittance economy whose informality had so successfully helped people to thrive at a time of crisis.

Similarly, support for rebuilding houses was mainly given through the Rural Housing Reconstruction Project, jointly developed by the Government of Nepal and major donors (World Bank 2015). In order to be eligible beneficiaries of this programme, applicants were requested to sign a legally binding participation agreement with their respective village district committee or municipality. The participation agreement, as it was referred to in official documents, outlined 'the entitlements and obligations of both parties regarding key details of the program such as payment, housing construction standards, and grievance redress mechanisms' (World Bank 2015, 5). It was upon signing the agreement that people started receiving technical and social support to rebuild their houses, in line with a newly formed National Building Code that fostered resilient buildings. A subsidy of NPR 200,000 (later adjusted to NPR 300,000 to cover inflation in building costs),[9] disbursed in three tranches, was granted to those who could provide full documentation of ownership and citizenship. Money was to be transferred through formal banking. A special provision, moreover, was detailed for those who had started rebuilding things on their own. Again, subsidy was made dependent on compliance with standards of construction, on the provision of full documentation of ownership and of access to official channels of economic integration. The ideals of donors could thus be engraved in governmental compensation schemes from the outset.

Such an approach, which had been envisioned and justified in the terms of an accountable and transparent procedure to compensate 'the right amount to the right people', was not devoid of troubles and inequalities. On the ground, earthquake victims who were living in remote rural areas had to travel long distances and spend thousands of rupees to reach bank branches usually situated in the regional headquarters; once there, long queues and delays in the transferring of money forced many to stay and wait in the headquarters for days, if not weeks. Moreover, an owner-driven reconstruction left out all renters and those incapable of providing satisfactory documents. It also opened up spaces of interference for middle men and brokers of all sorts to step in: local cadres of political parties interested in intersecting funds or unblocking situations in exchange for future votes; professional writers and *lekhapān* (notaries), mostly high-caste Bahun, acting as consultants and playing on their expertise of the law and on personal connections in bureaucratic offices; Catholic professionals sent to give consultancies in exchange for the recognition of theological efficiency.

In the new setting, ruptures that had only been latent before the earthquake were now accelerated owing to the conditions created by the seismic event. Bureaucracy entered into people's lives and intersected decisional processes imbued by doubt and uncertainty. As Haxby (2017) shows in his ethnography of households' strategies of recovery, joint estates were legally separated between competing brothers; previous cycles of reproduction of amity and moral values amongst household-ers were interrupted; and long-term, informal temporalities of affect were ruptured into a drier and better punctuated discourse on own-ership, documentation and bureaucracy. With money pouring in for reconstruction – and often even for reconstructing what used to be of no concern whatsoever for the legal owner – fluid processes of occupa-tion, informal renting, land usage and so forth were reduced and framed in the uncontradictory and exclusivist logics relating to ownership and documentation: this is mine, this is not. Infrastructural expansion, the decentralization of administrative structures and the fiscalization of the territory thus became 'instrumental effects' of a reconstruction project that never aimed only at rebuilding earthquake-affected areas – a hyper-bolic process of bureaucratic intensification reminiscent of the expand-ing states described by Ferguson (1990) and Scott (1998).

The earthquake also gave momentum to political processes that had been stalled for years. In less than five months after the first earthquake, then prime minister Sushil Koirala announced that an agreement had been reached amongst the four major parties for drafting a much-awaited new Constitution. With the so-called 'emergency phase' still ongoing, Nepal obtained what could not be obtained in the past decade. On 20 September 2015, the Constitution was promulgated, after the deal had eluded citizens well after the failure of the first Constituent Assembly in 2012. Seasoned commentators on Nepali politics began wondering why things had taken such a sudden turn. Some believed the government had found in constitution-drafting a desperate way for regaining state legiti-macy in troublesome times; others glimpsed in it a practical response to the ever-increasing pressures of international donors and development banks, whose pleas for stability and for a structural readjustment of fiscal policies and administration could not be left unanswered; the most criti-cal ones accused party leaders of chipping in on a popular piece of paper for drawing unwanted gazes away from all the troubles that had been festering in the rubble, while advancing personal agendas and exclusion-ary politics that would be more difficult to handle in normal times (Jha 2015; M. Thapa 2015). Whatever the reason may be, Nepal was given a new foundation when all others seemed to be failing.

The foundation came in the shape of a federal state. For the first time in the history of the country, Nepal was officially declared a federal democratic republic. Its territory was to be divided into seven provinces, whose boundaries were ideally drawn on the basis of a mixture of identity and capability criteria. Geographical continuity, language, culture and ethnicity were to be considered alongside administrative governability, potential for infrastructure development, availability of natural resources and economic interrelationships in the making of new borders. Thus formed, provinces could work in a more autonomous manner, while provincial elections would decide the 165 members of Parliament. This exercise in collaging and decentralization had been at the basis of previous failures in drafting the Constitution. Now, the earthquake seemed to have provided the right condition for expediting the process without much second thought.

The new Constitution was saluted with joy and hope by a substantial chunk of the population. Candlelit ceremonies were held in many seriously affected districts, soon becoming signals of an upcoming period of renovation; welcoming banners for a new Nepal were hung at the entrance gate of villages and neighbourhoods; and a touching ceremony was organized at Kasthamandap, one of the historic hubs of Kathmandu, with leaf plates burning around the image of a bygone Dharahara tower: this was circulated on all media. A sudden gust of national belonging rushed through the rubble, with top-tier politicians blowing in the wind their speeches of unity and renovation.

Yet, while pleasing donors and everyone who hoped for a refreshing wave of stability, critical stances towards such a 'fast-tracked' document were not absent. In fact, the Constitution was promulgated in a climate of resurgent ethnic politics. For weeks prior to the official announcement, people in the Southern plains of Nepal (Tarai) had been protesting against a state that, they felt, was profiting from a situation of emergency to erase years of struggle for recognition. Since Nepal had emerged as a unified nation at the end of the eighteenth century, the political economy of the country had been flourishing around a fundamental postulate: people from the hills are different from the people of the plains (Madeshi). For most of the past two centuries, the Gangetic soils of the Tarai had been more the agricultural goldmine for a hillcentric politics of extraction than an integrated part of Nepal's self-crafted national identity. The new Constitution was now further strengthening a hillcentric state ideology. Seen from the perspective of Madeshi leaders and critical analysts (Lal 2016), the introduction of unfavourable rules of citizenship, the demarcation of federal state borders so as to reinforce old patterns of dominance and the dissolution of equitable provisions contained in the former Interim Constitution of Nepal were all clear instances of the durability of exclusionary politics. The post-earthquake wind of unity thus turned incendiary.

As protests took place and people kept dying – more than 60 casualties would be counted at the end of the conflict – a blockade of the Nepal–India border (*nākābandi*) was enforced. In a characteristic convergence of institutional and street stereotyping in the country, Madeshi's quests for recognition were turned into a matter of international geopolitics. People started blaming Madeshi and Indian leaders indiscriminately, their responsibility for stalling essential goods in a post-earthquake emergency phase taken as a particularly serious issue.

With petrol and gas blocked at the Indian border, life in earthquake-hit areas became tangibly more difficult – if that was possible. In Kathmandu, one had to spend hours lining up in queues just to obtain a few gallons of petrol; kitchen stoves ran low on gas, and many restaurants had to shut down or adopt 'Modi-fied' menus (a play on words inspired by a widespread feeling of resentment towards the Indian prime minister); and hospitals and pharmacies ran short of medicine, as the blockade was now affecting the delivery of all kinds of goods. The *nākābandi* was also extensively used to explain why some things were stopping and why others had not started yet. Both the government and I/NGOs started complaining about the shortage of petrol and gas for justifying their inability to carry on with the recovery. Street beggars and unemployed youths soon took the chance to earn some money by queuing on demand. In the countryside and up the mountains, the situation was either slightly better or terribly worse. Old practices were recovered at the time of need. Homemade *chulos* – wood-burning stoves – reappeared in their dozens, at least where people could retrieve the precious red earth (*rāto māto*) of which they are made. Trees were cut and the price of wood went through a period of hyperbolic inflation. Some villagers profited from the situation to pump up their incomes.

At the same time, while temporary shelters had yet to be delivered and the reconstruction proper was still at a vestigial stage, fantasized images of future developments started appearing in the press. Pictures of engineeringly sound buildings, often legitimated with the stamp of the Nepal Engineering Association, were widely circulated on newspapers and social media; working plans of railways, highways and smart cities caught the imagination of many; projects for the reconstruction of 'model' villages mushroomed. Even the project of making Nepal a self-sufficient hydro-nation gained momentum along the lines of a post-earthquake ideology of risk reduction, economic growth and security – one that was backed up by the interests of development banks and donors (Lord 2016). If such images, inflected in the popular, future-looking grammar of *bikas* (development), had been part of life before the earthquake as well, now they were reformulated in the catchy terms of an ameliorative project of recovery and security. In the process, what had been daily practices of survival at the time of the crisis, especially in the countryside, were rearticulated in the grammar of commendable and yet short-term instances of resilience, to be enhanced and made more effective within a modernist logic of risk reduction suitable to the needs of a growing urban nation.

Conclusion

Aftermath refers to the second growth or crop in the same season, the new flush of grass after mowing, which is often quite different in its qualities to the first crop; but it is still grass. The second crop may grow unevenly as it races for the light. It may pale before establishing itself. Aftermath is a measure of a quality of time and growth. It is also popular to think about disasters leading to a *tabula rasa*, or blank slate. The term refers to society akin to the unformed and featureless mind found in the philosophy of John Locke.[10] Destruction wipes things clean so that they can be remade anew. Naomi Klein in her appropriately titled *Shock Doctrine* finds obvious fault with this idea, adopting a metaphor of her own. She describes the experiments of psychologists who thought that if the personality of a patient could be erased, then it could be built back again without fault or disorder.[11] To this end, patients were deprived of all routine and structure, and were subjected to irregular and disorienting sensory stimulation. Despite initial successes, the psychologists were often frustrated by the return of elements of the patient's original personality. So too, in Gujarat and Nepal, those who came to intervene did not find the featureless mind they might have hoped for. However, in both locations we can see nation-building, expanding states and intimate transformations that can be empirically tied to the earthquake. Remarkably, we can also see regime change in Gujarat and radical constitutional reform in Nepal, both of which have strong and clearly identifiable origins in the moment of the earthquake.

Aftermaths often appear to have similar structures characterized by the interaction of shock and stun with new intentions and plans. They cannot, however, be seen as a generic sociological condition, for the shocks and doctrines vary. An aftermath is a product of the longer history of the locality. The world does not implode into the moment of disaster to emerge afresh or ready to be remade in any old way. Older ideas will not disappear: old Bhuj was thrown into disarray by the earthquake, yet the national flag was still raised to mark Republic Day before the dust had settled. Likewise, post-earthquake grievances of blame and poverty in Nepal drew on well-established grammars of complaint and hierarchy in the country. In both moments, people found their way home despite the absence of streets and buildings; networks of amity and economic support did not vanish in the rubble; Bhuj was reconstructed from archival sources and the Madeshi were kept at the usual distance in the new federal setting. In sum, there was no clean slate in rupture.

Yet the sudden suspension of certainty that comes with an earthquake makes people dubious about the proper course of action. How to tame the sense of things being torn apart? In history, the sublime reach of catastrophe has led to speculation on the possible purpose of mass death and destruction in the grander scheme of things. In particular, the catastrophe of an earthquake has provided opportunity to reconsider how men should properly relate to their gods, and has prompted additional speculation on God's supposed intentions. We have described the promotion of neo-liberal Hindu nationalism in Gujarat and the formation of bureaucratic subjects in Nepal. In both locations, codes, regulations and new ways of ordering chaos and thought became the order of the day. The momentum to reform and restructure the state and relations between people and the state was central to disaster politics in Gujarat and Nepal. In Gujarat, the east moved on the west; in Nepal, highland moved on lowland, as spatial and identity politics entered the debate about rights and privileges of development. In both locations too we saw regime change and an intensification and occasional renewal of pre-disaster politics. These events were accompanied by the personal stories of grief, guilt and gain, and the difficulties of surviving. If one looks deep enough, there is a possibility for comparison in aftermaths.

The 1755 Lisbon earthquake is much written about by those seeking to understand the debate enlivened by the disaster about whether optimism or pessimism was the underlying philosophical condition of eighteenth-century Europe. Looking at the earthquake with hindsight, historians have wondered whether the shock of the disaster pushed the Enlightenment in certain godless directions. Some say it did; others believe the paradigm shift from God to rational science was already under way.[12] But what of the moral and philosophical content of the debates provoked by the earthquake? Do these have relevance for thinking about the earthquakes we have discussed? Can we think comparatively about the thoughts people have in the aftermath of a disaster? Or do the thoughts earthquakes provoke only belong to a particular place and time, in this case Lisbon and Europe of the mid-eighteenth century?

At the time of the tremors, Lisbon was a prosperous mercantile centre. The destruction of its inhabitants and wealth by an earthquake and the ensuing floods and fires reverberated across Europe. Lisbon was also known for its inquisitors and idolatry, which added a sharp edge to events in the aftermath. The Protestant clergy in northern Europe asserted that the earthquake happened because the people of Lisbon were Roman Catholics. The clergy of Lisbon, on the other hand, felt that the shock was the result of divine anger at the presence of certain Protestants in the town. The heretics were forcibly baptized and a splendid auto-da-fé was held, with a view to preventing further disaster.

Lisbon, too, like Gujarat and Nepal, boomed after the math of its destruction, and the new glory sat uneasily with the images of loss, wrath and human sacrifice that accompanied the initial news of the earthquake. The tugs and contradictions of the destruction and the prosperous aftermath detained some of the foremost thinkers of the age: Rousseau, Voltaire and Kant. They discussed the death of God, whether God's design for the world was the best of all possible designs and, if so, what place there was for the terror and destruction of an earthquake. Is chance or fate the general principle of universal operation? Is death a greater evil when it strikes at many people simultaneously, rather than removing them at intervals?

Their thought shows that earthquakes shake certainties as well as foundations, and, therefore, they necessarily became part of the discussions of theologians and philosophers. For the Christian theologians, earthquakes were instruments of fear, operating either as a routine and indiscriminate part of the divine order of things, or as divine instruments of punishment, which could be distributed when appropriate. Consequently, not only in Europe, but in India and Nepal, aftermaths have often spawned the rise of new religious forms, as the beleaguered have become zealots, transforming their fear, guilt, trauma, ecstasy or rapture into improved forms of devotion or into ritualized apologies for their wrongdoings. In Bode's Peru of the 1970s, the religious resurgence took the form of a battle between different currents of Christianity. The discussions that followed the Lisbon earthquake, although not restricted to that disaster by any means, marked another kind of critical shift and added momentum to thinking in the Enlightenment mode.

The Lisbon earthquake of 1755 broke Voltaire's faith in the doctrine of 'whatever is, is right'. In his first poem on the earthquake, he (1756) attacked the optimism represented by characters such as Pope: 'come, ye philosophers, who cry, "All's well", And contemplate this ruin of a world'.[13] Voltaire mocked: whatever happened must have happened for the best of all possible reasons! In Lisbon, the heirs of the dead will benefit financially; the building trade will enjoy a boom; animals will grow fat on meals provided by corpses trapped in the debris; an earthquake is a necessary effect of a necessary cause; private misfortune must not be overrated; an individual who is unlucky is contributing to the general good. Is this the best of all possible worlds? Is there not as much evil in these sentiments – Voltaire asked – as in the earthquake itself? For Voltaire, man could not hope for a safe life with benevolent protection of Providence rewarding virtuous behaviour. The saddening truth is that we know nothing of our origin, purpose or destiny. Nature has no message for us. God does not speak. The bodies of men are made for decay and our minds for grief.

Rousseau was unhappy with Voltaire's views on our fate. He said that at a personal level the optimism Voltaire attacked had helped him to endure the very things supposed to be unendurable. For Rousseau, man must recognize evil as the consequence of his own nature as well as that of the universe. A benevolent God desired to preserve man from evil, and of all the possible systems whereby God's creation might be ordered, God had chosen the one that contained the least evil and the most good. Put bluntly, said Rousseau, the reason why God had not done better for mankind was that God could not do better. Rousseau maintained that moral evil originated in man himself, not God, and that, even though physical evil is a necessary part of the creation, the majority of physical evils are man's own fault. According to him, it was not nature or God that had congregated 20,000 houses of six or seven storeys in Lisbon. If the inhabitants of the city had not lived in crowded and dangerous buildings, the damage would have been less. Had they left the city after the first shock, then they could have been saved. Instead, they stayed obstinately on the spot, worrying about their money and their possessions. For Rousseau, there was sociology in the disaster as well as theology and philosophy.

These lyrical discussions serve to show how earthquakes impose on the imagination in practical, sociological and philosophical registers. The philosopher sublimates the variegated doubts that an earthquake produces into a moment of epistemological, even theological, rupture. Is God dead, or is He simply incapable of catering for His worshippers? Is Evil a part of God or the unwanted offspring of humanity? In the same vein, we like to think, as the planner or the political leader embroiders narratives of blame and rehabilitation, and reassures the citizens who have been left to wonder about their future amidst rubble. In this sense, the doubt and hope of the Enlightenment philosophers no longer seem so profound. Their thoughts are the stuff of teashop chat on the streets of South Asia. The earthquake, wherever it takes place, is an opportunity to take ownership of the story and to turn abstract thoughts into concrete realities. These doubts and hopes are those that allow for the implementation of new building codes, bureaucratic citizenship and the renaming of prominent public spaces after once-obscure figures in nationalist history. The oscillation between life and death also allows the governments of India and China to develop their influence within Nepal through the creation of infrastructure and supply chains.

Our discussions of events in South Asia have also shown how earthquakes break, disorient and bereave. They have also allowed for the formation of new policy landscapes, new forms of citizens and governments. Earthquakes are opportunities for those with the composure and gall to see them as such. The long drag and conclusion of processes in Gujarat contrasts with the contingency and immediacy that still animates Nepal. In Nepal, we have seen the opportunism of fleet-footed international organizations seeking to make the world new.

Regime change and constitutional reform are not perhaps linked to earthquakes with any organic or scientific certainty. However, the failure of God, buildings and society to protect leads to the distinct sense of betrayal that comes with inevitable delays to post-earthquake reconstruction. In both Nepal and Gujarat, dramatic changes to government occurred at about the same time as people had come to terms with what had happened to them and were beginning to understand what needed to be done in order to make things better. The urge to rebuild individual lives and houses thus clashed with the ideas and plans of those who could ease recovery. Out of the crisis of judgement, new forms of narrative followed. Earthquakes allow for storytelling, and effective storytellers may find particularly receptive audiences given the conditions of particular uncertainty that earthquakes bring with them.

Notes

1. The edited works of Anthony Oliver-Smith and Susanna Hoffman (1999) and in reverse name order (2002) have been influential.
2. On syndromes and New Orleans see Adams et al. (2009).
3. This ascription of disaster-like qualities to the aftermath is commonly reported. The wave of aid in Sri Lanka was called the 'second tsunami', for example.
4. See, for example, Klein (1984) on famine relief and D'Souza (2006) on flood control in India.
5. Tirthankar Roy (2008) suggests that patterns of response during the period see the destruction of state capacity, which activates anarchic unregulated markets and private institutions,

until the state bounces back to take control. We see some resemblance of this pattern in Gujarat, with the additional influence of the international community and the partnership of state and private interests in reconstruction.

6. The Gujarat State Disaster Management Bill was passed as Act 20 of 2003. A national disaster management bill was passed in 2005.

7. Anthony Oliver-Smith (1986, 76) writing about the Peruvian earthquake and landslide of 1970. Rebecca Solnit (2010) sees the moment of post-disaster disorientation as a possible source of new politics. While sympathetic with the sentiment, the nationalist and cultural chauvinism evident in Gujarat were probably not the forms of utopia Solnit had in mind.

8. For critical approaches to the ideology of *bikas* in Nepal, see Pigg (1992, 1996); Fujikura (2013); Heaton-Shrestha (2004).

9. World Bank (2018).

10. John Locke (1632–1704), the Scottish Enlightenment philosopher, thought humans were born without innate ideas, and that knowledge is instead determined only by experiences derived from sensual perception (see Baird and Kaufmann 2008).

11. Naomi Klein (2007, 25–48) outlines this theory in a chapter provocatively entitled 'The Torture Lab: Ewen Cameron, the CIA and the Maniacal Quest to Erase and Remake the Human Mind'.

12. Recent historians such as Goldberg (1989), Larsen (2006), Paice (2008), Shrady (2008) and Wootton (2000) contribute to placing the earthquake and its debates in proper context. Kendrick (1955) remains the classic account of the English sources.

13. From Voltaire's poem on the Lisbon disaster; or an examination of the axiom 'All is well' (see 1988).

References

Adams, Vincanne, Taslim Van Hattum and Diane English. 2009. 'Chronic Disaster Syndrome: Displacement, Disaster Capitalism, and the Eviction of the Poor from New Orleans'. *American Ethnologist* 36 (4): 615–36.

Baird, Forrest E., and Walter A. Kaufmann. 2008. *Philosophical Classics: From Plato to Derrida*. Upper Saddle River, NJ: Prentice Hall.

Benadusi, Mara. 2013. 'The Two-Faced Janus of Disaster Management: Still Vulnerable, Yet Already Resilient'. *South East Asia Research* 21 (3): 419–38.

Bode, Barbara. 1989. *No Bells to Toll: Destruction and Creation in the Andes*. New York: Charles Scribner's Sons.

D'Souza, Rohan. 2006. *Drowned and Dammed: Colonial Capitalism and Flood Control in Eastern India*. New Delhi: Oxford University Press.

Ferguson, James. 1990. *The Anti-Politics Machine: 'Development', Depoliticization and Bureaucratic Power in Lesotho*. Cambridge: Cambridge University Press.

Freud, Sigmund. 1917. *Mourning and Melancholia*, The Standard Edition of the Works of Sigmund Freud, Vol. 14. London: The Hogarth Press.

Fujikura, Tatsuro. 2013. *Discourses of Awareness: Development, Social Movements and the Practices of Freedom in Nepal*. Kathmandu: Martin Chautari.

Ghimire, Sagar. 2017. 'Bank Accounts Must in Nepal for People Heading Abroad to Work'. *MyRepublica*. Accessed 30 May. https://myrepublica.nagariknetwork.com/news/bank-accounts-must-in-nepal-for-people-heading-abroad-to-work/.

Hacking, Ian. 1990. *The Taming of Chance*. Cambridge: Cambridge University Press.

Haxby, Andrew W. 2017. 'The Maintenance of Virtue over Time: Notes on Changing Household Lives in Post-Disaster Nepal'. *HIMALAYA, the Journal of the Association for Nepal and Himalayan Studies* 37 (2): 65–74.

Heaton-Shrestha, Celayne. 2004. 'The Ambiguities of Practising Jat in 1990s Nepal: Elites, Caste and Everyday Life in Development NGOs'. *South Asia: Journal of South Asian Studies* 27 (1): 39–63.

Hoffman, Susannna M., and Anthony Oliver-Smith. 2002. *Catastrophe and Culture: The Anthropology of Disaster*. Santa Fe: School of American Research Press.

Jasanoff, Sheyla 2010. 'Beyond Calculation: A Democratic Response to Risk'. In *Disaster and the Politics of Intervention*, edited by A. Lakoff, 14–40. New York: University of Columbia Press.

Jha, Hari Bansh. 2015. 'Nepal's New Constitution: An Analysis from the Madeshi Perspective'. *Kantipur*. Accessed 24 September. https://idsa.in/idsacomments/NepalsNewConstitution_hbjha_240915.

Kant, I. 1764. *Beobachtungen über das Gefühl des Schönen und Erhabenen*. Königsberg: Johann Jacob Kanter.

Kendrick, T.D. 1956. *The Lisbon Earthquake*. New York: J.B. Lippincot Company.

Klein, Ira. 1984. 'When the Rains Failed: Famine, Relief, and Mortality in British India'. *Indian Economic & Social History Review* 21 (2): 185–214.

Klein, Naomi. 2007. *The Shock Doctrine: The Rise of Disaster Capitalism*. London: Macmillan.

Lal, C.K. 2016. 'The Brute Majority'. *MyRepublica*. Accessed 20 September. http://admin.myrepublica.com/opinion/story/28487/the-brute-majority.html.

Larsen, Svend Erik. 2006. 'The Lisbon Earthquake and the Scientific Turn in Kant's Philosophy'. *European Review* 14 (3): 359–67.

Lenin, Vladimir. 1970. *Left-Wing Communism: An Infantile Disorder*. Peking: Foreign Languages Press.

Lifton, Robert Jay. 1967. *Death in Life: Survivors of Hiroshima*. London: Weidenfeld and Nicolson.

Lord, Austin. 2016. 'Citizens of a Hydropower Nation: Territory and Agency at the Frontiers of Hydropower Development in Nepal'. *Economic Anthropology* 3 (1): 145–60.

Mill, John Stuart. 1848. *Principles of Political Economy, With Some of Their Applications to Social Philosophy*. London: John W. Parker.

Oliver-Smith, Anthony. 1986. *The Martyred City: Death and Rebirth in the Andes*. Albuquerque: University of New Mexico Press.

Oliver-Smith, Anthony. 1996. 'Anthropological Research on Hazards and Disasters'. *Annual Review of Anthropology* 25 (1): 303–28.

Oliver-Smith, A., and S.M. Hoffman, eds. 1999. *The Angry Earth: Disaster in Anthropological Perspective*. New York: Routledge.

Paice, Edward. 2008. *Wrath of God: The Great Lisbon Earthquake of 1755*. London: Quercus.

Pigg, Symaco Lorraine. 1992. 'Investing Social Categories through Place: Social Representations and Development in Nepal'. *Comparative Studies in Society and History* 34 (3): 491–513.

Pigg, Symaco Lorraine. 1996. 'The Credible and the Credulous: The Question of Villagers' Beliefs in Nepal'. *Cultural Anthropology* 11 (2): 160–201.

Raj, Yogesh, and Bhaskar Gautam. 2015. *Courage in Chaos: Early Rescue and Relief after the April Earthquake*. Kathmandu: Martin Chautari.

Ratha, Dilip. et al. 2016. 'Migration and Remittances: Recent Developments and Outlook'. In *Migration and Development Brief* 26. Washington: The World Bank.

Roitman, Janet. 2013. *Anti-Crisis*. Durham, NC: Duke University Press.

Roy, Tirthankar. 2008. 'State, Society and Market in the Aftermath of Natural Disasters in Colonial India: A Preliminary Exploration'. *Indian Economic & Social History Review* 45 (2): 261–94.

Scott, James. 1998. *Seeing Like a State: How Certain Schemes to Improve the Human Condition have Failed*. New Haven, CT: Yale University Press.

Shrady, Nicholas. 2008. *The Last Day: Wrath, Ruin and Reason in the Great Lisbon Earthquake of 1755*. London: Penguin Books.

Simpson, Edward. 2013. *The Political Biography of an Earthquake: Aftermath and Amnesia in Gujarat, India*. London: Hurst.

Solnit, Rebecca. 2010. *A Paradise Built in Hell: The Extraordinary Communities that Arise in Disaster*. London: Penguin.

Thapa, D. 2015. 'The Honeymoon is Over'. *The Kathmandu Post*, 18 June.

Thapa, M. 2015. 'Nepal's Slippery Fast-Track'. *The Wire*, 13 June.

Voltaire. 2005. *Candide, or Optimism*. Translated by Tobias Smollett. London: Penguin.

Voltaire. 1988. 'Poème sur le désastre de Lisbonne'. in *The Riches of Rhyme: Studies in French Verses*, edited by C. Scott, 208–36. Oxford: Oxford University Press.

Wootton, David. 2000. 'Introduction'. In *Candide and Related Texts*, Voltaire, viii–xxxiii. Indianapolis, IN: Hackett Publishing.

World Bank, The. 2015. *Nepal Rural Housing Reconstruction Program: Program Overview and Operations Manual Summary*. Washington: The World Bank.

World Bank, The. 2018. 'Nepal: The World Bank Sign Three Agreements Totalling $440 Million'. Accessed 21 January. http://www.worldbank.org/en/news/press-release/2018/01/21/nepal-world-bank-sign-three-agreements-totaling-440-million.

Xu, Bin. 2014. 'Consensus Crisis and Civil Society: The Sichuan Earthquake Response and State–Society Relations'. *The China Journal* 71: 91–108.

Afterword: Some Reflections on Rupture

Joel Robbins

In keeping with the commitment to ethnographic complication rather than grand theorizing that marks the approach of this collection, I write this final reflection not to provide an overall synthetic reading of all the previous chapters, but rather to offer a few rather scattered thoughts on the notion of rupture. I come to this task as someone who has on the one hand been working at this topic for a long time (at least since an article published in 2003), but who on the other came to it not by the road marked 'revolution', but rather by the one named 'conversion'. At an abstract level, conversion is like revolution in that both are, at least in their fullest forms, processes of change undertaken in light of a story about how such change can work. That is to say, both are kinds of transformations rooted in cultural models of cultural rupture – in models, to borrow terms from Caroline Humphrey's chapter in this volume, that specify things to 'break from' as well as things to 'break toward'. Based in part on this similarity between revolution and conversion, there has been in the recent past, albeit fading a bit now, some movement toward erasing the distinction between these two paths to rupture, particularly on the part of continental thinkers such as Žižek (2003), Badiou (2003) and Agamben (2005). These figures, generally considered closer to political philosophy than to theology or other forms of religious thought, have taken St Paul's sudden and thorough conversion as a possible model for revolutionary process (see also Robbins 2010; Robbins and Engelke 2010). I hope that the similarities between revolution and conversion, along with this recent move toward holding these two types of change together, might mean that my reflections in what follows will be relevant to those interested in both kinds of rupture. Yet it will remain the case that even as I start with a brief discussion of one important work on revolution, I will focus my remarks mostly on some new developments in thinking about Christian conversion as a process of rupture.

My primary interest is in rupture considered as cultural process – that is to say, I am inclined to ask how ruptures in social life can arise out of conceptual resources shared by the people who experience or create them. It is this concern that motivates the observation I made in my opening remark that both conversion and revolution are changes undertaken in the light of stories about or models of change. One can, of course, imagine kinds of rupture that affect cultural and social life but do not arise from within it, situations of change in which people are simply overtaken by events or phenomena they neither find they can readily understand nor attempt to direct. But I want to set those kinds of ruptures aside to consider instead radical breaks that people bring about at least in part by deploying culturally meaningful tools.

An argument for rupture as culturally driven cultural change is easier to assert than it is to really work through, for in theoretical terms it is not as simple as one might imagine to construe rupture as a cultural process. This is so because culture is generally taken almost by definition to be, and in fact often is, a force for its own reproduction (Robbins 2007). Defined as structure or tradition, culture is all about steering social action along well-worn grooves, and this means rupture ought not to be part of its modus operandi. This is one of several reasons many contemporary anthropologists do not want to have anything to do with culture, being more interested in what the editors, in their introduction, describe as vitalist or life-affirming conceptualizations of human being that find notions of well-worn grooves, social forms or structures of any kind to be misguided at best and pernicious at worst. From this point of view, as the pioneering electronic composer Edgard Varèse put it, 'tradition is simply a bad habit' (cited in Stubbs 2018, 64). But I would argue that if we do not posit culture or some other force that pushes for reproduction, rupture itself becomes uninteresting – just the norm, or at most little more than a fancy name for an increase in the scale of processes of change that are always under way. To put this another way, vitalist or immanentist anthropologies, with their strong commitment to nominalist views of the world, render the question of rupture or change generally moot, since nothing ever stays the same in any case. To keep rupture firmly in focus, then, I propose to hang on to some conception of culture – a conception that sees it as a mechanism mostly of order and reproduction – and then try to account for how culture so conceived can sometimes foster radical change by means of processes that are not outside or in excess of culture, but are rather themselves cultural.

One hypothesis I want to explore is that if any given case of rupture is to be seen as a result of cultural processes, then it will need to involve at least in part shared conceptualizations of rupture itself. On this account, only cultures of rupture, or cultures that at least conceive of the possibility of rupture, produce ruptures that are culturally meaningful and of real interest to the people involved in them. This is a strong assertion, and I am more than willing to be wrong about it. But I want to float it here and see how far it might be able to take us.

The thought of a number of scholars has inspired this claim, most importantly Marshall Sahlins, whose work I have discussed in related terms elsewhere (Robbins 2016). But to launch my argument here, I turn first to another scholar strongly influenced by Sahlins, the historian William Sewell (1996). Writing of 'events' rather than the narrower notion of rupture (narrower not in terms of its purported effects, but only in the sense that revolutions might be seen as a subcategory of the broader category of event), Sewell insists in terms very close to my own 'that social relations are profoundly governed by underlying social and cultural structures and that a proper understanding of the role of events in history must be founded on a concept of structure' (1996, 842). In the superb 1996 article from which this quotation is taken, 'Historical Events as Transformations of Structures: Inventing Revolution at the Bastille', Sewell exemplifies his approach by considering a key event of the French Revolution. The taking of the Bastille on 11 July 1789, Sewell argues, was in the conception of the actors who undertook it no more than an effort to secure gunpowder stored in the former fortress so that they could better resist Louis XVI's attempt to retake Paris by military force. In its initial performance, it was not an event in the strong, socially transformative sense Sewell reserves for this term, but rather a familiar form of popular contention. It was only in the days that followed that the General Assembly transformed the taking of the Bastille into an event, a feat they accomplished by working out a cultural model of revolution as 'a rising of the sovereign people whose justified violence imposed a new political system on the nation' and then applying it to what had transpired (1996, 859). Initially applied retrospectively, this new notion of revolution immediately began to do prospective work by encouraging further radical transformation of French social life, and in time of course it became a shared cultural model for similar practices of cultural rupture the world over; or, as Reinhart Koselleck (2004, 50) puts it in an analysis that covers ground similar to that covered by Sewell, it 'became a *metahistorical concept* ... charged with ordering historically recurrent convulsive experiences' (emphasis in original). Inasmuch as it was the development and rapid cultural diffusion of the very notion of 'revolution' itself during the heat of the events of mid-July 1989 that pushed forward the rupture that became known as the French Revolution, one must accept that it was precisely the development and diffusion of a new cultural model of change that allowed for the production of a major rupture in French culture and social life, not some acultural force.

I find Sewell's article enormously helpful in thinking about rupture as a cultural process, but as I have already noted I came to an interest in rupture and discontinuity not through the study of revolutions, but rather by way of an interest in Christian conversion. It is to this topic I now want to return in an effort to explore some aspects of Christian notions of rupture that I think anthropologists (myself included) have neglected in the past. I hope that in doing so I might raise some more general questions about a few of the less remarked upon aspects of rupture as a cultural process.

Before launching into a broad argument about the nature of Christian notions of rupture, it might be useful very briefly to summarize the ethnographic experience that brought me to this topic in the first place. In the early 1990s, I carried out fieldwork among the Urapmin of Papua New Guinea. Only a little over a decade before I arrived in Urapmin, all of the adult members of the community had converted to a charismatic, spirit-filled form of Christianity in the midst of a revival movement that was then moving through their country. People in Urapmin consistently and frequently insist that their conversion changed their lives dramatically. As they often say when discussing aspects of their lives that were important before revival but are not any more, 'that was before, this is now'. And the list of things that were important to them before their conversion but not after it is long, attesting to the extent to which the revival did in fact count as a major rupture in their lives. Thus, for example, Urapmin no longer think their ancestors created the human world in which they dwell, and they no longer practise any of the many rituals directed at these ancestors. The cult houses in which Urapmin men used to practise such rituals have been torn down, and the paraphernalia involved in these rites, including the bones of the ancestors themselves, have been, as people put it, 'thrown out'. More than this, the complex system of taboos that used to govern who could eat what and that strictly regulated contact between the sexes is gone. Now, the Urapmin say, using a phrase borrowed from English, is 'free time': because God made everything and gave it to his children, people can eat whatever they want. And women and men no longer sleep in separate houses or walk on different paths through the community – they can be together all the time now if they want to be. All of this has changed, Urapmin say, because to follow any of the ancestral rules or customs is to live in a way that God does not approve – it is to sin. For a group of people strongly focused on following God's 'law' in order to reach heaven, it has been morally necessary to bring about these major ruptures in their social life in order to come into compliance with His commands, and the Urapmin are glad they have done so.

So far, so much rupture as straightforward radical discontinuity with the past. This is indeed how Urapmin talk about their conversion, and as I tried to suggest above, they are able to marshal plenty of evidence for a reading of their past framed in these wholly transformative terms. If you push the Urapmin to name anything traditional that might still matter to them and count as good, they will sometimes say that they still build houses mostly as they did before, and that these houses are good; and they will add that so are their gardens, which, though now watched over by God and not the ancestors, also look pretty much the same. But they are not inclined to expand the list of enduring and good traditional things much beyond these few items. On the surface, their model of rupture is one that holds out complete abandonment of traditional culture as the ideal; to quote Kirk Dombrowski (2001) writing about Native American charismatics in Alaska – Urapmin Christianity initially appears quite thoroughly to be a culture 'against culture'.

In a complicated way I will come back to later, I think the Urapmin are right in the way they understand the model of rupture at the heart of their Christianity as a matter of radically changing everything. But to understand the complication involved, it is best to start with some ways in which one might imagine that on the face of things Urapmin assertions are wrong about the kind of change Urapmin converts have actually accomplished. There are at least two major elements of Urapmin life in the early 1990s that might lead us to this conclusion. I have written about both in great detail elsewhere, so I will just mention them here. The first is that the morality that guides most of Urapmin social interaction is still much as it was before, despite the fact that this morality conflicts with the Christian moral understandings that are central to Urapmin religious thinking and that people regularly proclaim should govern everything that they do. In my book *Becoming Sinners* I argue that it is this conflict between their traditional and their Christian moral systems that accounts for people's deeply felt conviction that they are sinful (Robbins 2004). The second piece of evidence that not all vestiges of the past except houses and gardens are gone is that the Urapmin still believe all illnesses are caused by nature spirits, and they sometimes still practise modified forms of traditional sacrifice to these spirits in order to heal the afflicted. Urapmin are reluctant to practise these sacrifices, but nonetheless they do occasionally resort to them. I have in other places analysed these sacrifices and the controversy among the Urapmin that surrounds their practice in relation to the first point I made about lingering aspects of traditional Urapmin culture, for it is possible to see the sacrifices as exemplifications of the tenets of traditional Urapmin morality (Robbins 2009). But I do not need to rehearse that argument here. For present purposes, I merely want to note the continued existence of these two important elements of traditional Urapmin culture in the Urapmin Christian era in order to pose the questions of what their presence means for our understanding of the Christian model of rupture the Urapmin promulgate and for our judgement of their own success in living in the light of that model.

To answer these questions, I want to step back from the Urapmin for now and consider some recent work on Christian models of rupture more generally that reveal it to be more subtle than our first interpretation of the Urapmin version would lead us to believe. French historian Rémi Brague (2002, 54) notes that Christianity is at its core a religion of 'secondarity' – one that understands itself as appearing in the wake of a prior religion with which it has a complex relationship that is not in any simple terms one only of rejection. Christianity, after all, never wholly rejected the Jewish Tenakh, instead incorporating a version of it as its own 'Old Testament' and therefore requiring that its followers always have some or other understanding of Christianity's relationship with the religion that preceded it. In situations in which converts have had little contact with Christianity before, it is evident that part of what makes Christianity attractive to them is the way its self-conscious secondarity leads it to acknowledge that converts start from somewhere else and must forever negotiate a relationship with that origin. The demand that Christianity as a religion of secondarity sets up for such negotiation is a key feature of Christian models of rupture.

Along with Brague's model of Christian secondarity, there is also another, closely related, aspect of Christianity that drives forward processes of cultural rupture and gives them a distinctive Christian shape. The work of the theologian Katherine Tanner (1997, 97) is useful in laying this out. She argues that Christianity rarely attempts to construct an entire culture or create a whole society in its own terms. Instead, she notes, 'The majority view in Christianity for most of its history never favored efforts to make Christian social practices into the sort of group that modern anthropologists would think of as possessing its own way of life.' For this reason, she goes on to assert, Christians have often participated in the 'educational, economic, familial ... [and] political' institutions of the wider societies of which they have been a part (see also Brague 2002, 160–5). This point is helpful, for as with Brague, Tanner helps us to see why the existence of 'pre-Christian' or not wholly Christian aspects of a culture may not stand as evidence of the incomplete application of the cultural model of rupture that Christianity installs, but instead as fulfilments of it.

But Tanner does not end her argument on the point that Christian ruptures tend to leave some aspects of social life as they are. After making this claim, she develops the argument that Christians do not generally relate to these prior or non-Christian institutions in a manner of straightforward acceptance. Rather, in the spirit of Brague's continual negotiations between forms of Christianity and the older cultures they do not wholly discard, Tanner (1997, 116) suggests that Christians 'trope' on the prior social forms that endure in their lives, giving them new Christian meanings or otherwise bringing them in line with Christian concerns (1997, 116). This point brings her work into line with some of the best recent anthropological work on Christian rupture.

Consider, in this regard, Simon Coleman's (2006, 3) argument that at least some forms of Christianity, and Pentecostal and charismatic Christianity in particular, take the form of 'part cultures' that are designed so as to be able to relate to other cultures with which they come into contact not by endeavouring to replace them wholesale, but by coming into 'tension' with their values. Making a related point, Courtney Handman (2015) has argued that Christianity is a religion that tends to promote criticism of past and current social and religious practice to a central place in the lives of its adherents. This fact is responsible for the tendency of some of Christianity's forms to over and over again produce the ruptures we call schisms, even as in less dramatic cases this sacralized critical impulse keeps up the kinds of tensions between Christianity and aspects of the world it is breaking from that suggest that no rupture ever quite completes its work of making that world wholly anew.

Drawing on the work of Handman, Coleman, Tanner and Brague, we might say that Christianity is a religion that is inclined to create what we might usefully call duplex cultural formations. These are formations in which converts do not in fact completely discard their traditional cultures, or even transform all of their parts in ways that lead them to be unrecognizable in relation to their previous forms, but are rather ones in which Christians are enjoined constantly to take an evaluative position with regard to their previous traditions. In a recent book on Navajo Pentecostalism entitled *Upward, Not Sunwise* that stands as the most sophisticated recent anthropological interrogation of Christian notions of rupture that I have read, Kimberly Marshall (2016) adds a final, important, moving part to the Christian model of rupture as I have been laying it out here. An ethnomusicologist as well as an anthropologist, Marshall does this by arguing in detail that Christianity works by means of establishing what she calls 'resonant ruptures'. These are cultural formations in which, as in musical resonance, some vibrations amplify others without becoming identical to them (2016, 15). In cases of Christian rupture, this means that Christian forms resonate with older ones in ways that do not erase them, even as they assert dominance over them. This happens, for example, in the cases of both Urapmin traditional morality and sacrifice to the nature spirits – forms that are sometimes highlighted in Urapmin consciousness because of their entanglement with Christian concerns, but that are never able to reassert the taken-for-granted status they once had. The point that Marshall (2016, 8) makes, and that I am keen to borrow here, is that this kind of 'complicated nexus of continuity and rupture' does not mark cases in which Christian notions of rupture have failed to fully realize themselves. They are, rather, precisely the kind of enduringly dynamic kinds of ruptures Christianity aims to produce. It is because the Urapmin are fully caught up in just this kind of dynamism, a kind of dynamism that is captured in similar ways in all of the models of Christian rupture I have been discussing, that they are right to say that their conversion has changed everything about the way they live; nothing is left as it was, at the very least the ways Urapmin evaluate all aspects of their lives has changed; but this does not mean that no elements of their tradition are in any respect present in their lives. Tobia Farnetti, in his chapter on the lives of Japanese Catholics in this volume, offers a portrait of different version of these same kinds of dynamics, one that at once indicates how diverse they can be in practice and how recognizable they remain as species of a broader genus of Christian rupture.

What I have aimed to lay out here is a model of Christian rupture that on the one hand expects it to set up duplex cultural formations in which parts of the cultures from which people break remain in play even whilst they also remain in tension with the converts' new Christian understandings, and that on the other hand thrives on the energy these tensions produce, making of rupture a continuing ideal rather than a settled accomplishment. It is this kind of enduring impetus to continually work toward rupture that some Christians capture in such slogans as 'reformed and always reforming' or 'God has no Grandchildren' (i.e. each person and each generation has to experience the Christian rupture for themselves – it is an experience that cannot be inherited). My suggestion is that these kinds of dynamics are also in play in many changes guided by cultural models of revolution, beset as they are by the temptation to put new purifying measures in play in the wake of their initial success. But others will be more competent than I am to cash this point out empirically.

Among the many reasons that scholars are not always quick to group Christian conversion and revolution together as kinds of rupture, and this even in the wake of the recently flagging vogue for doing so in some corners of continental thought, is that in many times and places, and often as a matter of theological principle, Christian ruptures are seen by converts as involving individuals in the first and ultimately most important instance, while most scholars assume that revolutions are by nature collective (at least if they are those that succeed in driving radical change). Indeed, it is a bit of a critical cliché amongst politically minded secular thinkers that Christian conversion is ultimately quietest because it focuses only on individual change, and when Christians respond to this charge by asserting that making changes within individuals is the only way to change society more broadly, these same thinkers are inclined to feel that they are misguided. The Urapmin case I discussed above, which features a group of socially related people all undergoing individual conversions within a short span of time, and which also features the adoption of a version of Christianity that itself possesses a strong model of cultural change, somewhat sidesteps this issue in a way not all cases of conversion do. Situations such as that of the Danish Lutheran movement discussed by Morten Pedersen in his chapter in this volume fit the stereotype more closely and are perhaps more common. In this case the individual, personal and subjective nature of conversion and of ongoing faith is self-consciously crucial for participants' understandings of both their religious and their political lives in ways that point in a direction other than that of work toward radical social or cultural transformation (see also Bialecki 2009).

The recognition of tensions between conflicting evaluations of personal and cultural ruptures in some kinds of Christianity sets up a host of new questions for research in the study of change. Nicholas Lackenby (n.d.), who has worked with strongly committed and engaged Orthodox Christians in Serbia, has explored some of these questions in seeking to give strong personal senses of rupture their due in a situation in which people understand themselves to be transforming their lives by returning to an ancestral religion marked by a strong commitment to continuity. The study of the revival of Orthodox Christianity in post-socialist times more generally raises issues of the concatenation of rupture and continuity across the personal–social boundary with great clarity because, at least within the anthropology of Christianity, the Orthodox tradition, along with Catholicism, has often been held up as exemplary of forms of Christianity that do not value rupture (Hann and Goltz 2010, see Freeman 2017 for a review). Yet as Timothy Carroll (2017) nicely argues, there are serious limitations to the image of Orthodoxy as monolithically committed to continuity. This makes this tradition an excellent place to explore how personally experienced ruptures, whether as part of a 'return' to a religion that one never really practised before, as Lackenby explores, or by taking part in the disruptive presencing of the transcendent in Orthodox liturgy, as Carroll documents, intersect with a simultaneous investment in the continuity of what Lackenby calls the 'overarching historico-religious tradition'.

The question of how subjective experiences of rupture relate to broader movements either of rupture or continuity also raises a pressing problem for any theory of radical cultural change: how do personal desires for or commitments to change ever become effective cultural projects? This question besets discussions of revolution as much or more than it does those of conversion. In an important recent discussion of rupture in the anthropological literature on Christianity, Dena Freeman (2017) has begun to explore one potential answer to this question that is rooted in the relationship between the impetus provided by religious models of change and the practical openings to transformation afforded by people's political and economic situations. My goal here is not to evaluate her argument, but just to note that, along with work like Lackenby's, it indicates the extent to which a more nuanced understanding of the personal side of rupture could help us develop better answers than we have been able to offer in the past to the question of how personal and broader social and cultural ruptures relate to one another.

The matter of rupture as profoundly felt personal experience – of the undoubted presence of Pauline moments of intense personal disruption in some person's encounters with Christian or revolutionary models of change – suggests a perhaps unexpected connection between the study of rupture and another topic of broad contemporary concern within anthropology and the human sciences more generally. I have in mind here the study of trauma as the negative experience of the disruption of one's life and thought by the appearance within them of unassimilable phenomena that are often but perhaps not always violently imposed (Das 2007 is an already classic discussion; see Robbins 2013 for a brief review of some other important contributions to the literature on this topic). Revolution and conversion have in common with trauma the quality of constituting a life-altering force, and in neither are experiences of violence always absent as the old life is made to give way in the face of the new. The presence of these similarities leads us to the question of how it is possible to understand these two phenomena of rupture as different from trauma. This is a question that requires an answer if the study of conversion and revolution is not to become simply a subset of a broader investigation in which trauma is taken to be the kernel of all disruptive experience.

My own sense of this issue, and the brief sketch of an approach to it I will offer here, comes out of some recent reading in theology. The prominent German Lutheran theologian Eberhard Jüngel, who grew up in what became East Germany and taught there before moving to Switzerland and then, after German reunification, to West Germany, has lived through more than his share of radical changes. Perhaps drawing on his own background, and certainly drawing on the Lutheran tradition, he reckons Christianity as a religion based upon experiences of what he calls 'interruption', a phenomenon that fosters an 'experience with experience' that leads those who undergo it to re-evaluate all of the understandings that have previously constituted their lives. He is not alone in linking Christianity and religious experience more generally to interruption – indeed another prominent German theologian, in this case a Catholic, once offered 'interruption' as 'the shortest definition of religion' (Metz 2007, 158; see also Boeve 2007; Hart 2001). But Jüngel stands out for our purposes for having asked a necessary follow-up question to such a definition of interruption: what is it that distinguishes Christian interruptions from other kinds?

Jüngel answers that question by asserting that the Christian interruption is unique because it 'has the peculiarity of interrupting human experience *unequivocally to its benefit*' (Jüngel 2014, 209; original emphasis). For Jüngel, the Christian interruption is peculiar in this way because it is caused by the Christian God. In the terms in which he offers this explanation, it is unlikely to satisfy the demands of the kind of secular social scientific and humanistic thought that has shaped this collection (and that has shaped my own reflections here as well). But he may nonetheless point us in a fruitful direction that can also be explored in those terms. A younger theologian from the United States, Kevin Hector (2015), gets us closer to these terms when he argues that modern theology (a lineage that for him runs from Kant through Schleiermacher and Hegel to more recent figures such as Tillich) has been preoccupied with answering the question of what he calls 'mineness': this is the question of how it is that individual human beings – beings that are not themselves the most potent force in the universe or even in their own lives – can claim as their own and integrate into their senses of themselves experiences that profoundly interrupt them (he does not use Jüngel's term or cite him, but something like interruption is a fair gloss on the kinds of experiences he has in mind). On Hector's account, the philosophers and theologians he treats offer different answers to this question, all of which turn on some notion of 'faith' as a trust in the beneficial potential of disruptions that one experiences. This need not be faith in God per se, but only in the ability of radical disruption to improve one's life in its wake.

I think there is a lesson in Jüngel's and Hector's writings about how the possession of the kind of self-conscious models of change I have been discussing – models such as those of conversion and revolution – allow people to trust in the benign potential of changes they participate in bringing about but do not alone fully control. Put otherwise, having such models at hand allows people to have experiences of radical rupture that do not traumatize them. Such experiences do not confront people, as Jüngel (2014, 207) puts it, with the threat of the 'non-being' of the older self that is being transformed, but instead solicit their active engagement in change and by doing so become parts of that self's own life-projects. This quality of mineness that is critical to conversion and revolution as forms of practice is thus at least one key feature that sets them apart from many other types of change that people experience, including those that are traumatic in the currently accepted sense.

I have come to the end of my remarks. I know that I rest my argument here leaving many questions unanswered. Some of these may be theoretically consequential. For example, it is fair to ask where *new* cultural models of rupture come from, and if they themselves might have acultural causes (arising, for example, out of genuinely unprecedented experiences). There are some hints about this as regards the notion of revolution in Sewell's (1996) work and in Larry Hurtado's (1998) study of Christian origins, where he offers a theory of the advent of Christianity as a new religion that also looks to acultural causes to explain the rise of new Christian models of change. It is at least arguable that even models of rupture that have their own origins outside culture only become effective forces for change when they themselves achieve cultural status, and this would preserve the value of some of the arguments I have made here. But it is clear that these issues need further investigation.

A second important question I regrettably have to tackle in the same absurdly limited way is that of whether a culture of rupture – that is to say a culture that gives one or more models of rupture a central place in its conceptions of social life – is only working out its own reproduction when it generates ruptures that follow the lines its own models set out.

When cultures that are heirs to cultural models of revolution undergo revolutionary transformation, should this count as a rupture or is it just more of the same? If we answer that it is a rupture, then we might have to say that cultural processes of rupture by their very nature count simply as performative contradictions – claims to foster something new that are themselves nothing more than routine. I do not think this argument should rest here, but I will leave figuring out how to get beyond this position for another time.

References

Agamben, Giorgio. 2005. *The Time that Remains: A Commentary on the Letter to the Romans*. Stanford, CA: Stanford University Press.

Badiou, Alain. 2003. *Saint Paul: The Foundation of Universalism*. Stanford, CA: Stanford University Press.

Bialecki, Jon. 2009. 'Disjuncture, Continental Philosophy's New "Political Paul," and the Question of Progressive Christianity in a Southern Californian Third Wave Church'. *American Ethnologist* 36 (1): 110–23.

Boeve, Lieven. 2007. *God Interrupts History: Theology in a Time of Upheaval*. New York: Continuum.

Brague, Rémi. 2002. *Eccentric Culture: A Theory of Western Civilization*. South Bend, IN: St. Augustine's Press.

Carroll, Timothy. 2017. 'Theology as an Ethnographic Object: An Anthropology of Eastern Christian Rupture'. *Religions* 8: 1–21.

Coleman, Simon. 2006. 'Studying "Global" Pentecostalism: Tensions, Representations and Opportunities'. *PentecoStudies* 5 (1): 1–17.

Das, Veena. 2007. *Life and Words: Violence and the Descent into the Ordinary*. Berkeley: University of California Press.

Dombrowski, Kirk. 2001. *Against Culture: Development, Politics, and Religion in Indian Alaska*. Lincoln: University of Nebraska Press.

Freeman, Dena. 2017. 'Affordances of Rupture and Their Enactment: A Framework for Understanding Christian Change'. *Suomen Antropologi/Journal of the Finnish Anthropological Society* 42 (4): 3–24.

Handman, Courtney. 2015. *Critical Christianity: Translation and Denominational Conflict in Papua New Guinea*. Berkeley: University of California Press.

Hann, Chris, and Hermann Goltz. 2010. 'Introduction: The Other Christianity?'. In *Eastern Christians in Anthropological Perspective*, edited by Chris Hann and Hermann Goltz, 1–32. Berkeley: University of California Press.

Hart, Kevin. 2001. 'Absolute Interruption: On Faith'. In *Questioning God*, edited by J.D. Caputo, M. Dooley, and M.J. Scanlon, 186–208. Bloomington: Indiana University Press.

Hector, Kevin W. 2015. *The Theological Project of Modernism: Faith and the Conditions of Mineness*. Oxford: Oxford University Press.

Hurtado, Larry W. 1998. *One God, One Lord: Early Christian Devotion and Ancient Jewish Monotheism*. London: T&T Clark.

Jüngel, Eberhard. 2014. *Theological Essays II*. Translated by A. Neufeldt-Fast and J.B. Webster. London: Bloomsbury.

Kosellek, Reinhart. 2004. *Futures Past: On the Semantics of Historical Time*. Translated by K. Tribe. New York: Columbia University Press.

Lackenby, Nicholas. n.d. 'Notes on Repenting, Liturgy and (Dis)continuity amongst Serbian Orthodox Christians'. Unpublished paper presented at Workshop on Anthropology of Christianity, Cumberland Lodge, London.

Marshall, Kimberly Jenkins. 2016. *Upward, Not Sunwise: Resonant Rupture in Navajo Neo-Pentecostalism*. Lincoln: University of Nebraska Press.

Metz, Johann Baptist. 2007. *Faith in History and Society: Toward a Practical Fundamental Theology*. Translated by J.M. Ashley. New York: Crossroad.

Robbins, Joel. 2003. 'On the Paradoxes of Global Pentecostalism and the Perils of Continuity Thinking'. *Religion* 33 (3): 221–31.

Robbins, Joel. 2004. *Becoming Sinners: Christianity and Moral Torment in a Papua New Guinea Society*. Berkeley: University of California Press.

Robbins, Joel. 2007. 'Continuity Thinking and the Problem of Christian Culture: Belief, Time and the Anthropology of Christianity'. *Current Anthropology* 48 (1): 5–38.

Robbins, Joel. 2009. 'Conversion, Hierarchy, and Cultural Change: Value and Syncretism in the Globalization of Pentecostal and Charismatic Christianity'. In *Hierarchy: Persistence and Transformation in Social Formations*, edited by K.M. Rio and O.H. Smedal, 65–88. New York: Berghahn.

Robbins, Joel. 2010. 'Anthropology, Pentecostalism, and the New Paul: Conversion, Event, and Social Transformation'. *South Atlantic Quarterly* 109 (4): 633–52.

Robbins, Joel. 2013. 'Beyond the Suffering Subject: Toward an Anthropology of the Good'. *JRAI* 19: 447–62.

Robbins, Joel. 2016. 'How Long is a Longue Durée: Structure, Duration, and the Cultural Analysis of Cultural Change'. In *A Practice of Anthropology: The Thought and Influence of Marshall Sahlins*, edited by A. Golub, D. Rosenblatt, and J.D. Kelly, 40–62. Montreal and Kingston: McGill-Queens University Press.

Robbins, Joel, and Matthew Engelke. 2010. 'Introduction to Special Issue: Global Christianity, Global Critique'. *South Atlantic Quarterly* 109 (4): 623–31.

Sewell, William. 1996. 'Historical Events as Transformations of Structures: Inventing Revolution at the Bastille'. *Theory and Society* 25: 841–81.

Stubbs, David. 2018. *Mars By 1980: The Story of Electronic Music*. London: Faber and Faber.

Tanner, Kathryn. 1997. *Theories of Culture: A New Agenda for Theology*. Minneapolis: Fortress Press.

Žižek, Slavoj. 2003. *The Puppet and the Dwarf: The Perverse Core of Christianity*. Cambridge, MA: MIT Press.

Index

9/11 attacks 47

Acorn (environmental activist) 167, 169
adoption (cultural) 118, 132–33, 135
Adorno, Theodor 8, 153
aftermath 21, 198, 200–202, 205, 211–13, 215
Agamben, Giorgio 4, 32, 218
agency 72, 87, 101; linear time and 72; political 81, 84, 87; Protestantism and 100–101
alcohol drinking 64–65, 76, 98, 111–13, 129–33, 135–37
Alvarado, Velasco 194
Amazing China (2018 film) 59
Amr (Islamist militant) 178–80, 182, 184–85
anarchist groups 158, 167–68, 172
Angola 143–44
anti-coal movement 158, 160, 168
Arab Spring 20, 174–80, 183–89
Arendt, Hannah 7, 52
Arthur, Brian 149
Assad, Bashar al- 178–79, 180, 181, 185
Assad, Hafez al- 185
assimilation 117–18, 132–33, 137

Badiou, Alain 7, 12, 22–23, 176, 188
Bakongo (ethnic group) 141–43, 145, 154
Bannon, Steve 80
Bastille Day attack 28–29, 32, 48–49, 220
Belshazzar 147
Bey, Hakim 8, 169
Bialecki, Jon 180
Bible 120–22
Bicêtre (prison) 44–46
Bloch, Maurice 43
bloodletting and blood relics 13, 36, 38–42, 46, 48–49
Bo Xilai 60–61, 63, 68
Bode, Barbara 194–96
Brague, Rémi 223–24
Brandes, Georg 100–101, 105–6
Bryant, Rebecca 181
butterfly effect 169

capitalism 7, 20, 30, 158, 168–69, 194; "green" 168
Catholicism 16–17, 116, 119–25, 133, 137, 153, 195, 227; Mass ritual 120–21; morality 131; professionals 207. *See also* Christianity

CENA (Centre for the Study of Mandombe) 145–46
Chiang Kaishek 56, 60, 68
childhood 18–19
China: decolonization 52–53; historical rupture and repair 53; museums 14, 55, 58–67
Chongqing 60–63, 68
Christianity 23, 93–94, 103, 106, 117–18, 120, 122–24, 127–28, 132–36, 176, 213, 221–27, 229; alcohol and 135–36; assimilation of 117–18, 132–33, 137; as community 121–22; conversion to 17, 110, 118, 126–32, 176, 189–90, 219, 221, 226; social vs dogmatic understanding 122; themes within modern Japanese culture 134. *See also* Catholicism; Protestantism
Church of the Holy Family 116, 118–20, 124–25, 127–28
Ciavatta, David 49
Clinton, Hillary 77–79, 82, 85, 89
Coleman, Simon 224
colonialism 6, 52–53, 182, 189
Congo, Democratic Republic of 143–45, 147
conservatism 30, 95, 100–101, 112
conversion (religious) 16–17, 116–18, 125–27, 137, 176; cultural continuity and 126–32; to Kimbanguism 153; revolution and 218–19, 227–29; Urapmin 184, 221–22, 225–26
creative destruction 2
creativity 7–8, 142, 148–50, 152
creolization 136
Cuba 47
Cultural Radicals movement 99–100, 104, 106
Cultural Revolution 14, 54–55, 57, 59, 61, 63–64

Danner, Mark 82
de Baecque, Antoine 37, 39–41, 49
Deleuze, Gilles 4, 8, 22, 154, 188–89
democracy 6, 16, 30, 54, 70, 75, 81–83, 87, 182
Democratic Party (US) 76–77, 80, 87–88
Denmark 93, 102; freedom-notions 101; youth rebellion (1968) 105
dentō 124
development banks 198–99, 201, 208, 211
dialectic 8–9, 11, 48, 56–57, 67, 136
Disobedienti 158
Dombrowski, Kirk 222

drinking. *See* alcohol drinking
Dubuffet, Jean 147–49, 151
Dumont, Louis 107–9, 113, 132

earthquakes 21, 193–98, 200–203, 205–6,
    208–9, 211–16
Eisenstein, Paul 10
emancipation 8, 52–53
encompassment 119, 132–37
environmental activism: anti-coal movement
    158, 160, 168; critiques of capitalism
    168–70; forest occupations 160–67;
    summit protesting 158
European Coal and Steel Community 160
exclusion 7, 71
executions. *See* guillotine
existentialism 94, 103, 111–13

Fabian, Johannes 71
Fan Jianchuan 14, 53, 55, 58–60, 63–64,
    66–67
forest occupation 157–72
Foucault, Michel 34–36
Francis Xavier 119
Free Syrian Army (FSA) 178, 183
freedom 6–7, 10, 16, 33–34, 54, 73, 94, 96,
    100–101, 104, 106–7, 112, 194; Danish
    concepts 101
Freeman, Dena 227
French Revolution 17, 34, 42, 47–48, 158–59;
    anthropological approach 32–34;
    Bastille Day attack 28–29, 32, 48–49,
    220; executions, Louis XVI 13, 28–29,
    33, 35–45, 49; executions, Princesse de
    Lamballe 35–37; executions, Robespierre
    42; familial order and 33; Furet's
    interpretation 30; Germany and 108;
    guillotine as emblematic 27; as nonlinear
    process 13; September Massacres 35, 37,
    49; universality 34–35
frigjorthed (uninhibitedness) 101, 106
Frost, Robert 147
Furet, Francois 30–31, 47

geometry 142, 149, 152
Germany 108, 161
Gluckman, Max 3, 159
grand narratives 5, 11–12, 15
Great Leap Forward (China) 53
Grundtvig, N.F.S 100–103, 106, 108–9
Grundtvigianismen 100, 102, 106
guillotine 13, 27–31, 33, 35, 37–41, 43,
    45–49, 155
Gujarat 193–94, 197–98, 200–202, 205,
    211–13, 215–16
Guo Songming 54
Guomindang 56, 62

Handman, Courtney 224
Hardt, Michael 8–9, 168

heat 74
Hector, Kevin 228–29
Hegel, G.W.F 8, 34–35, 228
historical nihilism 14, 53–56, 67
historicity 34, 88
Holloway, John 8–9
Hunt, Lynn 33, 47
Hurtado, Larry 229

iconicity 81
inculturation 133
Islam 23, 99, 185, 189; jihadism 175–79, 181,
    183–85, 187–89
Islamic State 178, 185

Jacobinism 30, 44
Japan: concepts of religion and tradition 124–
    25; prevalance of Christianity 122–24
Jiang Zemin 54
jihadists 175–79, 181, 183–85, 187–89

Kant, Immanuel 34–35, 38, 193, 213, 228
Kante, Souleymane 141
Keane, Webb 100
Khaled (Islamist militant) 174–75, 178–87
Kierkegaard, Søren 16, 93–94, 100–101,
    103–4, 106–10, 114
Kimbangu, Simon 141, 143–44, 146, 154
Kimbanguism 143–44, 146, 153–54
Kinshasa 145–47, 149–50, 152
Klein, Naomi 168, 193, 211
Kohn, Eduardo 81, 83, 89
Koirala, Sushil 208
Kounios, John 148–49
Krarup, Søren 93–95, 110–11

Laborit, Henri 149
Lackenby, Nicholas 226–27
Lamballe, Marie-Louise Therese, Princess de
    35–37
Latour, Bruno 32
Leonardo da Vinci 147, 152
Lévi-Strauss 149
life-affirmation 5–6, 8–9, 11
liminality 2, 21, 33, 48
Lisbon Earthquake 212–13
Llull, Ramon 142, 148
Locke, John 211, 216
Lorenz, Edward 169
Louis XVI of France 13, 28–30, 33, 35–45, 49
Lutheranism 16, 94–95, 100, 106, 228. *See
    also* Protestantism; Tidehverv
Lynx (environmental activist) 163–65, 169

madness 45, 148, 200
Mahara, Krishna Bahadur 206
Manchester School 3–4, 159
Mandombe language 17, 141–47, 149–50,
    152–55
Mao Zedong 54–57, 60, 63–65

Maoism 57, 66
Marat, Jean-Paul 32, 41
Marie-Antoinette 36–37
Marshall, Kimberly 225
Marshall, Ruth 190
Martin, Jean-Clément 47
Mass (Catholic) 120–21
Matamoros, Fernando 8–9
Mayer, Arno 31–32
McGowan, Todd 10
Minkowski, Eugene 155
Modern Breakthrough 100, 104–6
modernity 2, 5, 11, 23, 134; genesis as rupture 158; grand narrative 5, 23
Moeran, Brian 130
Monkey Town 167, 172
museums 14, 55, 58–67
Muslim Brotherhood 181

nationalisms 6, 53, 60, 84, 89, 102, 127, 198–99, 204, 216
natural disasters 1, 21, 193–205, 207, 209, 211–15
negation 1, 7–9
Negri, Antonio 4, 8, 168
Nepal 21, 193–95, 197, 199–201, 203, 205–13, 215–16
New Life movement 60
Nietzsche, Friedrich 106
N'kamba 143–44, 146
normativity 9

Obama, Barack 75, 77, 80–82
Occupy Movement 164
ontology 89
outsider artists 148
Owen (environmental activist) 162–63

Paglia, Camille 130
Paine, Robert 154
Paris Commune 38
Paul the Apostle 176, 180, 188, 218
Pinel, Philippe 44–46
populism 1, 6, 11–12, 57, 70, 81, 88–89, 189
power: everyday 87, 196; majoritarian 28, 31, 79; political 72, 87; predator-prey 83; presidential 75, 84–86; sacred 39; state 53, 71, 83, 86–87, 201–2; Trump's personal 81–83
Prendergast, Christopher 29
prophecy 17, 140–41, 143, 154
Protestantism. See also Lutheranism; Tidhedverv

Raahauge, Agnete 98
race and racism 6; Nordic race as God's chosen 102
Rambo, Lewis 116
red culture movement 61–62
relativism 15, 70–71, 79, 88

repair 13–14, 21, 52–53, 55–57, 59–61, 63–65, 67, 140
repetitions 15, 22, 64–65, 82, 149, 154, 177, 181, 188–89
replication 65
resilience 205–6, 211
revolution 7, 34, 47, 53, 93, 179, 185–86, 188, 218–21, 226–29; China 56–57, 67; Cuba 47; as distinct from rupture 13, 27; emancipation and 53; as expression of desire 8; as failure of modernity 7; historical stasis and 185; jihadist 184; Middle East 176–78; modernity and 7, 9, 29; rebellions and 159; religious conversion and 218–19, 227–29; sacrifice and 42; temporal boundaries 27; terror as dialectic interaction 31; theological rupture and 94, 110, 113; theoretical treatments 33
Robbins, Joel 116–17, 125, 176, 184
Robespierre, Maximilien 28, 38, 42, 48, 151
Rousseau, Jean-Jacques 28, 30, 193, 213–14
Ruefle, Mary 74, 76
Ruhr (Germany) 159–60
rupture: as central element of culture 229; Christian concepts 221–29; as contemporary concept 11–12; as cultural process 219–21; defined, as singular splitting movement 27; defines, as radical discontinuity 1; as distinct from revolution 13, 27; double 17, 64, 150; dual aspect 1; as ethnographic practice 12–13; existential 16; ideals emerging from 6; models of 222, 229; as modernist concept 10–11; multiple 14, 187–88; pace of 170–71; political 7, 10, 15–16, 38, 46, 71, 73, 75, 77, 79, 81, 83, 85, 87, 89; political, distinct from revolution 27; as repair 52; as repetitive rhythm 187; revolutionary 8, 27, 38, 53; scale of measurment 167–70; as self-transformation 117; as singular break 20; as tipping point between continuity and change 176
Rural Housing Reconstruction Project 207
Russian Revolution 38
RWE (energy company) 157, 160, 168

Sahlins, Marshall 220
Said, Behnam 187
Said, Edward 177
schizophrenia 155
Schumpeter, Joseph 2
Scott, David 7, 88
September Massacres 35, 37, 49
shichi-go-san 125
Shinto institutions 125
Shong Lue 141, 152
shūkyō 124
skill-sharing 159, 161–62, 164

slow rupture 158–59, 167–69, 171
smoking 96–99, 174
sneaking 20–21, 159, 161–65, 167–71
Solnit, Rebecca 193, 216
Soviet Union 44
Spinoza, Baruch 1, 152–53
Starhawk (environmental activist) 170, 172
state power 71, 83, 86–87, 201
Stengers, Isabelle 4, 159, 170, 172
Stewart, Charles 14
Stoler, Ann 181
Stone, Essy 82
Strathern, Marilyn 5, 170
syncretism 136
Syria 20, 174, 176–77, 179–82, 184, 186

Tackett, Timothy 31
temporal ruptures 116, 118, 126
temporary autonomous zones 8, 169
terror 1, 7, 11, 17, 31, 45–46
Terror of the French Revolution 13, 17, 29–32, 34–39, 42, 44–49, 213
Tidehverv movement 94–101, 103–4, 106–7, 109–13
time and temporality 5, 86, 88, 126, 128, 155, 158, 169–70, 176, 181–82, 186, 208; colonial temporality 21; elasticity of rupture 15; ethnographic 74; future-oriented temporality 53; guillotine as temporal cutting mechanism 13; heat and energy 15, 74; language-time 73; legal pluralism and 89; linear conception 72–74, 176; in periods of crisis 14, 72; religious 94, 110, 116, 118, 125; repair versus obsolescence 63; rupture as constant present 16; rupture as temporal tear 80; rupture/repair paradox 57, 67; slow rupture 170–71; temporal scale-shifting 14, 18, 20–21; temporal undecidability 71; thermodynamic 73–74

Tischle, Sergio 8–9
Tokyo 116, 119, 122, 124, 126, 130–31, 133–34, 136
trees 20, 158–59, 161, 167, 171, 186, 210
Trump, Donald 15, 71–72, 75, 186; binary morality 83–84; charisma and personal appeal 81–83, 85; electoral campaign 75–79; Hillary Clinton and 78; policies 76, 80; policies, Obama and 75, 80; voter base 77–79, 81–82, 84; white nationalism and 80
Tsing, Anna 11
Turner, Victor 2

Uchimura Kanzō 137
United States 77, 87–88, 175, 182, 206, 228; 2008 Presidential election 81; 2016 Presidential election 70, 75–76, 79–82, 86–89, 197, 209
Urapmin (ethnic group) 117–18, 129, 132–33, 136–37, 221–23, 225–26

Valéry, Paul 148
Voltaire 193, 213–14

Wabeladio Payi, David 17–18, 141–42, 145–54
Wahnich, Sophie 31–32, 38, 43, 47–49
Wang, Sam 89
Wang Hui 53
Wang Yangming 60, 63
Weber, Max 1, 23
Weibo 59
white nationalism 80, 89
Willis, Elizabeth 85

Xi Jinping 14, 53–54, 56–57, 59–63, 68, 190

Žižek, Slavoj 7, 11

Lightning Source UK Ltd.
Milton Keynes UK
UKHW021849300719
347103UK00006B/173/P